Michael Herbert teaches Accounting and Business Studies at South Devon College of Arts and Technology. He was Chief Examiner for the Associated Examining Board's GCE in Business Studies at ordinary level from 1979 to 1988.

His other publications include *Practical Accounts 1* and *Accounting O Level Studyguide* (with George Bright).

Pan Study Aids for GCSE include:

Accounting

Biology

Chemistry

Commerce

Computer Studies

Economics

English Language

French

Geography 1

Geography 2

German

History 1: World History since 1914

History 2: Britain and Europe since 1700

Human Biology

Mathematics

Physics

Sociology

Study Skills

PAN STUDY AIDS

ACCOUNTING

Michael Herbert

A Pan Original
Pan Books   London, Sydney and Auckland

First published 1988 by Pan Books Ltd,
Cavaye Place, London SW10 9PG

9 8 7 6 5 4 3 2 1

© Michael Herbert 1988

ISBN 0 330 29411 3

Text design by Peter Ward
Text illustration by M L Design
Photoset by Parker Typesetting Service, Leicester
Printed and bound in Spain by
Mateu Cromo SA, Madrid

CONTENTS

6　　　　Contents

INTRODUCTION TO GCSE

From 1988, there will be a single system of examining at 16 plus in England and Wales and Northern Ireland. The General Certificate of Secondary Education (GCSE) will replace the General Certificate of Education (GCE) and the Certificate of Secondary Education (CSE). In Scotland candidates will be entering for the O grade and standard grade examinations leading to the award of the Scottish Certificate of Education (SCE).

The Pan Study Aids GCSE series has been specially written by practising teachers and examiners to enable you to prepare successfully for this new examination.

GCSE introduces several important changes in the way in which you are tested. First, the examinations will be structured so that you can show *what* you know rather than what you do *not* know. Of critical importance here is the work you produce during the course of the examination year, which will be given much greater emphasis than before. Second, courses are set and marked by six examining groups instead of the previous twenty GCE/CSE boards. The groups are:

Northern Examining Association (NEA)
Midland Examining Group (MEG)
London and East Anglian Group (LEAG)
Southern Examining Group (SEG)
Welsh Joint Examinations Council (WJEC)
Northern Ireland Schools Examination Council (NISEC)

One of the most useful changes introduced by GCSE is the single award system of grades A–G. This should permit you and future employers more accurately to assess your qualifications.

GCSE	GCE O Level	CSE
A	A	–
B	B	–
C	C	1
D	D	2
E	E	3
F	F	4
G		5

Remember that, whatever examinations you take, the grades you are awarded will be based on how well you have done.

Pan Study Aids are geared for use throughout the duration of your courses. The text layout has been carefully designed to provide all the information and skills you need for GCSE and SCE examinations – please feel free to use the margins for additional notes.

PREFACE

This book has been written to help anyone studying for the new GCSE Accounting examination. In the first three chapters special attention is paid to the balance sheet, the concept of profit and double entry book-keeping. Mastering these areas provides essential groundwork for the topics that follow. You are advised to work through these chapters very carefully before proceeding, whatever the stage of your accounting knowledge.

Each chapter contains a number of self-checks which are designed to test you on the section you have just read. For convenience the solution and comments on these self-checks follow immediately. To maximise the benefit of these, you are advised to have paper and pencil ready at all times and to attempt the question honestly, not looking at the solution until you have finished. At the end of each chapter there are exercises covering the work that has preceded that chapter. Most of these exercises relate directly to that chapter. However, as accounting is an integrated subject you will find that concepts and techniques mastered in the early parts of the book will still be called upon in later chapters. Some of these exercises are questions from specimen papers provided by the various GCSE boards. Answers or guidance are provided to most numerical questions at the end of the book. These answers and guidance are solely the author's responsibility unless stated otherwise.

The Syllabus Grid provides you with some help in identifying topics covered by the various examining boards. This does not, however, replace the need to obtain an actual syllabus from the board whose examination you decide to take. You are also advised to obtain a full specimen paper and, when the first examinations have taken place, to supplement this with past examination papers. Boards differ in regulations regarding matters such as use of calculators and the type of accounting paper provided. You are advised to acquaint yourself with these regulations well before the date of your examination. To assist I include on page 10 the addresses of the examining boards.

ACKNOWLEDGEMENT

I would like to thank the following GCSE examining bodies for permission to reproduce questions from their specimen papers:

London and East Anglian Group
University of London School
Examinations Board
Stewart House
Russell Square
London WC1B 5DP
Tel (01) 636 8000

Midland Examining Group
University of Cambridge Local
Examinations Syndicate
Syndicate Buildings
1 Hills Road
Cambridge CB1 2EU
Tel (0223) 61111

Northern Examining Association
Joint Matriculation Board
Manchester M15 6EU
Tel (061) 273 2565

Northern Ireland Schools Examinations Council
Northern Ireland Schools
Examinations Council
Beechill House
42 Beechill Road
Belfast BT8 4RS
Tel (0232) 704666

Southern Examining Group
Associated Examining Board
Stag Hill House
Guildford
Surrey GU2 5XJ
Tel (0483) 506506

Welsh Joint Education Committee
Welsh Joint Education
Committee
245 Western Avenue
Cardiff CF5 2YX
Tel (0222) 561231

SYLLABUS GRID

TOPICS	LEAG	MEG	NEA	NISEC	SEG	WJEC
Accounting concepts & conventions	✓	✓	✓	✓	✓	✓
Books of original entry	✓	✓	✓	✓	✓	✓
Ledger and trial balance	✓	✓	✓	✓	✓	✓
Capital and revenue distinction	✓	✓	✓	✓	✓	✓
Final accounts – sole trader	✓	✓	✓	✓	✓	✓
Final accounts – partnership	✓	✓	✓	✓	✓	✓
Final accounts – clubs	✓	✓	✓	✓	✓	✓
Final accounts – ltd companies	✓	✓	✓		✓	✓
Manufacturing accounts	✓	✓	✓	✓	✓	✓
Incomplete records	✓	✓	✓		✓	✓
Adjustments and provisions	✓	✓	✓	✓	✓	✓
Bank reconciliation statements	✓	✓	✓	✓	✓	✓
Control accounts	✓	✓	✓	✓	✓	✓
Valuation of assets	✓	✓	✓	✓	✓	✓
Cash budgets		✓		✓		
Analysis and interpretation	✓	✓	✓	✓	✓	✓
Departmental accounts	✓					
Purchase of business	✓					
Value added tax	✓		✓		✓	
Errors and suspense accounts	✓	✓	✓		✓	✓
Break-even analysis				✓		
Household accounts and personal money management	✓	✓		✓		

BUSINESSES AND BALANCE SHEETS

CONTENTS

1.1 INTRODUCTION

The course you are following will deal mainly with the accounts of businesses. To understand business accounts, and to pass an examination, you must understand something about businesses.

There are many different forms of business organization, ranging from a small shop, which has a local market and may well have only one owner, to a large multi-national company which often has a world-wide market and probably thousands of owners or shareholders. We can identify features that are common to all businesses. These features will provide a framework which will help you to gain greater understanding of what you are doing.

1 Businesses exist to make a profit for their owners by selling products or services.
2 Assets are needed to enable the business to operate.
3 Finance will be required to provide the assets the business needs.
4 Accounts must be kept to record profits and losses, assets used and the finance provided. This applies to all businesses. Government departments engaged in collecting taxes may require evidence of any business transaction. Failure to provide such evidence could result in a tax inspector making a much higher tax demand than the owner expects. The onus is then on the owner to show that he should not be taxed so highly. To do that he will need evidence in the form of accounts. If the business has failed to fulfil a legal requirement, for example to complete a VAT return on time, it is likely to face prosecution. Therefore, most businesses keep accounts.

To begin with, we will consider only those businesses involved in selling goods which are owned by one person. These are known as **sole traders, sole owners** or **sole proprietors**. Later, we will consider those businesses which provide services and also those which are owned by more than one person, such as partnerships and limited companies. We will also look at the accounts of clubs and societies as well as considering how accounting knowledge can be adapted to meet the needs of simple household accounts.

1.2 BALANCE SHEET STRUCTURE

A balance sheet is a statement of the assets and sources of finance of a business at a particular date. The following summary of a balance sheet emphasizes the relationship between the assets and sources of finance.

Balance sheet of John Smith, retailer, as at 31 December 1986

Assets employed	£	Sources of finance	£
Fixed assets	40,000	Owner's capital	30,000
Current assets	10,000	Long term liabilities	15,000
		Current liabilities	5,000
	50,000		50,000

The relationship is one of equality.

The value of the assets employed = The sources of finance

All assets employed in a business must be financed in some way. Before developing this relationship we must make certain that the terms contained in it are fully understood.

Assets are the possessions or advantages belonging to a business on which a money value can be placed. **Fixed assets** are those which are relatively permanent. They are employed to help the business make a profit but it is not normally intended to make a profit on their purchase and sale. The main examples are premises, machinery, furniture, fixtures and fittings, equipment and motor vehicles. **Current assets** are those which are constantly changing in value as the business seeks to make a profit. Cash in hand, cash at bank, debtors and stock are the main examples. Stock is short for stock-in-trade. It is made up of the items the business deals in, i.e. what it buys and sells to make a profit. A debtor is someone who owes money to the business. It is an asset because most people pay their debts.

Current assets are also known as **circulating assets**. Cash is used to buy stock which is sold to customers on credit or for cash. If the sale is on credit the customer becomes a debtor to the business until payment is made. Cash received is then available to purchase further stock and so the process continues.

The classification of an asset as fixed or current will depend on the use to which it is being put in a business. For example, the cars for sale on a garage forecourt will be part of the stock of that business. The owner of the garage will want to make a profit on them. They are a current asset. However, a motor vehicle owned by a retail shop that is used to make deliveries would be classified correctly as a fixed asset since, in that business, it is being used in the pursuit of profit without any intention of making a profit on the vehicle itself. The vehicle will be a relatively permanent asset belonging to the retail shop.

Figure 1.1 Circulating assets

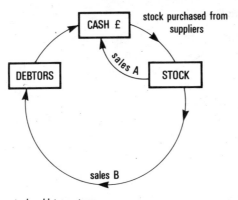

stock sold to customers
A for immediate cash
B on credit for cash settlement later

Owner's capital is the finance provided by the owner, in this case John Smith. This figure will not remain the same. The amount he puts into the business when he starts operating may be added to by investing further sums whenever he wishes. He might also take assets from the business from time to time for his private use; this is known as **drawings** and reduces his capital. Drawings is short for withdrawal of capital. The profits made belong to the owner and these will also increase his capital. Losses will have the reverse effect and reduce the owner's capital.

Liabilities are amounts owing by the business to providers of finance from outside the business. The distinction between long term and current liabilities is one of time. **Current liabilities** are those due to be repaid within one year. **Long term liabilities** are those which do not have to be repaid for at least one year. Loans from banks and finance companies are common examples of long term liabilities while amounts due to suppliers, who are usually called trade creditors, are current liabilities. A creditor is someone to whom the business owes money. You must not confuse this with the term 'debtor' which refers to someone who owes money to the business. Remember it is the length of time of repayment which is the essential distinction, not the supplier of the loan. Thus, a bank loan taken out for three months should be regarded as a current liability while a three year bank loan will be classified as a long term liability.

  Bank overdrafts sometimes cause a classification problem. Some businesses make use of one of these for much longer than a year. They are always counted as current assets, however, as the bank can recall the amount due whenever it wishes.

ENTITY CONCEPT

We have classified liabilities and owner's capital as two types of sources of finance for a business. Some teachers and books describe the owner's capital itself as a liability. This can be justified because of a very important principle in accounting. This principle is known as the **entity concept**. It requires us to treat the business as having a separate existence from its owner. Thus, if we regard the owner as separate from the business it is possible to state that the business owes its owner money. The amount owed is, in fact, the amount of capital he has invested in the business. Nobody is going to suggest that the owner of any business is not very closely involved with its performance. This is particularly true of a small business owned by one person. The entity concept does not seek to deny this relationship. What it does is remind us that from an accounting viewpoint we should consider the owner as a separate 'person' from the business. From a practical point of view it is a timely reminder that no businessman should mix up his private bank account with that of his business.

> **SELF-CHECK ▶**
> **1.2**

John Tate, a retailer, had the following assets and sources of finance on 31 May 1987: cash £900, premises £40,000, mortgage on premises (twenty years) £20,000, furniture and fittings £7,000, debtors £850, trade creditors £1,500, stock £6,000, bank £3,600, equipment £2,600, capital £39,450.

Put this information into a balance sheet using the headings we have defined.

> **SOLUTION ▶**

Balance sheet of John Tate, retailer, as at 31 May 1987

	£	£		£
Fixed assets			**Owner's capital**	39,450
Premises	40,000		**Long term liabilities**	
Furn & fittings	7,000		Mortgage	20,000
Equipment	2,600		**Current liabilities**	
		49,600	Trade creditors	1,500
Current assets				
Stock	6,000			
Debtors	850			
Bank	3,600			
Cash	900			
	11,350			
		60,950		60,950

Note

1   The balance sheet heading must contain the three essential items: name of the statement, name of the business or owner, and the exact date.

2   I have omitted the general headings for the two sides, i.e. assets and sources of finance. This is usually done because it is obvious which side is which from the contents.

3   Since there is more than one fixed and current asset I have shown sub-totals for these groups. If there had been more than one current or long term liability I would have done the same on the finance side.

4   The assets are arranged in order of permanence which is usual in the UK. The most permanent asset is premises, followed by the other fixed assets. The least permanent is cash. Cash is also the most liquid of the assets. Some countries follow the **order of liquidity**. Liquidity refers to the ease with which something can be turned into cash. To follow the order of liquidity the current assets would come first with cash as the first item. The fixed assets would come afterwards with premises being the last item.

5   The order on the finance side matches the order on the assets side. Finance that is the most permanent, i.e. the owner's capital, comes first, followed by the long term liabilities. Current liabilities, which are the least permanent source of finance, are placed last.

6   The totals of the two sides are always shown level, even if one side is longer than the other.

7   This is only one style of balance sheet layout. It is called a **horizontal balance sheet** because it shows the assets and sources of finance side side. You may have come across horizontal balance sheets which show the assets on the right and sources of finance on the left. Indeed for many years this was the normal practice in the UK. While this is not necessarily wrong, it is not as logical as displaying the assets on the left. This will be explained later. It is also possible that you have seen **vertical balance sheets** in which the finance is shown beneath the assets. These will be introduced later. For the time being, however, we will stick to the horizontal style, because this method emphasizes best of all the relationship between the assets and sources of finance that was established earlier. Let's return to that now.

1.3 THE ACCOUNTING EQUATION

This is the name given to the equation that states the relationship between the assets and sources of finance of a business.

The value of the assets employed = The sources of finance

This equation can be simplified to:

Assets = Capital + Liabilities

It is also known as **the book-keeping equation**. You must know it and be able to apply it. You are often required to calculate one missing figure when the rest of the figures are given.

If you were given the information that Tom's capital was worth £12,000 and that he had liabilities of £8,000 it is fairly easy to calculate that his assets must be worth £20,000.

Assets = Capital (£12,000) + Liabilities (£8,000)

▶ Suppose that you are told that Jerry's assets are worth £50,000 and that he has liabilities of £10,000. What is the value of his capital?

▶ The answer is £40,000. This may appear obvious to you because the figures are so straightforward. It is important, however, that you are able to change the equation around to fit the circumstances. Firstly, because the figures given are rarely that easy. Secondly, because the process is an important one that you will meet in other areas.

To move items from one side of an equation to another you must remember to change the sign of the item moved. This means that a plus sign becomes a minus and a minus becomes a plus.

Thus **Assets = Capital + Liabilities** becomes
Assets − Liabilities = Capital
Applying this to the figures given above we get
Assets (£50,000) − Liabilities (£10,000) = Capital (£40,000).

Suppose that Pat's assets are valued at £60,000 and she has capital of £18,000. We are able to write an equation to calculate her liabilities. When moving capital to the other side of the equation remember the rule that an item in an equation without a negative or minus sign in front of it is regarded as a plus. Hence the basic book-keeping equation Assets = Capital + Liabilities becomes
Assets − Capital = Liabilities
and Pat's liabilities can be calculated as £60,000 − £18,000 = £42,000.

SELF-CHECK ▶
1.3

Test you ability to apply the basic book-keeping equation by completing the following table:

	Assets	Capital	Liabilities
	£	£	£
(a)	12,500		3,750
(b)		2,680	14,150
(c)	32,870		12,680
(d)	45,960	16,790	
(e)	25,400		29,800

SOLUTION ▶

(a) capital £8,750 (b) assets £16,830 (c) capital £20,190 (d) liabilities £29,170 (e) deficiency of capital £4,400.

COMMENT ▶ Using the equation correctly should have given you few problems with the first four. However, you may not have come across a business that has liabilities greater than its assets and (*e*) may have caused concern. A business that has liabilities greater than its assets is said to be insolvent and the condition is known as one of insolvency. Many people refer to this position as one of bankruptcy and regard the owner as bankrupt. This is not correct. Bankrupt is a legal term that applies when a court of law has examined the accounts of the owner of a business and declares a state of bankruptcy. The owners of many businesses that are insolvent will find themselves in court being declared bankrupt. Some, however, are able to rescue their business and return it to a healthy position (perhaps by obtaining additional finance from other sources). In accounting therefore it is important to use the term insolvency to describe the position when total liabilities of a business are greater than total assets. As far as applying the equation is concerned the only problem is that you have to remember the minus sign.

$$\text{Assets } (\pounds 25,400) - \text{Liabilities } (\pounds 29,800) = \text{Capital } (-\pounds 4,400).$$

There is a capital deficiency of £4,400.

1.4 TRANSACTIONS INVOLVING ASSETS AND LIABILITIES

Balance sheets are normally drawn up at intervals of six or twelve months. It is important to realise, however, that every transaction a business makes affects its assets and/or its finance. An example will help to make this clear. The following is a balance sheet relating to the business of Tom Rice before he begins trading on 1 May 1987. In illustrations like this headings within the balance sheet will usually be omitted to save space.

Balance Sheet of Tom Rice as at 9 a.m. on 1 May 1987

Premises	£20,000	Owner's capital	£30,000
Furniture	5,000	Loan – Webber	4,000
Stock	9,000	Trade creditors	1,000
Bank	1,000		
	£35,000		£35,000

During the day he made the following transactions:
(*a*)   10.00 a.m. Withdrew £400 from the bank for use as cash.
(*b*)   11.00 a.m. Paid £100 for a new desk for his office.
(*c*)   11.30 a.m. Bought £500 stock on credit.

(*d*)   2.00 p.m. Sold his old office desk worth £50 for £50 cash.
(*e*)   2.30 p.m. Paid one of his creditors £300 by cheque.
(*f*)   3.00 p.m. Obtained a bank loan of £4,000 which was used immediately to repay Webber.

It is important that you learn how to analyse the effects of transactions on a balance sheet. We will take each in turn and see how the balance sheet would be affected. The transactions will be repeated for ease of reference.

(*a*)   10.00 a.m. Withdrew £400 from the bank for use as cash. Asset bank will be reduced by £400 and asset cash will be increased by £400.

Balance Sheet of Tom Rice as at 10 a.m. on 1 May 1987

Premises	£20,000	Owner's capital	£30,000
Furniture	5,000	Loan – Webber	4,000
Stock	9,000	Trade creditors	1,000
Bank	600		
Cash	400		
	£35,000		£35,000

(*b*)   11.00 a.m. Paid £100 cash for a new desk for his office.
Asset furniture will increase by £100 while asset cash decreases by £100.

Balance Sheet of Tom Rice as at 11 a.m. on 1 May 1987

Premises	£20,000	Owner's capital	£30,000
Furniture	5,100	Loan – Webber	4,000
Stock	9,000	Trade creditors	1,000
Bank	600		
Cash	300		
	£35,000		£35,000

(*c*)   11.30 a.m. Bought £500 stock on credit.
Asset stock will increase by £500 while trade creditors also increase by £500.

Balance Sheet of Tom Rice as at 11.30 a.m. on 1 May 1987

Premises	£20,000	Owner's capital	£30,000
Furniture	5,100	Loan – Webber	4,000
Stock	9,500	Trade creditors	1,500
Bank	600		
Cash	300		
	£35,500		£35,500

(*d*)   2.00 p.m. Sold his old office desk worth £50 for £50 cash. Asset cash increases by £50 while asset furniture is reduced by £50.

Balance Sheet of Tom Rice as at 2 p.m. on 1 May 1987

Premises	£20,000	Owner's capital	£30,000
Furniture	5,050	Loan – Webber	4,000
Stock	9,500	Trade creditors	1,500
Bank	600		
Cash	350		
	£35,500		£35,500

(*e*)   2.30 p.m. Paid one of his creditors £300 by cheque. Asset bank decreases by £300 while the liability to trade creditors also decreases by £300.

Balance Sheet of Tom Rice as at 2.30 p.m. on 1 May 1987

Premises	£20,000	Owner's capital	£30,000
Furniture	5,050	Loan – Webber	4,000
Stock	9,500	Trade creditors	1,200
Bank	300		
Cash	350		
	£35,200		£35,200

(*f*)   3.00 p.m. Obtained a bank loan of £4,000 which was used immediately to repay Webber.

The liability of the loan due to Webber for £4,000 is replaced by a liability to the bank for the same amount.

Balance Sheet of Tom Rice as at 3 p.m. on 1 May 1987

Premises	£20,000	Owner's capital	£30,000
Furniture	5,050	Loan – bank	4,000
Stock	9,500	Trade creditors	1,200
Bank	300		
Cash	350		
	£35,200		£35,200

All of these transactions have one thing in common. Each one has **two** effects on the balance sheet. This concept is known as **duality** or the dual nature of a transaction. Because of it the balance sheet totals remained equal even though they sometimes changed in amount. We can summarise the effects of the above transactions in the form of a table:

Diagram 1.2 The effect of transactions on assets and liabilities

Transaction	Effects on assets	Effect on liabilities
(a)	+ –	No effect
(b)	+ –	No effect
(c)	+	+
(d)	+ –	No effect
(e)	–	–
(f)	No effect	+ –

A transaction that results in an increase in one asset and a decrease in another asset such as (a) leaves the balance sheet totals unchanged. Similarly a transaction that increases one liability and decreases another such as (f) leaves the balance sheet totals unchanged. When a transaction increases an asset and a liability at the same time as in (c) or decreases an asset and a liability as in (e) the balance sheet balances at different totals.

It is important that you are able to analyse the effects that transactions have on a balance sheet. Examination questions are often asked on this area and understanding it helps a great deal with a topic that we will be looking at shortly.

SELF-CHECK ▶
1.4

C. Legg started business on 1 April with £50,000 in the bank, all of which came from his own savings. Show his balance sheet on that date and then again after the following transactions have taken place. You do not need to use proper headings within your balance sheets.

2 April	Bought premises by cheque for £30,000.
3 April	Bought second-hand equipment for £3,000 and paid by cheque.
4 April	Purchased stock on credit from Wholesales Ltd for £5,000.
5 April	Sold £500 worth of the equipment for £500 cash.
6 April	Paid £2,000 by cheque to Wholesales Ltd.

SOLUTION ▶

Balance Sheet of C. Legg as at 1 April

Bank	£50,000	Capital	£50,000

Balance Sheet of C. Legg as at 2 April

Premises	£30,000	Capital	£50,000
Bank	20,000		
	£50,000		£50,000

Balance Sheet of C. Legg as at 3 April

Premises	£30,000	Capital	£50,000
Equipment	3,000		
Bank	17,000		
	£50,000		£50,000

Balance Sheet of C. Legg as at 4 April

Premises	£30,000	Capital	£50,000
Equipment	3,000	Trade creditor	5,000
Stock	5,000		
Bank	17,000		
	£55,000		£55,000

Balance Sheet of C. Legg as at 5 April

Premises	£30,000	Capital	£50,000
Equipment	2,500	Trade creditor	5,000
Stock	5,000		
Bank	17,000		
Cash	500		
	£55,000		£55,000

Balance Sheet of C. Legg as at 6 April

Premises	£30,000	Capital	£50,000
Equipment	2,500	Trade creditor	3,000
Stock	5,000		
Bank	15,000		
Cash	500		
	£53,000		£53,000

1.5 TRANSACTIONS AFFECTING CAPITAL

There are four types of transaction that will have an effect on an owner's capital and therefore on the balance sheet:

1 The owner of a business might increase his investment in the business by introducing additional assets from his private resources.

2 The owner might decrease his investment by withdrawing assets from the business and transferring them to his private use.

3 Making a profit will increase the value of the assets of a successful business. This profit belongs to the owner and is therefore added to the owner's capital.

4 Making a loss will decrease the value of the assets of an unsuccessful business. This loss has the opposite effect of reducing the owner's capital.

Let's see how each of these transactions affects the capital of T. Rowe.

Balance Sheet of T. Rowe as at 1 May 1987

Stock	£ 5,000	Capital	£15,000
Bank	12,000	Creditors	2,000
	£17,000		£17,000

1 2 May Rowe pays £2,000 into the business bank account from his private account. The asset bank will increase in value by £2,000 while the owner's investment has increased by this amount. Therefore the owner's capital is increased by this amount. We will call such an increase an **input** of capital.

Balance Sheet of T. Rowe as at 2 May 1987

Stock	£ 5,000	Capital	£17,000
Bank	14,000	Creditors	2,000
	£19,000		£19,000

2 3 May Rowe takes out £500 from the business to use outside the business (perhaps he wants to book a holiday and realises that he has left his private bank account too short of funds).

This will reduce the business bank balance by £500 and also reduce Rowe's capital by the same amount. **Drawings** is the name given to this kind of reduction of capital. It is short for withdrawal of capital.

Balance Sheet of T. Rowe as at 3 May 1987

Stock	£ 5,000	Capital	£16,500
Bank	13,500	Creditors	2,000
	£18,500		£18,500

Let's look now at the effect of profits and losses on the owner's capital. We will be looking at profits and losses in a lot more detail later. For the moment we will only consider the relatively straightforward situations when some of the stock of the business is sold for more than it is worth and a profit is made, or for less than it is worth when a loss is made.

3 4 May Rowe sold an item of stock worth £1,000 for £2,000 which was received by cheque. The asset stock will be reduced by £1,000 while another asset, bank, increases by £2,000. This means that the value of the assets will have increased by £1,000, the amount of the profit. This profit belongs to the owner and it is added to the owner's capital.

Balance Sheet of T. Rowe as at 4 May 1987

Stock	£ 4,000	Capital	£17,500
Bank	15,500	Creditors	2,000
	£19,500		£19,500

4   5 May Rowe sold an item of stock worth £700 on credit for £500. This time the asset stock is reduced by £700 while another asset, debtor, increases by only £500. Thus the value of the assets has reduced by £200, the amount of the loss. This loss also belongs to the owner and has the effect of reducing the value of his capital.

Balance Sheet of T. Rowe as at 5 May 1987

Stock	£ 3,300	Capital	£17,300
Debtor	500	Creditors	2,000
Bank	15,500		
	£19,300		£19,300

SELF-CHECK ▶
1.5

J. Harvey had £6,000 worth of stock and £1,000 in cash on 1 March 1988. He had no other assets and no liabilities. Draft a balance sheet to show his position on that date and then draft a balance sheet to show the effect of each of the following separate transactions.

2 March	Harvey withdrew £100 cash from the business for private use.
3 March	Sold £2,000 worth of stock for £3,000 cash.
4 March	Sold £3,000 worth of stock for £2,800 cash.
5 March	Harvey invested a premium bond win of £1,000 cash in the business.

SOLUTION ▶

Balance Sheet of J. Harvey as at 1 March 1988

Stock	£6,000	Capital	£7,000
Cash	1,000		
	£7,000		£7,000

Balance Sheet of J. Harvey as at 2 March 1988

Stock	£6,000	Capital	£6,900
Cash	900		
	£6,900		£6,900

Balance Sheet of J. Harvey as at 3 March 1988

Stock	£4,000	Capital	£7,900
Cash	3,900		
	£7,900		£7,900

Balance Sheet of J. Harvey as at 4 March 1988

Stock	£1,000	Capital	£7,700
Cash	6,700		
	£7,700		£7,700

Balance Sheet of J. Harvey as at 5 March 1988

Stock	£1,000	Capital	£8,700
Cash	7,700		
	£8,700		£8,700

1.6 CAPITAL STATEMENTS

We will now examine the way in which an owner's capital can change over a period of time. For example, we know from Smith's balance sheet in section 1.2 that the amount of finance he has invested in the business on December 31 1986 is £30,000. This situation might have been reached in a number of different ways. Here is one of them:

	£
1 Jan. 1984 Smith started business by investing his life savings	20,000
Year ended 31 Dec. 1984 Smith made a loss	5,000
Capital was reduced to	15,000
During the year ended 31 Dec. 1985	
Smith invested into the business a legacy he received	7,000
He also made a profit of	2,000
Capital was increased to	24,000
During the year ended 31 Dec. 1986	
Smith made a profit of	12,000
This would have increased his capital to	36,000
But in that year he also withdrew for his private use	6,000
Therefore at 31 Dec. 1986 Smith's capital stands at	30,000

From this it is possible to write an equation that summarises all the changes that can take place in an owner's capital:

> Initial capital (IC) − Losses (L) + Inputs (IN) + Profits (P) − Drawings (D) = Final capital (FC)

Initial capital is the capital at the start of any period of time.

Input is the investment by the owner of additional assets in the business.

Drawings are the withdrawal of assets from the business by the owner for his private use.

Profits from trading successfully result in an increase in the value of the assets of the business. As the business belongs to its owner such a profit increases the owner's capital.

Losses from trading unsuccessfully result in a decrease in the value of the assets of the business. As the business belongs to its owner such a loss decreases the owner's capital.

Final capital is the owner's capital at the end of any given period of time.

Thus a loss has the oposite effect to a profit and an input has the opposite effect to drawings.

►   Let's check the equation by using the information below:

	£
IC	20,000
−L	5,000
	15,000
+IN	7,000
	22,000
+P	14,000 (£2000+£12,000)
	36,000
−D	6,000
FC	30,000

It shows us that an owner's capital at the beginning of any period of time will be increased by making a profit or investing additional finance of his own into the business. It will be reduced by making a loss or withdrawing assets from the business for his private use. Understanding this equation will enable you to calculate any item that is missing from it provided that you have all the information about the other items. Usually the equation is needed to calculate an owner's capital at the end of a particular financial period, that is, his final capital.

SELF-CHECK ▶
1.6

Jean Bull started business on 1 January 1987 with owner's capital of £19,000. During the year that followed she earned profits of £8,000. Each month she withdrew £200 to assist her living expenses. In December she received £2,000 from the sale of some shares on the Stock Exchange and decided to invest this in her own business. Calculate her capital on 31 December 1987.

SOLUTION ▶

Capital on 31 December = £26,600.

COMMENT ▶

You may have been able to get this right by feeding the information into your calculator and pressing the right buttons for addition and subtraction. It is a good idea, however, to write down the process involved in obtaining the solution. This will help you to avoid careless errors. If you do still make a mistake, however, it will mean that the examiner marking your paper will be able to see that you did at least known *how* to answer the question. There are marks for correct method in nearly all examinations. These can only be earned if you show the examiner your method. Start your work from this book with the resolution that every exercise you complete will contain enough explanation to enable an examiner to award you marks for your method even if you make mistakes with the calculations. That's the end of the sermon on method but let's look at the way this solution might have been shown:

Initial capital £19,000 + Input £2,000 + Profits £8,000 − Drawings £2,400 = Final capital £26,600.

It is important to lay out the answer in a way that satisfies the question. The above question required you to calculate and this answer would be sufficient for the purpose. Suppose, however, you were required to draw up a statement to show the owner's final capital. Do not be put off by the term 'statement'. A statement is a numerical or verbal explanation. It requires a more formal answer than a mere calculation but if you are already in the habit of giving a brief explanation of your work then it should not cause you much bother. A statement should always contain a heading and it should be easy to read. Here is a possible answer to the above question if a statement had been requested.

Statement of Jean Bull's capital as at 31 December 1987

	£
Capital at 1 Jan. 1987	19,000
Add additional capital invested	2,000
	21,000
Add profits for 1987	8,000
	29,000
Less drawings during 1987	2,400
Capital at 31 Dec. 1987	26,600

This statement contains all the essentials of any statement that you will be asked to prepare during your course. The figures are labelled and each calculation made clear as to whether it is an addition or subtraction. There is a heading explaining exactly what the statement contains and the heading includes the important requirements of date and the name of the person or business.

1.7 VERTICAL BALANCE SHEETS

At the end of section 1.2 it was stated that it was possible to have different styles of layout for the balance sheet. The style we have used so far has been horizontal with assets to the left of the finance. The balance sheet has reflected the accounting equation:

Assets = Capital + Liabilities

It could be written in even more detail as:

Fixed assets   Capital
+ Current assets   =   + Long term liabilities
                        + Current liabilities

Look again at the balance sheet of John Tate retailer as at 31 May 1987 which is on page 18. This gives you a good picture of a balance sheet in the horizontal layout. Now look at the balance sheet opposite which uses the same figures to obtain a slightly different result.

Balance Sheet of John Tate, retailer, as at 31 May 1987

	£	£	£
Fixed assets			
Premises		40,000	
Furniture and fittings		7,000	
Equipment		2,600	
			49,600
Current assets			
Stock	6,000		
Debtors	850		
Bank	3,600		
Cash	900		
		11,350	
Less current liabilities			
Trade creditors		1,500	
Working capital			9,850
Total assets less current liabilities			59,450
Financed by:			
Long term liabilities			
Mortgage		20,000	
Owner's capital		39,450	
			59,450

This is an example of a vertical balance sheet. Compare it with the balance sheet on page 18 and see what differences you can spot. This is what you should have noticed:

1 Instead of the accounting equation being written horizontally across the page, it has been written down the page. The two totals are directly underneath each other instead of being side by side.

2 The totals are different. This is because the equation has been changed.

$$\begin{array}{rl} \text{Fixed assets} & \text{Capital} \\ + \text{ Current assets} = & + \text{ Long term liabilities} \\ & + \text{ Current liabilities} \end{array}$$

has become

$$\begin{array}{rl} \text{Fixed assets} & \text{Capital} \\ + \text{ Current assets} = & + \text{ Long term liabilities} \\ - \text{ Current liabilities} & \end{array}$$

34   **Accounting**

Remember it is possible to change any item in an equation to the other side of the equation provided you remember to change the sign of the item that is changed. Thus when + current liabilities moves to the other side of the equation it becomes − current liabilities.

3   There is a new item within the balance sheet. The sub total for current assets less current liabilities is here labelled working capital. It is also sometimes known as net current assets because that is what the current assets are worth net when any outstanding current liabilities are settled.

You are probably already wondering why it is necessary to have more than one style of balance sheet layout. The answer to that is that we are currently in a state of transition from the horizontal style which predominated for many years to the vertical style which, though of more recent origin, has become more popular. You will therefore meet both types of layout and must be able to understand them. There are, indeed, variations on both the horizontal and vertical layouts. However, if you can understand those shown here then you should not have too much difficulty with any slight variations. The most likely of these variations you will find involves the horizontal balance sheet. Until comparatively recently many of these were written with the assets to the right of the finance. This makes no difference to the equation that it represents as you should realise and the information it provides is exactly the same. To prove it here is the balance sheet of Tate once again:

Balance Sheet of John Tate, retailer, as at 31 May 1987

	£		£	
Owner's capital	39,450	Fixed assets		
Long term liabilities		Premises	40,000	
Mortgage	20,000	Furn & fittings	7,000	
Current liabilities		Equipment	2,600	
				49,600
Trade creditors	1,500			
		Current assets		
		Stock	6,000	
		Debtors	850	
		Bank	3,600	
		Cash	900	
				11,350
	60,950			60,950

If you come across a balance sheet written like this it is not incorrect. It is the way that horizontal balance sheets have been written for many years. Although it is likely that newer textbooks will use a vertical layout or a horizontal layout with assets to the left of the liabilities this does not necessarily make the older books wrong.

VERTICAL OR HORIZONTAL LAYOUTS?

Which type of layout should you adopt in your coursework and examination? As far as coursework is concerned you will obviously be guided by your teacher or lecturer. In examinations too sometimes guidance is given. For example, a question might tell you to prepare a balance sheet in vertical style. Here there is no problem deciding what is required. It might, however, be a little less direct and tell you to prepare a balance sheet which shows the total of working capital. This, of course, is an indirect way of telling you to use vertical layout since, as we have seen, only this layout includes a figure within the balance sheet for working capital or current assets less current liabilities. Often, however, no instructions are given as to the method you should use. The advice I would give you is the same as I give my own students. As the vertical layout has become the preferred layout in the accountancy profession then it is better to opt for that format. You will get lots of practice at preparing balance sheets in this book and this is a good place to start.

SELF-CHECK ▶
1.7

From the following information prepare a vertical balance sheet of Peter Dark as at 31 January 1988.

Owner's capital £42,530, premises £40,000, stock £6,800, debtors £1,900, trade creditors £2,350, cash £180, furniture and fittings £3,000, delivery vehicle £2,000, mortgage £5,000, bank overdraft £1,000, loan ABC Finance (3 years) £3,000.

SOLUTION ▶

Balance Sheet of Peter Dark as at 31 January 1988

	£	£	£
Fixed assets			
Premises		40,000	
Furniture and fittings		3,000	
Delivery vehicle		2,000	
			45,000
Current assets			
Stock	6,800		
Debtors	1,900		
Cash	180		
		8,880	

Current liabilities

Trade creditors	2,350	
Bank overdraft	1,000	
	———	
		3,350
		———
Working capital		5,330
		———
Total assets less current liabilities		50,530
		———

Financed by:

Long term liabilities

Mortgage	5,000	
Loan – ABC Finance	3,000	
	———	
		8,000
Capital		42,530
		———
		50,530
		———

COMMENT ▶

It takes a little while to learn how to use the columns to get the clearest layout and practice will make perfect. It is useful to think in terms of the final column containing only the sub-totals for fixed assets, working capital, long term liabilities and owner's capital. The final column is thus a clear representation of the equation:

$$\text{Fixed assets} + \text{Working capital} = \text{Long term liabilities} + \text{Capital}$$

The other columns can then be used to calculate the figures needed to appear in the final column.

The individual items that might have caused you greatest problems were the ones involving the liabilities. A bank overdraft is always regarded as a current liability because it is recallable by the bank at very short notice. The loan from ABC Finance is long term because any loan longer than one year is regarded as long term and this is stated to be a three year loan. A mortgage is a long term loan usually secured on the premises of the business. It is possible, of course, that the mortgage is due for repayment within the next few months but this is not very likely when the length of many mortgages runs into many years. When no time period is specified it is best therefore to regard it as a long term liability.

1.1 Complete the following table:

	Assets	Capital	Liabilities
	£	£	£
(a)	14,560		3,850
(b)		12,670	16,950
(c)	42,875		16,688
(d)	45,960	16,790	
(e)	26,466		39,506

1.2 Judy Smith, a restaurant owner, had the following assets and sources of finance on 1 May 1988: Cash £950, premises £50,000, bank loan (5 years) £15,000, furniture and fittings £8,000, debtors £150, trade creditors £750, stock £3,000, bank £6,600, equipment £3,600.
(a) Calculate the owner's capital.
(b) prepare a balance sheet in good style using
(i) horizontal layout
(ii) vertical layout.

1.3 G. Wiggs started business on 1 June with £10,000 in the bank, all of which came from his own savings. Show his balance sheet on that date and then again after the following transactions have taken place.

2 June — Bought equipment by cheque for £3,000.
3 June — Bought second-hand fittings for £1,000 and paid by cheque.
4 June — Purchased stock on credit from Wholesales Ltd. for £6,000.
5 June — Sold £600 worth of the fittings for £600 cash.
6 June — Paid £2,000 by cheque to Wholesales Ltd.

1.4 S. Davis had £7,000 worth of stock and £2,000 in cash on 1 March 1988. He had no other assets and no liabilities. Draft a balance sheet to show his position on that date and then draft a balance sheet to show the effect of each of the following separate transactions.

2 March — Davis withdrew £500 cash from the business for private use.

3 March	Sold £3,000 worth of stock for £5,000 cash.
4 March	Sold £4,000 worth of stock for £3,800 cash.
5 March	Davis invested a legacy of £2,500 cash in the business.

1.5 Eric Evans started business on 1 January 1988 with owner's capital of £25,000. During the year that followed he earned profits of £16,000. Each month he withdrew £350 to assist his living expenses. In August he won £12,000 on the football pools and decided to invest £8,000 of this in the business. Prepare a statement to show his capital on 31 December 1988.

1.6 From the following information calculate the owner's capital and prepare a vertical balance sheet of Jean Peters as at 31 May 1988: Premises £50,000, stock £7,850, debtors £1,950, trade creditors £4,355, cash £286, furniture and fittings £6,500, equipment £3,500, bank overdraft £2,100, finance company loan (2 years) £8,000.

1.7 Balance Sheet of A. Tree as at 30 June 1984

	£	£
Fixed assets		50,000
Current assets	30,000	
less current liabilities	20,000	
W.C.		10,000
		60,000
Financed by:		
Capital		60,000

What is the amount of the working capital in the above balance sheet?
(NISEC Specimen Paper)

MEASURING PROFIT

CONTENTS

2.1 MAKING A PROFIT

There are a large number of different types of business in the UK and there are several different ways of classifying them. For example, businesses may be classified according to how they are owned. Sole traders, partnerships, limited companies, public limited companies, and co-operatives are types of businesses in the private sector of the economy. This means that they are owned by private individuals or, in the case of sole traders, one private individual. Public corporations or nationalised industries are types of businesses in the public sector of the economy. This means that they are owned by the state. In *GCSE Accounting* we only have to deal with the accounts of firms in the private sector.

The variety of businesses within the private sector is even more evident when you consider the many different goods they produce and services they provide. Some employ thousands of workers while others employ none – the owner or owners doing all the work themselves. Some use assets costing millions of pounds while others require assets which cost much less. Despite this variety there are some features which unite them all.

One is that they are all seeking to survive in a competitive environment. There are very few monopolies in the private sector that do not have to concern themselves about what their competitors are doing. In order to survive businesses need to make a profit. The objective of making a profit is thus a key concern of the management of all businesses. Measuring this profit is an important part of the role of the accountant.

SELF-CHECK ▶
2.1

(a)   List four types of business which exist in the private sector.
(b)   Name one feature common to them all.

SOLUTION ▶

(a)   Sole traders, partnerships, limited companies, public limited companies, and co-operatives.
(b)   Making a profit is the answer relevant to this section though, of course, there are others, e.g. survival.

2.2 CALCULATING PROFIT

Although the word 'profit' has been used quite a few times already in this book (and it will be used even more from now on) we have not yet tried to say exactly what the word means. We will start with a simple definition.

▶ The profit of a business is the difference between the total revenue or income earned and the total expenses paid during a period of time.

We will examine this definition in a little more detail:

The **period of time** over which profit is measured is usually a year because the tax authorities demand that kind of information on an annual basis. However, there is nothing to prevent the profit of a business being calculated monthly, weekly, or even daily if it is thought worthwhile. Sometimes it may even be thought useful to know the profit on a single transaction.

Calculating the **difference between revenue earned and expenses paid** should not cause any problem. It must be recognised that the revenue earned may sometimes be less than the expenses paid. In this case a loss has been made. Thus:

	£		£
Revenue	10,000	Revenue	20,000
Less Expenses	4,000	*Less* Expenses	25,000
Profit	6,000	Loss	5,000

The important thing is the relationship between the revenue and the expenses. A high revenue will not necessarily mean a high profit, or indeed any profit at all, as can be seen from the above examples.

The problem with calculating the profit lies with deciding what figures to use for revenue and expenses. It is not as simple as it might seem. All money coming into a business is not revenue. Neither is all money flowing out of the business expenses. To know what counts as revenue and expenses it is necessary to distinguish between capital and revenue expenditure; and also between capital and revenue receipts.

SELF-CHECK ▶   Learn the definition of profit and test yourself.
2.2

2.3 CAPITAL AND REVENUE EXPENDITURE

Capital expenditure is the purchase of assets which are intended to be used over a relatively long period of time, i.e. fixed assets. Common examples are premises, machinery, furniture and fittings, equipment and motor vehicles. They will be used by the business to help make a profit over a number of years. Some may last longer than others. For example you would expect premises to be of use to the business for longer than a motor van. What matters is that these assets are purchased not with the intention of making a profit on them but to assist with the profit making activities of the firm. Anything a business buys which is to be used for longer than a year can usually be classified as a fixed asset and therefore is regarded as capital expenditure.

Profit is generally measured over one year time intervals. Clearly it would not be fair to take the cost of buying an asset that is going to last longer than a year (usually many years) from the earnings of only one year. Thus we exclude capital expenditure from our profit calculation.

Revenue expenditure is the spending which relates to benefits which are not intended to last for longer than one year. Expenditure on all items except the purchase of fixed assets can therefore be regarded as revenue expenditure. We have only come across one item in this book so far that could be correctly termed revenue expenditure and that is the purchase of stock. The term stock is used to describe items owned by a business that it intends to resell. Buying and selling stock is a short term rather than a long term activity and in our balance sheets we have classified stock as a current asset. It would be quite correct, therefore, to include any spending on stock in our calculations of profit.

There are many transactions that a business is involved in that do not involve the purchase of an asset. All businesses that own property will have to pay rates to their local council in return for the services they receive such as refuse collection, street lighting and road repair. They will pay insurance premiums in order to insure their motor vehicles in case of accident. They will pay wages to their employees in return for their labour. If they borrow money from a bank then they will have to pay interest on the loan. All these transactions involve the benefit of a service for which the business has to pay. The benefit is immediate or short term and they are counted as revenue expenditure. There are many more but the extra ones you will meet most often are:

▶ Rent, advertising, transport, fuel, telephone, postage, lighting, heating.

SELF-CHECK ▶
2.3

Ron Yates owns a garage. Some of his items of expenditure are listed overleaf. Complete the table by putting a tick in those columns that are relevant to each item.

Expenditure		Capital	Revenue	Used in measuring profit
		£	£	£
(a)	Purchase of petrol for resale		✓	✓
(b)	Purchaser of car for resale		✓	✓
(c)	Purchase of new ramp	✓		
(d)	Purchase of till	✓		
(e)	Advertising		✓	✓
(f)	Rates		✓	✓
(g)	Purchase of breakdown vehicle	✓		
(h)	Repairs to garage roof		✓	✓

SOLUTION ▶

You should have ticked both revenue and profit columns for (a), (b), (e), (f) and (h) because all items of revenue expenditure affect the calculation of profit. None of these involve the purchase of a fixed asset to last for a long period. The petrol and car will be sold as quickly as possible in order to make a profit. These items form part of the stock of the business while they are still on sale. Advertising and rates are paid to enjoy benefits over a short period of time. Item (h) is the one that may have given most difficulty because it does involve a fixed asset, i.e. the premises. Repairs are undertaken when an asset is damaged and has to be restored to its value before the damage took place. It does not involve the purchase of a fixed asset and is therefore regarded as revenue expenditure.

Items (c), (d) and (g) are items of capital expenditure and therefore only the capital column should have been ticked. The purchase of the till and ramp are clearly long term fixed assets but the breakdown vehicle may have given you more cause for thought. The breakdown vehicle is a good illustration of the fact that it is the intended use of an asset that matters when it comes to classifying it as stock or fixed asset. Garages use breakdown vehicles to enable them to tow in cars that cannot be driven. The intention is not usually to sell them to make a profit. Thus such an asset would be regarded as a fixed asset designed for relatively long term use in the business.

COMMENT ▶

It should now be clear that all items of revenue expenditure have a direct effect on the calculation of profit. It is those items that we will fit into our equation:

Total revenue less total expenses = Profit

You must not think that the capital expenditure has no effect on profit. The quality and quantity of the fixed assets used in a business will obviously affect the ability of any business to make a profit. For example a garage without the necessary equipment to meet the Department of Transport requirements will not be able to carry out

MoT tests and will thus lose a valuable source of custom. The effect on profits is of a long term nature lasting as long as the fixed assets themselves. It would not be right to take the cost of a fixed asset purchased for, say, £10,000 which will last ten years from one year's earnings to find the profit made in that year.

DEPRECIATION

There is a way to spread the cost of a fixed asset over its working life to ensure that a portion of the cost is counted in calculating profit each year that the fixed asset is being used. This is known as **depreciation** which can be defined as the process by which a fixed asset declines in value over its life. At this stage it is only necessary to know what the term depreciation means and to recognise that it is a way of ensuring that a fair amount of the cost of the fixed asset appears in the calculation of profit each year it is being used. For example depreciation on the fixed asset that cost £10,000 and which was thought likely to last ten years could be calculated as £1,000 per annum and this amount counted each year against the earnings of that year to find the profit. Depreciation will be dealt with in much more detail later. For the time being it is sufficient that you recognise depreciation as revenue expenditure and that it counts in the calculation of profit.

Although fixed assets are usually purchased with the intention of using them over a fairly long time period, the time will come when some of them are sold. They will then require consideration in the profits equation. For example, a fixed asset valued at £1,000 by the business may be sold for only £800. A loss of £200 has been incurred in selling the asset. In other words the asset has depreciated in value by £200 more than we thought. This loss should be counted in calculating expenses.

2.4 CAPITAL AND REVENUE RECEIPTS

A capital receipt is finance invested in the business either by the owner or an outside person. It the owner has invested the money from his own private resources we call it an input of capital. If an outside person or organisation is responsible then the liabilities of the business are increased because the money has to be repaid one day. Suppose Ron Yates decided to invest a further £10,000 of his own money in the business and paid this amount into the business bank account in 1988. Would it be fair to include this amount to calculate profit for that year? Clearly not, as the business is not earning any revenue but is being given extra finance to use. The same would be true if the £10,000 invested was from a loan by the bank.

The only receipt that should count in calculating profit is a **revenue receipt** which is also known as a receipt of income. Revenue or income is money received from the normal profit making activities of the firm. In a business that sells goods the value of its sales will be the major item of revenue. Other businesses such as lawyers or estate agents receive fees for their services rendered. Whatever the business, it is also possible that some additional income may be received in addition to what is normally received from trading. For example, the owner of a café may receive rent for letting out the flat above the café. Such additional income will usually be relatively small when compared to the income from the normal activities of the business.

Just as the sale of a fixed asset at a loss requires the loss to be counted as revenue expenditure so the sale of a fixed asset at a profit requires this profit to be counted as revenue received. For example, a fixed asset valued by a business at £1,000 might fetch £1,300 when sold. The profit on sale of £300 would be added to the revenue receipts. In effect the depreciation taken from the value of the asset over its working life has been found to be £300 too much and this is now being allowed for.

**SELF-CHECK ▶
2.4(a)**

First write down the definition of profit that we adopted in 2.2. Try to do it without looking back if you can. Then say whether each of the following statements is true or false.

1 Both capital and revenue expenditure must be included in the calculation of a firm's profit.
2 Neither receipts of capital nor receipts of income should be included in the calculation of a firm's profit.
3 The purchase of a delivery vehicle by a retail shop is an example of capital expenditure.
4 Wages paid to employees are examples of revenue expenditure.
5 Repairs to damaged equipment are an example of capital expenditure.
6 A win on the football pools by the owner of a business that is then invested in the business is an example of a revenue receipt.
7 The sale of a meal by a café owner results in the receipt of revenue.
8 Profit or loss on the sale of a fixed asset should count in calculating profit.

SOLUTION ▶

Statements 3, 4, 7 and 8 are true; 1 is false because although revenue expenditure is included capital expenditure is not; 2 is false because, while receipts of income are included, capital receipts are not; 5 is false because it is assumed that repairs merely restore an asset to its value before it was damaged – there is thus no increase in the value of the asset; 6 is false because this is an example of a capital receipt.

COMMENT ▶

Writing down the definition should have helped you to decide whether the statements were true or false. Let's re-write it now.
▶ The profit of a business is the difference between the total revenue earned and the total expenses paid during a period of time.

What has been emphasised in the last few sections is what should count as revenue earned and expenses paid. Capital items should not be included.

We can now simplify our profit equation to read:

▶ Revenue receipts less revenue expenditure = profit for that period.

SELF-CHECK ▶
2.4(b)

The following information refers to the restaurant of Liz Fry for the year ended 31 December 1988:

	£
Sales revenue	50,000
Cost of food and drinks sold	12,000
Purchase of equipment	2,000
Insurance	500
Rent and rates	5,600
Gas and electricity	2,900
Employees' wages	11,000
Depreciation on fixed assets	1,600
Loan from bank	4,000
Advertising	300
Telephone expenses	200
Drawings	5,000
Postage	100

Select the items that you need and then prepare a statement to show her profit for the year.

SOLUTION ▶ Statement of Liz Fry's profit for the year ended 31 December 1988

	£	£
Revenue receipts:		
Sales of food and drinks		50,000
Revenue expenditure:		
Cost of food and drinks sold	12,000	
Insurance	500	
Rent and rates	5,600	
Gas and electricity	2,900	
Employees' wages	11,000	
Depreciation	1,600	
Advertising	300	
Telephone expenses	200	
Postage	100	
		34,200
Profit		15,800

COMMENT ▶ Did you remember to follow the procedure suggested in Self check 1.6 for preparing a statement? The items used in the above statement all have one thing in common. They are all **revenue** items. The items *not* used are all **capital** items. The purchase of equipment for this kind of business is a fixed asset which will last for a number of years and thus should not be written off against one year's profits. However, the depreciation on the fixed assets may include some depreciation on this new equipment and this is correctly inserted in the statement. The loan from the bank is not included because that is the receipt of capital into the business from an outside source. Even if the owner himself had put extra finance into the business during the year we would not have counted it. Drawings by the owner are excluded for the same reason. Including drawings is a very common mistake and it is a good one to have made now – provided that you do not make it again!

▶ A reminder: drawings is a reduction of owner's capital not a reduction of profit.

It is perfectly possible for an owner to withdraw assets from the business even if no profit has been made. It is the owner's business after all. Of course if she continued to do so for any length of time there would be few assets left and eventually no business.

2.5 THE DUAL NATURE OF TRANSACTIONS INVOLVING REVENUE AND EXPENSES

In chapter one it was pointed out that all transactions involving assets and liabilities have two effects on the balance sheet. After any transaction a new balance sheet can be prepared and it will still balance – the assets must always equal the sources of finance.

Transactions involving revenue expenditure and revenue receipts also have two effects on the business. For example, the benefit of an employee's labour is received in return for the payment of wages and the benefit of street lighting is received in return for the payment of rates. The same is true of transactions involving the receipt of revenue. Rent is received by a property owner in return for allowing someone else the use of part of the property, e.g. a flat above a restaurant.

The dual nature of these transactions can be shown in a balance sheet. Here is a summary of the position of J. Toms' business on 1 May.

Balance Sheet of J. Toms as at 1 May

Total fixed assets	£30,000	Capital	£29,000
Stock	1,000	Creditors	2,900
Bank	900		
	31,900		31,900

2 May   Toms pays £100 by cheque for an advertisement in the local newspaper.

One effect of this transaction is that the money in Toms' bank account will go down by £100. The second effect may not be quite so obvious. The effect is on the owner's capital. Taken by itself, no revenue has been received but a revenue expenditure of £100 has been paid. Because Revenue less Revenue expenditure = Profit, this transaction means that a loss of £100 has been made:

	£
Revenue	000
less Revenue expenditure	100
Loss	100

Profits are to the owner's advantage while losses are a disadvantage. We have already seen in section 1.5 that profits result in an increase in owner's capital while losses cause it to fall. In this case therefore owner's capital is reduced by £100.

Balance Sheet of J. Toms as at 2 May

Total fixed assets	£30,000	Capital	£28,900
Stock	1,000	Creditors	2,900
Bank	800		
	£31,800		£31,800

3 May   Toms' receives £50 rent by cheque for allowing a neighbouring business to use a garage that he does not require.

Again the first of the two effects is fairly straightforward. The asset bank will rise by £50. This time the second effect will probably not cause you to think quite so hard. Receiving a revenue without incurring any other expenses that day will mean he will have made a profit of £50. This profit will cause the owner's capital to increase by £50.

Balance Sheet of J. Toms as at 3 May

Total fixed assets	£30,000	Capital	£28,950
Stock	1,000	Creditors	2,900
Bank	850		
	£31,850		£31,850

In the real world of business, transactions like the ones above will be taking place frequently. Businessmen will therefore not normally look at any one such transaction in isolation from others. What will concern them is that after a period of time all the transactions taken together result in an overall profit rather than a loss and that this profit should be as good as they can achieve. These separate transactions have been examined in isolation from others solely to emphasise the dual nature of transactions involving revenue and revenue expenditure.

SELF-CHECK ▶ 2.5

The following information relates to the assets and liabilities of G. Patel, a retailer, on 1 April 1988:
Premises £20,000; equipment £1,575; motor vehicle £2,000; stock £5,450; bank £4,985; trade debtors £1,256; trade creditors £650; expense creditors £254; loan (5 years) £5,000.
During April the following transactions took place:

(a)   Stock costing £1,000 was bought on credit.
(b)   Stock which cost £700 was sold for £1,200 on credit.
(c)   Expenses of £250 were incurred and have not yet been paid.
(d)   The motor vehicle was sold for £1,750, received by cheque.
(e)   £100, one month's interest on the loan, was paid by cheque.
(f)   Patel repaid £500 of the loan by cheque.
Draw up Patel's balance sheet on 30 April, taking into consideration all the above information.

SOLUTION ▶ Balance sheet of G. Patel as at 30 April 1988

	£	£	£
Fixed assets			
Premises		20,000	
Equipment		1,575	
			21,575
Current assets			
Stock		5,750	
Debtors		2,456	
Bank		6,135	
		14,341	
Less current liabilities			
Trade creditors	1,650		
Expense creditors	504		
		2,154	
Working capital			12,187
Total assets less current liabilities			33,762
Financed by:			
Owner's capital			29,262
Long term liabilities			
Loan (5 years)			4,500
			33,762

COMMENT ▶ There are various ways of tackling this question. For safety and to illustrate clearly the dual nature of transactions it is probably a good idea to start by drafting in rough the balance sheet as it would have appeared on 1 April. To do that you need to calculate the capital using the book-keeping equation. (Capital is often left for candidates to find so look out for this.) You should discover that the opening capital is £29,362.

Then you can analyse each transaction making certain that you cover all the effects and incorporate the changes into a well presented balance sheet like the one above.

(a)   Stock +£1,000; Trade creditors +£1,000.
(b)   Stock −£700; Debtors +£1,200; Capital +£500 (profit).
(c)   Expense creditors +£250; Capital −£250 (loss).
(d)   Motor vehicle −£2,000; bank +£1,750; Capital −£250 (loss).
(e)   Bank −£100; Capital −£100 (loss).
(f)   Bank −£500; Loan −£500.

It is worth emphasising that complicated transactions sometimes have more than two effects but when the effects are put together the result is two net effects. For example in (b) the assets increase by £500 which is the same as the increase in the capital. It is important to recognise the difference between repaying a loan (or part of it) and paying interest on the loan. Interest is paid in return for the use of the money lent; it is revenue expenditure which affects the owner's capital through its effect on profits and losses. Repayment of a loan directly affects the loan item in the balance sheet by reducing it. If you handled this self-check satisfactorily you might like to consider other possible ways of tackling it. Remember, though, you must show your workings!

EXERCISES

2.1   Jill Berry owns a shop. Some of her items of expenditure are listed below. Complete the table by putting a tick in those columns that are relevant to each item.

Expenditure		Capital	Revenue	Used in measuring profit
		£	£	£
(a)	Purchase of stock for resale		✓	✓
(b)	Purchase of van for deliveries	✓		
(c)	Rent		✓	✓
(d)	Purchase of new till	✓		✓
(e)	Advertising		✓	✓
(f)	Purchase of new display cabinet	✓		
(g)	Staff wages		✓	✓
(h)	Repairs to broken window		✓	✓

2.2
State whether the following items are capital receipts or revenue receipts:
(a) Owner borrows £5,000 from the bank.
(b) Cash sales for the day £400.
(c) Owner invests a premium bond win of £1,000 in the business.
(d) £10 rent received for subletting garage.

2.3
The following information refers to the business of Jane Tozer for the year ended 31 December 1988:

	£
Sales revenue	70,000
Cost of stock sold	22,050
Purchase of fixed assets	6,000
Rent and rates	6,665
Heating and lighting	3,250
Wages and salaries	16,000
Depreciation on fixed assets	3,460
Loan from bank	4,000
Advertising	300
Telephone expenses	366
Drawings	9,000
Repairs to premises	1,250

Select the items that you need and then prepare a statement showing the profit or loss for the year.

2.4
Abdul Majid trades as a retailer. The following information is known about his assets and liabilities on 1 January 1986.
Premises £10,000; motor vehicle £1,500; stock £2,140; cash or bank £300; trade debtors £850; trade creditors £200; expenses creditors £40; loan (final repayment due 1990) £1,000.
During January the following transactions took place:
(a) Stock costing £800 was bought on credit.
(b) Stock which cost £600 was sold for £900 on credit.
(c) £650 was received from debtors and paid into the bank account.
(d) The motor vehicle was sold for £1,250, payment being by cheque.
(e) The annual repayment instalment due on the loan was made, reducing the outstanding debt to £800.
(f) Expenses of £360 were incurred and are still outstanding.

QUESTIONS

1 Draw up Abdul Majid's balance sheet at 31 January 1986, taking into account all the above information.
2 Using the list given above identify
   (*a*)   one fixed asset.
   (*b*)   one current asset and explain how they differ.
3 How is working capital calculated?
4 What is the amount of Majid's working capital at 1 January 1986?

(MEG specimen paper)

2.5

Harry Jones has recently commenced business as a garage owner, selling petrol and dealing in new and second-hand cars. He purchases the following during the first month's trading. Indicate by placing a tick in the columns provided whether the items are Capital or Revenue expenditure.

Item		Capital	Revenue
(*a*)	Garage building and showroom	✓	
(*b*)	Petrol pumps (leased)	✓	
(*c*)	New cars for sale	✓	✓
(*d*)	Breakdown lorry	✓	
(*e*)	50,000 litres of petrol		✓
(*f*)	Salaries of staff		✓
(*g*)	One car for salesman	✓	
(*h*)	Spare parts for salesman's car		✓

(WJEC specimen paper)

DOUBLE ENTRY
BOOK-KEEPING

CONTENTS

3.1 THE LEDGER

In the first two chapters a new balance sheet was drafted after each transaction to emphasise the principle of duality. This would not be a practical way of recording large numbers of transactions so a simpler and more convenient method is needed. One such method is provided by the double entry system of book-keeping and it is used by many businesses, especially the larger ones.

The main book used to record transactions is called the ledger. At one time all ledgers were books in the form of bound volumes. Although these are still used by some businesses today many firms now use loose-leaf ledger paper or ledger cards and an increasing number are turning to computer-based systems. Whatever the means of recording transactions the principles are basically the same. We are going to concentrate on understanding the principles involved by considering ledgers kept by manual means. More will be said about computers later.

ACCOUNTS

The ledger contains records of transactions in the form of accounts. The word 'account' is usually abbreviated to 'a/c' and means 'a record of'. Each asset, source of finance, expense and revenue will usually have its own account. The layout of a traditional ledger account looks like this:

5

Dr							Cash account			Cr
Date	Details		Folio	£	p	Date	Details		Folio	£ p

Note

▶ Each page in the ledger is divided clearly into two sides.

▶ The left-hand side is known as the debit side but is usually abbreviated to 'Dr'. The right-hand side of the account is known as the credit side and is abbreviated to Cr. The word 'credit' has different meanings in other contexts. When referring to ledger accounts, though, it simply means the right-hand side of the account.

▶ The name of the account is written at the top of the page, which is numbered for reference purposes. The cash account above is on page 5 of the ledger. Some accounts will require more pages than others. A loose-leaf system will provide useful flexibility in such circumstances. The columns on the debit side are the same as on the credit side. There is space to record the date, brief details and the amount of money involved in a transaction. The folio column is used mainly to provide a cross reference system. This will be demonstrated later. You may be given ledger paper by your teacher or you may have to draw your own. If you have not seen ledger paper you should be able to find some in most good stationers.

SELF-CHECK ▶
3.1

A businessman keeps a record of his stock on page 23 of his ledger. Without looking at the above example, draw an outline for this account and label the columns.

SOLUTION ▶

Apart from the name (stock account) and the page number (23), your outline should be the same as the outline of the cash account. It is especially important that you get in the habit of labelling the left-hand side of the account 'Dr' and the right-hand side of the account 'Cr'.

COMMENT ▶

The word debit is often used to mean disadvantage while credit is used to mean advantage. For example, politicians may often be heard outlining the pros and cons of a particular policy by saying '. . . on the credit side . . . while on the debit side . . .'. It is very important that in accounting we avoid any possible confusion of terms. You should not think that debit is necessarily a disadvantage nor that credit is an advantage. In accounting it is much better to think of debit as simply meaning the left-hand side of a ledger account while credit means the right-hand side.

We will now turn to the principles involved in keeping a ledger. In this book I have used the balance sheet to explain the effects of a number of different transactions on the business. This approach is known as the balance sheet approach and it will be used to demonstrate how to keep a ledger.

3.2 ASSETS AND SOURCES OF FINANCE

Tom Jolly has just started his own retailing business and he has decided to use a ledger system to record his transactions. One way of beginning is to write down the state of his business on the day that he decides to start his ledger. The easiest way to show this clearly is by means of a balance sheet.

Balance Sheet of Tom Jolly as at 1 July 1988

Assets	£	Sources of finance	£
Premises	35,000	Owner's capital	32,000
Furniture and fittings	4,000		
Stock	3,000	Liabilities	
Bank	900	Loan – Busifinance Ltd	12,000
Cash	1,100		
	44,000		44,000

The next step is to open an account for each item in the balance sheet. The value of each asset is placed on the debit side of its own account while the value of each source of finance is placed on the credit side of its account. The date will be that of the balance sheet from which the figures have been taken and in the details column each entry will be described by the term 'balance'. For the time being we will not bother giving each account a page number as the folio column for cross referencing will be dealt with later in Chapter 10. Apart from the fact that they would not be condensed on one page the ledger accounts will then appear as below. For convenience we are not going to use the pence column for the time being.

Dr				Cr
		Premises a/c		
1988				
1 July	Balance	35,000		
		Furniture and fittings a/c		
1 July	Balance	4,000		
		Stock a/c		
1 July	Balance	3,000		
		Bank a/c		
1 July	Balance	900		

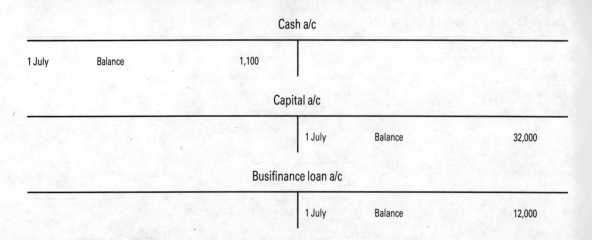

Cash a/c

1 July	Balance	1,100			

Capital a/c

			1 July	Balance	32,000

Busifinance loan a/c

			1 July	Balance	12,000

SELF-CHECK ▶
3.2

What is the relationship between the total value of debit balances and credit balances in Tom Jolly's ledger on 1 July?

SOLUTION ▶

The debit balances **equal** the credit balances. You probably said this without needing to add them up. If the total assets are equal to the total sources of finance then the debit balances (assets) must equal the credit balances (capital and liabilities).

COMMENT ▶

As we used a horizontal balance sheet to state the position of Tom Jolly's business on 1 July it probably seemed quite natural to enter the assets on the left-hand side of their accounts while sources of finance are entered on the right-hand side of their accounts. Do not let this lead you into the conclusion that a balance sheet is a kind of ledger account. It most certainly is not! As stated elsewhere, a **balance sheet** is a statement of the assets and sources of finance of a business at a particular date. A **ledger account** is an individual record of transactions affecting one aspect of the business.

If you have not encountered horizontal balance sheets of the type preferred (with assets on the left and finance on the right) you are more likely to find opening ledger accounts a little confusing. You will be used to seeing the assets on the right of the balance sheet and sources of finance on the left. You must not let this affect where you put the opening balances for assets and finance. In the ledger all opening entries for assets **must** be shown on the debit side of their own account while the opening entries for sources of finance **must** be shown on the credit side of their accounts. This rule must always be followed though, as we have seen, the balance sheet may be correctly written in a number of different ways.

The fundamental rules of book-keeping will now be introduced. It is absolutely essential that you master these rules as all of the GCSE syllabuses require very good knowledge of them.

3.3 ENTERING TRANSACTIONS FOR ASSETS AND FINANCE

An asset is represented in its own account by a debit balance. If something happens to increase the value of this asset we show it by making another debit entry. If the asset is reduced in value a credit entry is made in that account.

Example

We know that on 1 July Tom Jolly possessed furniture and fittings worth £4,000. Suppose that on 2 July he purchased some new shop fittings for £1,000 by cash and on 3 July sold some of his old fittings at their book value of £200 and received cash. **Book value** means their value according to his books. In other words, he did not make a profit or loss on the sale. Let's analyse these transactions in terms of the effect they will have on Tom's balance sheet.

▶ On 2 July furniture and fittings will increase in value by £1,000 while the asset cash will decrease in value by the same amount.

▶ On 3 July furniture and fittings will decrease in value by £200 while the asset cash increases in value by the same amount.

This should serve to remind you once again of the important fact that any transaction will affect the balance sheet twice. This dual aspect is shown in the ledger by making two entries for each transaction – one for each item affected. There will be a debit entry in one account and a corresponding credit entry in another account. **Double entry book-keeping** is the term used to describe this method of making entries in the ledger.

After the entries have been made to record the above transactions the furniture and fittings account and the cash account will look like this:

Furniture and fittings a/c

| 1 July | Balance | 4,000 | 3 July | Cash | 200 |
| 2 July | Cash | 1,000 | | | |

Cash a/c

| 1 July | Balance | 1,100 | 2 July | Furn. & fittings | 1,000 |
| 3 July | Furn. & fittings | 200 | | | |

The £1,000 worth of new fittings has been entered on the debit side of the account for furniture and fittings because this asset has increased in value by that amount on 2 July. At the same time a credit entry of £1,000 has been made in the cash account because this asset has fallen in value by that amount. The £200 worth of old fittings sold are entered on the credit side of the furniture and fittings account because this asset has decreased in value by that amount on 3 July. At the same time a debit entry has been made in the cash account because this asset has increased by that amount.

The description for each transaction is simply the name of the *other* ledger account involved. Thus, in the furniture and fittings account you would not find the description 'furniture and fittings' in the details column.

Sources of finance, whether liabilities or capital, are shown in their own accounts by credit balances. If something happens to increase the value of one of these we show it by making another credit entry. If the source of finance is reduced in value a debit entry is made in that account.

Example

On 1 July Tom Jolly owed Busifinance Ltd. £12,000. Suppose that on 6 July he obtained a further loan of £3,000 from Busifinance and received a cheque for this amount. Then, on 5 August he found that he was able to repay £1,000 of the loan and did so by cheque. Analysing these transactions shows us that:

▶ On 6 July the liability to Busifinance Ltd. increases by £3,000 and the asset bank also goes up in value by that amount.

▶ On 5 August the liability to Busifinance decreases by £1,000 and the asset bank also goes down in value by that amount.

You know now that we will reflect the **dual** nature of each of these transactions by **two** entries in the relevant ledger accounts and that this is called **double entry book-keeping**. After the entries have been made the relevant accounts will look like this:

Busifinance loan a/c

5 Aug	Bank	1,000		1 July	Balance	12,000
				6 July	Bank	3,000

Bank a/c

1 July	Balance	900		5 Aug	Busifinance	1,000
6 July	Busifinance	3,000				

The extra loan of £3,000 has been entered on the credit side of the Busifinance account because the liability to that company has increased by that amount. At the same time a debit entry has been made in the bank account because this asset has increased in value by that amount.

The £1,000 repaid to Busifinance Ltd is entered on the debit side of that account because the liability to them is reduced by that amount. At the same time a credit entry is made in the bank account because the asset bank will decrease in value by that amount.

BANK ACCOUNT ENTRIES

A word of warning here on possible confusion with entries that affect the bank account. Some readers, especially those who have accounts with one of the banks, might expect an increase in the amount of money in the bank to be shown by a credit entry and a decrease by a debit entry. This is because they have seen bank statements which show this. It must be remembered, however, that bank statements are a record of transactions from the bank's point of view not from the client's. As far as a bank is concerned, a client with money in an account is a liability because the money is owed to the client by the bank. Hence from the bank's point of view the rules they follow are those relating to liabilities, i.e. when money is paid into the account the liability of the bank to the client increases and a credit entry is made in the client's account to reflect this. Conversely when money is drawn out the liability is reduced and a debit entry is made in the client's account. We will examine this in more detail in section 9.7.

CREATING A DRAWINGS ACCOUNT

As it is a source of finance, the rules for entering changes in the owner's capital are the same as for liabilities. A credit entry records an increase and a debit entry a decrease. Suppose that on 6 August Tom Jolly invested a further £1,000 of his private wealth into his business by making a payment into the business bank account. The entries to record this would be:

>**Debit**   Business bank account
>**Credit**   Capital account.

If he decided to withdraw any assets from the business for his private use these drawings would reduce his capital. The entries needed to record this would be:

>**Debit**   Capital account
>**Credit**   Asset account affected (usually cash or bank but could be any other asset).

Most business owners make regular withdrawals from the business because they are usually dependent on their business for their ordinary living expenses. This might be done on a regular weekly or monthly basis and therefore could lead to a large number of debit entries in the capital account. To prevent the capital account from becoming overcrowded an extra account is often introduced for these entries. It is called the **drawings account** and should be thought of as a division of the capital account. All the debit entries will then be made in this account and at the end of the financial period the total can be transferred to the capital account. This will have the same effect as if the capital account had been debited directly with each individual entry.

Example

Suppose that during the half year ended 31 December 1988 Tom made no further investments of private wealth into his business but withdrew £500 per month living expenses. At the end of the six month period his accounts would look like this:

Capital a/c

1988				1988			
31 Dec	Drawings		3,000	1 July	Balance		32,000
31 Dec	Balance	c/d	30,000	6 Aug	Bank		1,000
			33,000				33,000
				1989			
				1 Jan	Balance	b/d	30,000

Drawings a/c

1988			1988		
31 Jul	Bank	500	31 Dec	Transferred to capital account	3,000
31 Aug	Bank	500			
30 Sep	Bank	500			
31 Oct	Bank	500			
30 Nov	Bank	500			
31 Dec	Bank	500			
		3,000			3,000

Before checking on your ability to enter transactions in ledger accounts for assets and sources of finance it is worth summarising the rules to be applied.

Debit	Any asset account	Credit
1. Opening value for that asset 2. Increases in the asset's value	Deductions in value of that asset	

Debit	Any source of finance account	Credit
Deduction in value of that source of finance	1. Opening value of that source of finance 2. Increases in value of that source of finance	

SELF-CHECK ▶ 3.3

From the following information open ledger accounts. Then enter the transactions opening new accounts when necessary.

Balance Sheet of Henry Small as at 1 May 1988

Premises	£40,000	Capital	£60,000
Equipment	5,000	AJK Supplies	4,000
Motor vehicles	6,000		
Stock	7,000		
Bank	6,000		
	£64,000		£64,000

2 May	Purchased equipment for £500 by cheque.
3 May	Purchased £400 stock from AJK Supplies on credit.
4 May	Sold £1,000 of old equipment at book value for a cheque.
5 May	Withdrew £200 from the bank for use as cash.
6 May	Paid AJK Supplies £900 of amount owing by cheque.
7 May	Sold £500 worth of stock for £600 cash.

SOLUTION ▶

Dr   Cr

Premises a/c

1 May	Balance	40,000			

Equipment a/c

1 May	Balance	5,000	4 May	Bank	1,000
2 May	Bank	500			

Motor vehicles a/c

1 May	Balance	6,000			

Stock a/c

1 May	Balance	7,000	7 May	Cash	500
3 May	AJK	400			

Bank a/c

1 May	Balance	6,000	2 May	Equipment	500
4 May	Equipment	1,000	5 May	Cash	200
			6 May	AJK	900

Capital a/c

			1 May	Balance	60,000
			7 May	Cash	100

AJK Supplies

6 May	Bank	900	1 May	Balance	4,000
			3 May	Stock	400

Cash a/c

5 May	Bank	200			
7 May	Stock	500			
7 May	capital	100			

COMMENT ▶

Compare your solution with the one above carefully noting any differences and referring to the rules for guidance where necessary. Most of the transactions were straight forward but you will have needed to open an account part way through in order to record the receipt of cash. Note that this account does not have an opening balance because the account did not exist at the date of the balance sheet. The first entry in this account is therefore not described as 'balance' but as 'bank' because that is where the corresponding double entry is to be found. The transaction that was designed to make you think hardest was the sale of £500 stock for £600 cash on 7 May. If you did not analyse this transaction in terms of its effect on the balance sheet you may only have debited the cash account with the £600 received and credited the stock account with the reduction in stock of £500. In that case you will have omitted the effect on the owner's capital. The owner has made a profit of £100. Profit belongs to the owner and the capital account is the one that is used to record the relationship of the owner to the business. As capital is a source of finance we follow the rules and credit the capital account to record an increase. Businesses that buy and sell will make a large number of entries to record stock changes. In order to prevent this account becoming overcrowded we will use a different method in section 3.5. We will also find another way to record profits and losses.

3.4 ENTERING TRANSACTIONS FOR REVENUE EXPENDITURE AND REVENUE RECEIPTS

REVENUE EXPENDITURE ENTRIES

The dual effect of transactions involving revenue expenditure and receipts on the balance sheet was noted in section 2.5. When keeping ledger accounts we show this effect by making two entries in the ledger accounts affected. You are probably already thinking 'one debit entry and a corresponding credit entry' and you are right. That is what double entry book-keeping is all about. Let's look at the expenses entries first.

On 1 March Ann White had a number of assets which included £750 in a bank account. On 2 March she paid £100 to advertise her business by cheque.

We analysed the effect of this kind of transaction on the balance sheet in 2.5 by showing that the asset bank would be reduced in value by the £100 paid and that the owner's capital would also be reduced by that amount. The reduction in owner's capital is to reflect the loss that is taking place on this transaction:

	£
Revenue	000
less Revenue expenditure	100
Loss	100

We could clearly record this in the ledger by the following entries:

Credit Bank account – because the asset bank is being reduced.

Debit Capital account – because the loss reduces the owner's capital.

There are some good reasons why the debit entry in the capital account would not be a good idea. One is that the capital account would rapidly fill up with the very large number of expenses that are being incurred weekly or even daily by most businesses. In order to prevent the capital account becoming overcrowded we make the debit entry in an expense account instead – opening a new expense account for all items of revenue expenditure. Thus the entries in Ann's accounts will be **credit** bank account and **debit** advertising account and the accounts will look like this:

Dr			Bank a/c		Cr
1 March	Balance	750	2 March	Advertising	100

			Advertising a/c		
2 March	Bank	100			

The amount of money in the bank has been reduced by a credit entry in the bank account for £100 and the revenue expenditure is recorded by making a debit entry in the advertising account for that amount.

REVENUE RECEIPT ENTRIES

Now let's take a look at the entries needed to record the receipt of revenue. Suppose that Ann had £90 cash on 1 March and received £50 cash for renting out the flat above her business to a tenant on 5 March. We analysed the effects of this kind of transaction on an owner's balance sheet in 2.5 by explaining that the asset cash would increase by £50 and at the same time the owner's capital would increase by the same amount. The increase in the owner's capital is to reflect the profit that is being made on this transaction.

Again we could clearly record this transaction in the ledger by these entries:

Debit   cash account to record the increase of that asset.
Credit   capital account to record the increase in owner's capital.

However, for the reason we have already given, instead of making a credit entry in the capital account we will make the credit entry in a new account which will be called rent received. The relevant accounts will then look like this:

Dr			Cash a/c		Cr
1 March	Balance	90			
5 March	Rent received	50			

Rent received a/c

	5 March	Cash	50

The amount of money in the form of cash has been increased by a debit entry for £50 while the revenue receipt is recorded by making a credit entry in the rent received account for that amount.

It is important that accounts for revenue received should have the word 'received' in their title. Rent is an expense if you are paying it but an income if you are receiving it. As most businesses have a greater number of expenses than incomes we assume that 'rent' on its own means the expense of rent. To make it clear that an income has been received it is necessary to open an account for 'rent received'.

REDUCTION OF EXPENSES AND REVENUE

Occasionally it is necessary to show a reduction of an expense or revenue received. Suppose for example that Ann was unhappy with the quality of the print used in the advertisement for which she had paid £100 on 2 March. Ann's complaint resulted in a refund of £20 by cheque on 7 March.

The value of Ann's bank account will increase by the £20 received. Therefore a debit entry will be made in that account. The expense of advertising is reduced by the refund. Therefore, the entry in this account must be on the credit side. After this has been done the advertising account will look like this:

Advertising a/c

2 March	Bank	100	7 March	Bank	20

In a similar way refunds may sometimes be given to people from whom revenue has been received. For example, suppose that after Ann had received the £50 rent for the use of the flat her tenant complained that it was cold. Ann agreed to reduce the rent to £45 per week until a new heater could be fitted and in the meantime returned £5 in cash to the tenant on 8 March. Ann will have to make a credit for £5 in her cash account to reduce the value of that asset. She will also have to make a debit entry in the rent received account. This will have the effect of reducing that revenue account by £5 and it will now look like this:

Rent received a/c

8 March	Cash	5	5 March	Cash	50

Before checking your ability to enter transactions involving expenses and revenue we can add the rules to the ones we have already summarised for assets and sources of finance.

Debit	Any expense account	Credit
1. Opening value of that expense 2. Increases in the expense	Decreases in the expense	

Debit	Any revenue account	Credit
Decreases in the revenue	1. Opening value of that revenue 2. Increases in the revenue	

I have already said how important it is to master the rules of double entry book-keeping. This really cannot be emphasised enough. It is not enough just to be able to make entries in ledger accounts when a number of transactions are given. Many questions test understanding by giving you a completed ledger account and asking for an explanation of each of the entries within. Mastering the rules is not just achieved by learning them. Practice in applying them to a large number of exercises is the real key to knowledge.

SELF-CHECK ▶ 3.4

Jean Dacy has £1,000 in her business bank account on 1 April. Open a ledger account with this balance and then enter the following transactions completing all the entries in the other accounts you will need to open.

2 April	Paid rates by cheque £250.
3 April	Paid employee's wages by cheque £120.
4 April	Received £40 rent from a tenant by cheque.
5 April	Received rates rebate of £30 by cheque from local council.
6 April	Withdrew £50 by cheque for private use.

SOLUTION ▶

Dr				Bank a/c			Cr
1 April	Balance		1,000	2 April	Rates		250
4 April	Rent received		40	3 April	Wages		120
5 April	Rates		30	6 April	Drawings		50

Rates a/c

2 April	Bank	250	5 April	Bank	30

Wages a/c

3 April	Bank	120			

Rent received a/c

			4 April	Bank	40

Drawings a/c

6 April	Bank	50			

COMMENT ▶

With this kind of exercise it is essential that you start the first account with the balance on the correct side. If you did so, and provided you have learnt the book-keeping rules, you should not have had too much of a problem. When dealing with expenses and revenues it is usually best to think of the kind of entry needed in the asset account first. Once you have established the fact that a cheque received increases the bank balance and requires a debit entry to show this, you should be immediately thinking that a credit entry is needed in another account to complete the double entries. This reinforces your knowledge that credit entries are needed in income or revenue accounts to record the receipt of income. You might be tempted to describe the transaction of 5 April as rate rebate in the bank account. This is acceptable provided it does not then tempt you into opening a rent rebate account to record the other entry. This is not really necessary as it leads to an increase in the number of accounts to be handled for no good reason. It is quite acceptable to show the expense of rates on the debit side of the account and any rebates you might be lucky enough to receive on the credit side.

Reminder

We have established a framework that will enable you to decide how to enter a large number of transactions in the ledger. From time to time we will increase the number and variety of transactions that you will have to record. The basic framework will always give you a clue as to where to start whenever a transaction appears difficult or unusual. It is worthwhile bringing together in one handy table the framework we have established. (Use this when you need a clue as to how to start dealing with the entries needed to record transactions in the ledger.)

Reasons for making an entry in its **own** account

Debit	Credit
1 Opening asset value	1 Opening value of a source of finance
2 Increasing asset value	2 Increase of a source of finance
3 An expense	3 An income
4 Increase in an expense	4 Increase in an income
5 Reduction of a source of finance	5 Reduction of an asset
6 Reduction of an income	6 Reduction of an expense

There is a nice logic to this arrangement and it will repay some study and thought. Provided you can sort out your assets from your sources of finance, and your expenses from your incomes, it should prove very useful.

3.5 PURCHASES, SALES AND RETURNS OF STOCK

Many businesses are involved in buying and selling. Sometimes goods that are bought or sold are later returned. Consequently the stock account often has a large number of transactions recorded in it. To keep things simple and prevent the stock account from becoming overcrowded four additional accounts are used to record the different events that change the amount of stock. These are: **purchases account**, **purchases returns account**, **sales account** and **sales returns account**. They may be thought of as subdivisions of the stock account. Whatever kind of entry you would have made in the stock account to record its increase or decrease will be made in the relevant one of these instead.

PURCHASES

Purchase of stock increases the amount of this asset and therefore needs a debit entry. This will now be made in the purchases account instead of the stock account. The account in which the corresponding credit entry is made will depend on the method of payment.

If payment is made immediately the credit entry will be made in the cash or bank account showing the reduction of one of these assets. If the goods (as stock is sometimes called) are bought on credit then the credit entry wil be made in the account of the supplier, who is a creditor to the purchaser. This shows the increase of a liability.

Example

On 1 April a greengrocer bought £150 of vegetables on credit from Freshveg Ltd. The entries in the greengrocer's accounts would look like this:

Purchases a/c

1 April	Freshveg Ltd	150		

Freshveg Ltd

			1 April	Purchases	150

PURCHASES RETURNS OR RETURNS OUTWARD

Sometimes goods which have been bought are later returned by the purchaser. This usually happens when something is found to be wrong with them. These purchases returns are also known as returns outwards because they are being sent **out** from the firm which bought them.

Suppose the greengrocer mentioned above discovered that £20 of the vegetables he had purchased were not of the right quality. On 2 April he sent them back to the supplier. The real value of his purchases is now £130 (£150 less £20 returned). Also he owes Freshveg Ltd only £130. We can show the reduction of the liability by making a debit entry in the supplier's account. Before introducing these new accounts the reduction in stock resulting from the return would have been made in the stock account. Now we can use the returns outward or purchases returns account. The accounts will now look like this:

Purchases a/c

1 April	Freshveg Ltd	150	

Returns outward a/c

			2 April	Freshveg Ltd	20

Freshveg Ltd

2 April	Returns out	20	1 April	Purchases	150

The account for Freshveg Ltd shows that £130 is now owing. To obtain the real value of the purchases we have to look at both the purchases account and the returns outward account. Together they show that the net value of the purchases is £130 (£150 less £20).

SALES

Sales of stock decrease the value of this asset and therefore it needs a credit entry. This will now be made in the sales account instead of in the stock account. The account in which the corresponding debit entry will be made will depend on how the stock was sold. If sold for money it will be in either the cash or bank account, showing an increase in the value of one of these assets. If the goods were sold on credit then the person to whom they were sold owes that sum to the business, i.e. he is a debtor and his account will be debited.

Example

On 1 May the greengrocer sold £20 of fruit to the Palace Hotel which was allowed monthly credit. The entries in the greengrocer's ledger would look like this:

Sales a/c

	1 May	Palace Hotel		20

Palace Hotel a/c

1 May	Sales	20		

SALES RETURNS OR RETURNS INWARD

When goods that have been sold are returned later for a valid reason, entries must be made to record the event. These sales returns are called returns inward because the goods are coming back **in** to the firm that sold them.

Suppose that on checking the fruit they had purchased the Palace Hotel found that £8 of it was not of the required quality. On 2 May this was returned to the greengrocer. A credit entry will now have to be made in the account of the Palace Hotel as this return reduces the amount owed. The Palace Hotel is a debtor and a credit entry in a debtor's account has the effect of reducing the value of that asset.

Before introducing these new accounts the corresponding debit entry would have been made in the stock account. Now we can use the returns inward or sales returns account. The accounts will now look like this:

Sales a/c

	1 May	Palace Hotel	20

Returns inward a/c

2 May	Palace Hotel	8			

Palace Hotel a/c

1 May	Sales	20	2 May	Returns inward	8

The account for the Palace Hotel shows that £12 is owed to the greengrocer. To obtain the real value of the sales we have to look at both the sales account and the returns inward account. Together they show that the net value of the sales is £12 (£20 less £8).

Correctly used, the four accounts we have just considered enable the stock account to be reserved for the valuation of stock which is made at stocktaking time. This depends on no other entries being made in the stock account. One other transaction that should be mentioned here is the withdrawal of stock from the business by the owner for his private use – called drawings of stock. In the last chapter it was stated that the entries needed to show the withdrawal of an asset from business by an owner for his private use were:

Debit – drawings a/c

Credit – the account of the asset taken out of the business.

If a credit entry is made in the stock account to record this then the balance in the stock account will not be its valuation at the time of stock taking. To preserve the stock account for this use the credit entry should therefore be made in the purchases account.

**SELF-CHECK ▶
3.5**

Ace Electrics is a wholesaler which has J. Biggs, a DIY retailer, as one of its customers. On 1 March Joe Biggs owed £160 from the previous month. The following transactions then took place:

| 2 March | Ace Electrics supplied Joe with £170 of materials on credit. |
| 3 March | Biggs returned materials worth £40 because they were not of the type he had ordered. |

Show how the above would be recorded in the ledger of:

(a)   Ace Electrics

(b)   J. Biggs

Note

When you are doing this kind of exercise it is important to be absolutely clear from whose point of view you are considering the transaction. Begin by labelling clearly for (a) Ace Electrics' books. Then consider the transactions solely from this company's point of view. When you have done this put a new heading and consider the transactions from J. Biggs' viewpoint.

SOLUTION ▶   (a)   Ace Electrics' books

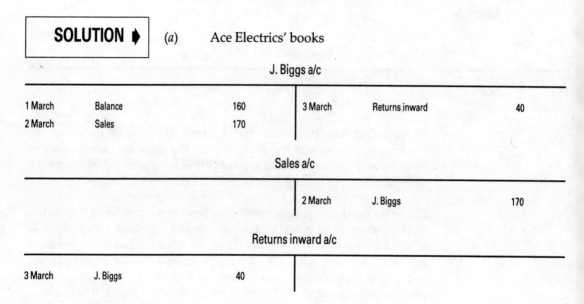

J. Biggs a/c

| 1 March | Balance | 160 | 3 March | Returns inward | 40 |
| 2 March | Sales | 170 | | | |

Sales a/c

| | | | 2 March | J. Biggs | 170 |

Returns inward a/c

| 3 March | J. Biggs | 40 | | | |

COMMENT ▶ It is most important to begin correctly. Ace Electrics will have an account for Biggs as he is their customer. It will have a debit balance on 1 March showing that the £160 owing from last month is an asset. The sale on 2 March increases the asset and the return on 3 March reduces it. The other accounts affected are sales, because Ace Electrics sold Biggs goods, and returns inward, because goods that had been sold have been returned to the firm.

(b)   J. Biggs' books

Ace Electrics a/c

| 3 March | Returns out | 40 | 1 March | Balance | 160 |
| | | | 2 March | Purchases | 170 |

Purchases a/c

| 2 March | Ace Electrics | 170 | | | |

Returns outward a/c

| | | | 3 March | Ace Electrics | 40 |

COMMENT ▶ Biggs will have an account for Ace Electrics because they are his supplier. It starts with a credit balance showing that, from Biggs' point of view, there is a liability of £160 on 1 March. The transaction of 2 March was a purchase as far as Biggs was concerned and increases the amount he owes by £170. When he makes the return on 3 March, however, he owes Ace Electrics £40 less and is able to show the reduction of the liability by making a debit entry. The other accounts affected are purchases, because Biggs bought the goods, and returns outward, because part of what he purchased has been sent back to the supplier.

The fact that from the wholesaler's point of view a sale has taken place and from that of the retailer a purchase has been made serves to emphasise the importance of being clear from the start from whose viewpoint you are considering the transaction. Similarly returns inward from the wholesaler's viewpoint are returns outward when considered from the position of the retailer. Do not forget that some businesses use the terms **purchases returns** for **returns outward** and **sales returns** for **returns inward**.

3.6 TRADE DISCOUNT, CASH DISCOUNT AND PERCENTAGES

TRADE DISCOUNT

Trade discount is a reduction in price allowed by a supplier and received by a customer when they are both involved in the same trade. For example, when you buy materials from a builders' merchant you pay a higher price than would a builder who was a regular customer. He would receive trade discount whereas you would not. As far as the ledger is concerned trade discount will not be recorded. It is deducted before any entries are made.

Example

The catalogue or list price of a bag of cement might be £5.00. A builder receiving ten per cent trade discount will be charged only £4.50, the 50p trade discount being ten per cent of £5.00. The merchant will make a credit entry of £4.50 in his sales account and debit the builder's account with the £4.50 due from him. The builder would debit his purchases account and credit the account of the merchant with the amount owed to him. Again only £4.50 would be shown in the accounts. Trade discount is deducted **before** any entries are made.

CASH DISCOUNT

Cash discount is a reduction in price allowed by a supplier and received by a customer in return for prompt payment. This kind of discount is recorded in the ledger.

DISCOUNT ALLOWED

A retailer called Ben Wilson owed RJK, a wholesaler, £200 for a purchase made on 18 May. The wholesaler has a policy of allowing debtors to deduct three per cent cash discount for settlement within seven days of a statement being sent. This was sent on 31 May and Wilson paid by cheque on 4 June. In RJK's ledger the accounts would look like this:

Sales

			18 May	B. Wilson	200

B. Wilson

18 May	Sales	200	4 June	Bank	194
			4 June	Discount allowed	6

Discount allowed

4 June	B. Wilson	6			

Bank

4 June	B. Wilson	194			

The debit entry in Wilson's account shows the amount sold to him on 18 May. When Wilson settles the account on 4 June he does not pay £200 and then claim his discount. It is much more convenient for him and the wholesaler if he deducts the discount and writes a cheque for the balance. Cash discount of three per cent on an amount due of £200 means that he is entitled to deduct £6 discount. He therefore sends a cheque for £194. The wholesaler will credit Wilson's account with this amount and debit his bank account. At the same time he will have to record the fact that he has allowed the discount of £6. A credit entry for £6 in Wilson's account will have the effect of wiping out the remainder of the amount due in his account. A debit entry of £6 in an account for discount allowed will complete the entries. Discount allowed is another expense account. It represents the expense of supplier's incurred in order to encourage prompt payment.

DISCOUNT RECEIVED

From the point of view of the customer who receives the discount in return for prompt payment cash discount is certainly not an expense.

It is regarded as an income. Using the above facts we can see how they would have been recorded in Wilson's ledger:

RJK

| 4 June | Bank | 194 | 18 May | Purchases | 200 |
| 4 June | Discount received | 6 | | | |

Purchases

| 18 May | RJK | 200 | | | |

Bank

| | | | 4 June | RJK | 194 |

Discount received

| | | | 4 June | RJK | 6 |

When Wilson purchases the goods on 18 May a credit entry is required in the account of the wholesaler, RJK. From Wilson's point of view RJK is a creditor. When he makes the payment of £194 by cheque a credit entry in the bank account reduces the value of this asset and a debit entry in RJK's account reduces the amount of the liability. As he knows that he is entitled to the discount by paying before the due date he is able to remove the £6 from RJK's account by a debit entry and credits an account for discount received.

As with returns it is absolutely essential that you are clear about from whose viewpoint you are recording the transaction. In a relationship between a purchaser and a seller, a discount allowed by the seller is a discount received by the purchaser.

PERCENTAGES

Discounts are usually expressed as a percentage of the amount due. It is therefore essential that you understand how to calculate them. You will almost certainly have learnt how to calculate percentages before but let us revise the basic method because from past experience it has been found that some students often find it difficult.

▶ 'Per cent' means 'per hundred'. Whatever percentage is involved is written as a fraction of 100. Three per cent is therefore written $\frac{3}{100}$.

▶ The next step is to multiply this figure by the amount you are calculating the percentage of. In the above example this could have been written like this:

$$\frac{3}{100} \times \frac{200}{1} = 6$$

The calculation may be done by calculator for some examinations. However, the figures involved are rarely difficult, and it is essential that you understand what you are doing.

SELF-CHECK 3.6

T. Smith purchased £150 of goods on credit from RJK on 22 March. He paid for them by cheque on 29 March and was prompt enough to be able to deduct the two per cent discount that applied. Show how this information would have been recorded in:
(a)   the ledger of T. Smith and
(b)   the ledger of RJK.

SOLUTION

(a)   Smith's ledger

RJK

| 29 March | Bank | 147 | 22 March | Purchases | 150 |
| 29 March | Discount received | 3 | | | |

Purchases

| 22 March | RJK | 150 | | | |

Bank

| | | | 29 March | RJK | 147 |

Discount received

| | | | 29 March | RJK | 3 |

(b)   RJK's ledger

T. Smith

| 22 March | Sales | 150 | 29 March | Bank | 147 |
| | | | 29 March | Discount allowed | 3 |

Sales

		22 March	T. Smith	150

Bank

29 March	T. Smith	147	

Discount allowed

29 March	T. Smith	3	

COMMENT ▶ The key to this is to make certain that you recognise that a purchase by Smith is the equivalent of a sale by RJK, a payment of money by Smith is equivalent to a receipt of money by RJK and discount received by Smith is the equivalent of a discount allowed by RJK. Clear labelling of whose ledger you are showing in each case will help to prevent confusion.

3.7 BAD DEBTS

Debtors are an asset because the majority of people who are allowed credit pay their debts. When it becomes impossible to collect a debt that is due it is said to be a bad debt. It is then necessary to remove that debt from the asset account. This is known as 'writing off' the debt. A debt that cannot be collected is clearly no asset. Bad debts can therefore be seen as an expense incurred when allowing credit. We remove the debt from the debtor's account by making a credit entry. The corresponding debit entry will be in an expense account called bad debts.

Example

Tim Jones, who for a short and unsuccessful time was a retailer, owes a wholesaler £180. The wholesaler has been unable to collect the money and has just heard that it is unlikely he ever will. After writing off the debt the accounts in the wholesaler's ledger will look like this:

Tim Jones

4 Jan	Sales	180	Oct	Bad debts	180

Bad debts

10 Oct	T. Jones	180		

SELF-CHECK ▶
3.7
On 4 March 1988 Rex Hunt purchased goods on credit for £200 from RJK. He had failed to pay by 31 December of that year so RJK decided to write off the debt. Show the entries needed to record this information in RJK's books.

SOLUTION ▶

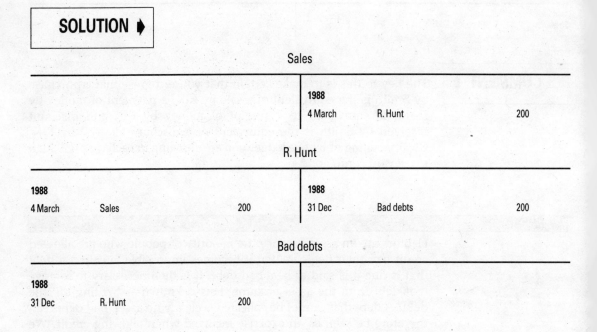

Sales

			1988		
			4 March	R. Hunt	200

R. Hunt

1988			1988		
4 March	Sales	200	31 Dec	Bad debts	200

Bad debts

1988					
31 Dec	R. Hunt	200			

COMMENT ▶
Although the information was given in terms of Hunt's purchase of goods, when you come to enter the information in the books of RJK you must remember that it is a sale from the wholesaler's point of view.

3.8 VALUE ADDED TAX

Value added tax (VAT) is charged by the government on sales (outputs) of certain goods and services. There are three categories of supplies:
(a)   Standard rated – the current rate is 15%.
(b)   Zero rated – no tax is currently charged but these items could be taxed if the government changed its policy.
(c)   Exempt – these are not intended to be taxed.
The tax is collected by the seller of the goods. At the time of writing,

all firms with a turnover (net sales) greater than £21,300 must register for VAT. This amount is adjusted each year in line with inflation.

Example

A VAT registered trader makes a standard rated sale on credit for £200 (excluding VAT) to N. Clark on 3 May. He will charge Clark £200 + 15% of £200 = £230. The ledger account entries will look like this:

N. Clark a/c

3 May	Sales	200			
3 May	VAT	30			

Sales a/c

			3 May	N. Clark	200

VAT a/c

			3 May	N. Clark	30

The full £230 must be debited to Clark's account because it is the trader's responsibility to collect this amount from him. It will not all belong to him, however, because the £30 tax has to be paid to H.M. Customs and Excise when the next payment is due. This amount is therefore entered in the VAT account where it represents a liability until it is paid. £200 counts as sales revenue for the trader, so only this amount should be shown in the sales account. If the sale was for cash or cheque, the debit entries would be in the cash or bank account.

It is likely that the trader will also be paying VAT to his suppliers on his purchases (inputs). He will need to keep a record of this because he is allowed to deduct the amount of VAT he has paid to suppliers from the amount he collects from customers before paying the difference to the government.

If £100 of standard rated goods (excluding VAT) are purchased on credit from Newsupplies Ltd. on 4 May the entries will be:

Newsupplies Ltd.

			4 May	Purchases	100
			4 May	VAT	15

Purchases a/c

| 4 May | Newsupplies | 100 | |

VAT a/c

| 4 May | Newsupplies | 15 | |

The full amount of £115 will have to be paid to Newsupplies. As the seller of the goods, it is their job to collect the tax from the purchaser. It is essential that only the cost of the goods, i.e. £100 is shown in the purchases account. The £15 VAT paid is shown as a debit entry in its account because that amount can be reclaimed by the trader from the government. In other words the government is a debtor to the trader for this amount. If the purchase was by cash or cheque the credit entries would be in the cash or bank account.

The debit entries in the VAT account will offset the credit entries. If there is a credit balance in the account at the time of the next VAT return then the amount of the balance is paid to the government. It is a liability balance. If there is a debit balance in the VAT account (this is less likely) the goverment will be in debt to the trader for this amount and will pay him what is due.

SELF-CHECK ▶ 3.8

Show the ledger account entries to record the following transactions in a trader's books. Assume that the standard rate of VAT is 15% and that it applies to both transactions.
7 May   Purchases of goods £300 (ex VAT) on credit from T. Honey.
8 May   Sale of goods £400 (ex VAT) on credit to K. Davies.

SOLUTION ▶

T. Honey

| | | | | 7 May | Purchases | 300 |
| | | | | 7 May | VAT | 45 |

Purchases

| 7 May | T. Honey | 300 | |

K. Davies

8 May	Sales	400			
8 May	VAT	60			

Sales

			8 May	K. Davies	400

VAT

7 May	T. Honey	45	8 May	K. Davies	60

EXERCISES

3.1

From the following information open ledger accounts. Then enter the transactions, opening new accounts when necessary.

Balance Sheet of Joy Spencer as at 1 May 1988

Premises	£33,000	Capital	£65,000
Equipment	15,000	Trade creditors	6,750
Debtors	5,500		
Stock	17,000		
Bank	1,250		
	£71,750		£71,750

2 May	Purchased equipment for £1,500 by cheque.
3 May	Purchased £950 stock from AJK on credit.
4 May	Sold £2,000 of old equipment at book value for a cheque.
5 May	Opened a bank account by paying in £500 cash.
6 May	Paid £300 of amount owing to trade creditors by cheque.
7 May	Sold £500 worth of stock for £500 cheque.

3.2

John Dean has £1,560 in his business bank account on 1 April. Open a ledger account with this balance and then enter the following transactions, completing all the entries in the other accounts you will need to open.

2 April	Paid rates by cheque £250.
3 April	Paid employees' wages by cheque £620.
4 April	Received £60 rent from a tenant by cheque.
5 April	Paid insurance £120.
6 April	Paid tenant rent rebate of £10.
7 April	Received insurance rebate of £12.
8 April	Withdrew £100 from bank for private use.

3.3

DIY Supplies is a wholesaler which has Bill Lewis, a retailer, as one of its customers. On 1 June Bill owed £250 from the previous month. The following transactions then took place:

3 June	Bill purchased £458 of materials from DIY Supplies on credit.
6 June	Bill returned materials worth £75 because they were unsuitable.
9 June	Bill settled the amount due on 1 June. He was entitled to 4% cash discount.

Show how the above would be recorded in the ledger of:
(a) DIY Supplies
(b) Bill Lewis.

3.4

Prepare accounts to show the following information in
(a) the ledger of Zoe Clough
(b) the ledger of Peter Blake.

1 April	Zoe Clough owed Peter Blake £450.
3 April	Zoe purchased £356 of goods on credit from Blake.
5 April	Zoe paid the amount due on 1 April by cheque and was prompt enough to deduct the 2% discount that applied.
6 April	Zoe returned £20 worth of wrongly-sized goods to Blake.

3.5

On 3 May Tom Scott purchased £450 of goods on credit from DIY Supplies. He paid £150 in cash on 29 May but made no further payments. The outstanding amount was written off as a bad debt on 31 August.

Show how all the above information would be recorded in the ledger of DIY Supplies.

3.6   State the entries needed to record the withdrawal of stock by the owner of a business for his private use.

3.7   Show the VAT account entries to record the following transactions in a trader's books. Assume that the standard rate of VAT is 15% and that it applies to all transactions.

5 January   Sales of goods £280 (ex VAT) on credit to B. Dale.
7 January   Purchase of goods £120 (ex VAT) on credit from T. Rees.
8 January   Sale of goods £260 (ex VAT) on credit to H. Davies.
9 January   Purchase of goods £140 (ex VAT) on credit from D. Wilkins.

THE TRIAL BALANCE

CONTENTS

The last chapter concentrated on the rules of double entry book-keeping and their application to a variety of transactions. Now we are going to look at a simple way of making a preliminary check on the accuracy of the entries made in the ledger. We will do this by balancing the accounts and then extracting a trial balance. When we have done this it will be possible for us to look at what we should do if errors have been made.

4.1 BALANCING ACCOUNTS

The balance of an account is the difference between the two sides. This is the most significant figure in the account because it tells us the value of the asset, liability, expense or income of which the account is a record. When the debit side is greater it is termed a debit balance. When the credit side is greater it is called a credit balance. Look at the following account in the ledger of J. Turner.

Cash

1 March	Bank	1,000	7 March	Northern Foods	400
5 March	R. Evans	100	9 March	Insurance	50

It is possible to calculate the balance after each one of the entries and say what this means:

1 March	Debit balance of £1,000. Turner has £1,000 cash. This asset has been created by drawing £1,000 cash from the bank.
5 March	Debit balance of £1,100. Turner has £1,100 in cash. His cash balance increased by the £100 he received from Evans.
7 March	Debit balance of £700. Turner has £700 in cash. His cash balance was reduced by the £400 paid to Northern Foods.
9 March	Debit balance of £650. Turner has £650 cash. His cash balance was reduced by the £50 paid for insurance.

None of these balances appear in the above account but they are all calculated from the information contained in it. Sometimes it is useful to show the balance in the account. This is what the above account would look like if it was balanced on 10 March after all the transactions had been made:

Cash

1 March	Bank		1,000	7 March	Northern Foods		400
5 March	R. Evans		100	9 March	Insurance		50
				10 March	Balance	c/d	650
			1,100				1,100
11 March	Balance	b/d	650				

This, in stages, is how it is done:

1 Find the difference between the two sides on the date the account is being balanced.
2 Place the difference on the side of the account that is **smaller**. It is described as balance c/d, which means that the balance is to be carried down. The date is that on which the account is being balanced.
3 Total the two sides, drawing the lines carefully so that the the two totals are level with each other. As the difference between the two sides has been added to the smaller side both sides will now be equal.
4 Enter the balance on the side to which it really belongs, i.e. the side that was originally bigger. It is described as the balance b/d, which means that the balance has been brought down. It is dated one day after the balance carried down figure. The folio column is used for the c/d and b/d. The significance of dating the balance to be carried down one day earlier than the balance which is brought down is that the account is shown as being temporarily closed at the end of business on one day and then reopened, with the same amount, when business begins next day.

When there is only one entry in an account, that amount is the balance or difference between the two sides. It may seem unnecessary to go through the process of balancing such an account. However this is still done by some people and it does serve as a means of showing that all the accounts have been looked at and brought up to date at the same time. For example this is what one such account might look like after it has been balanced on 30 June.

Equipment

4 Feb	Bank		700	30 June	Balance	c/d	700
1 July	Balance	b/d	700				

The procedure is the same as above except that there is no need to total the two sides. When the balance to be carried down is inserted on the smaller, credit, side both sides are immediately equal. Underlining the two figures is enough to show that they are totals.

SELF-CHECK ▸ 4.1

The following account appears in the ledger of Amanda Piper.
(a)   Balance it at the close of business on 14 May and state what this balance means.
(b)   Describe the transaction that has resulted in each entry.

Freshveg Ltd.

2 Jan	Returns out	10	1 Jan	Purchases	85
7 Jan	Bank	72	8 Jan	Purchases	25
7 Jan	Discount received	3			
14ᵗʰ Balance c.d.		25			1/ 0
		100			25
			8ᵗʰ Balance b.d.		

(c)   What percentage rate of discount applies in this case?

$$\frac{3}{75} \times \frac{100}{1} \quad \% \qquad \frac{}{85} \quad 4.\%$$

SOLUTION ▸

(a)

Freshveg

2 Jan	Returns out		10	1 Jan	Purchases		85
7 Jan	Bank		72	8 Jan	Purchases		25
7 Jan	Discount received		3				
14 Jan	Balance	c/d	25				
			110				110
				15 Jan	Balance	b/d	25

The credit balance of £25 in the account of Freshveg Ltd means that Amanda Piper owes Freshveg £25.

(b)   1 Jan   Piper purchased £85 of goods on credit from Freshveg.
2 Jan   Piper returned £10 of goods to Freshveg.
7 Jan   Piper paid £72 by cheque to Freshveg after deducting £3 cash discount for prompt payment.
8 Jan   Piper purchased more goods on credit from Freshveg for £25.

(c)   4%. If £72 is being paid and £3 discount received the amount that is being settled is for £75. $\frac{3}{75} \times \frac{100}{1} = 4\%$.

COMMENT ▶

Questions that require you to explain what transactions have resulted in entries in a particular ledger account test your understanding and are very popular. It is advisable to begin your explanation with the name of the person who is keeping the account. Remember that each description in the account tells you the name of the other account affected. This should help you to tell the story of the account correctly.

4.2 VERTICAL LEDGER ACCOUNTS

In this book we have used the traditional horizontal layout for ledger accounts. Descriptions for debit entries appear to the left of descriptions for credit entries. When accounting machines or computers are used a vertical style is normal with all descriptions in the same column. The cash account on page 92 would look like this in vertical style:

Cash account

Date	Description	Dr	Cr	Balance
1 March	Bank	1,000		1,000 dr
5 March	R. Evans	100		1,100 dr
7 March	Northern Foods		400	700 dr
9 March	Insurance		50	650 dr

One obvious advantage of this method is the automatic balancing that takes place after each entry. This is done speedily by a computer or machine. Usually its importance is not thought sufficient to calculate it after each entry when the accounts are handwritten in this layout.

SELF-CHECK ▶
4.2

Rewrite the account of Freshveg Ltd from Self-check 4.1 using vertical layout.

SOLUTION ▶

Freshveg Ltd

Date	Description	Dr	Cr	Balance
1 Jan	Purchases ·		85	85 cr
2 Jan	Returns outward	10		75 cr
7 Jan	Bank	72		3 cr
7 Jan	Discount received	3		0
8 Jan	Purchases		25	25 cr

COMMENT ▶

The changing balance has been shown after each entry as it does help to tell the story of the account. Usually you are free to prepare your ledger accounts in whichever way you prefer. It is advisable, however, to have some practice dealing with both types of layout as an examination question may use either and then ask you to explain or perhaps complete the account in that style. Although the horizontal layout will be retained for the explanations, some more exercises using vertical accounts will be included to make certain you get enough practice at dealing with them. If you do make use of vertical accounts and are writing them by hand you are advised not to complete the running balance column after each entry as it would be very time-consuming under examination conditions. Just show the balance on the date that it is requested.

4.3 PREPARING A TRIAL BALANCE

Study the following diagram which is virtually self-explanatory:

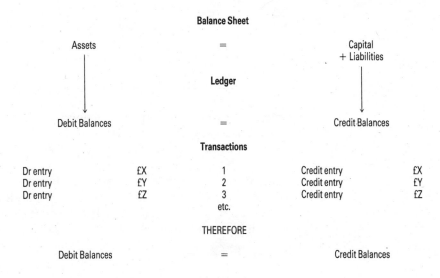

We begin with the balance sheet which reflected the book-keeping equation, i.e. total value of the assets must equal the total value of the sources of finance. In the ledger each asset was shown as a debit balance in its own account and each source of finance as a credit balance. Therefore the debit balances must equal the credit balances. When transactions are entered in the ledger additional accounts may be opened, but whatever the transaction it will involve a debit entry in one account and a credit entry of the same amount in another account. Therefore after any number of transactions the debit balances should still equal the credit balances.

Checking that the debit balances do, in fact, equal the credit balances is done by making a list of all the balances. This is known as a trial balance and usually takes the following form:

Trial Balance of Helen Berry as at 31 March 1988

Accounts	Dr balances	Cr balances
	£	£
Premises	15,000	
Furniture and fittings	3,000	
Bank	2,075	
Capital		19,000
Busifinance		2,000
Purchases	1,500	
AKJ		400
Sales		250
Cash	90	
Purchases returns		100
Discount received		20
N. Timms	100	
Insurance	25	
Rent received		20
Totals	21,790	21,790

The above trial balance provides enough evidence to prove that the transactions have been entered correctly in the ledger. The total debit balances equal the total credit balances. When preparing a trial balance the stage at which most problems occur is that of balancing the accounts. Remember to take special care at this stage. If the total of the debit side of an account is greater than the total on the credit side then it is a debit balance. If the credit side is greater than the debit it is a credit balance.

SELF-CHECK ▶
4.3

Mike Bishop opened a petrol service station on 1 May 1988. He had £1,000 in the bank, £200 in cash, £8,000 worth of stock and machinery and equipment worth £12,000. He had borrowed £4,000 from Petrofinance for nine months and provided the rest of the finance for himself.

1 Draft a balance sheet in vertical style to show Mike's position on 1 May 1988, taking care to calculate the figure for owner's capital.
2 Open a ledger account for each item and enter the opening balances.
3 Enter the following transactions in the ledger, opening new accounts when necessary.
4 Prepare a trial balance on 7 May to check the accuracy of your transactions.

2 May	Cash sales £600.
3 May	Cash sales £550; purchases £1,200 on credit from PB Ltd.
4 May	Cash sales £720; paid £1,500 into the bank.
5 May	Cash sales £680; paid rent £160 by cheque.
6 May	Cash sales £540; purchases £200 on credit from Greas-oils Ltd.
7 May	Paid amount due to PB Ltd. less 3% discount by cheque.

SOLUTION ▶

Balance Sheet of Mike Bishop as at 1 May 1988

	£	£
Fixed assets		
Equipment and machinery		12,000
Current assets		
Stock	8,000	
Bank	1,000	
Cash	200	
	9,200	
Less current liabilities		
Petrofinance Ltd.	4,000	
Working capital		5,200
Total assets less current liabilities		17,200
Financed by:		
Owner's capital		17,200

LEDGER

Equipment and machinery

1 May	Balance		12,000			

Stock

1 May	Balance		8,000			

Bank

1 May	Balance		1,000	5 May	Rent		160
4 May	Cash		1,500	7 May	PB Ltd.		1,164
				7 May	Balance	c/d	1,176
			2,500				2,500
8 May	Balance	b/d	1,176				

Cash

1 May	Balance		200	4 May	Bank		1,500
2 May	Sales		600	7 May	Balance	c/d	1,790
3 May	Sales		550				
4 May	Sales		720				
5 May	Sales		680				
6 May	Sales		540				
			3,290				3,290
8 May	Balance	b/d	1,790				

Capital

				1 May	Balance	17,200

Petrofinance Ltd

				1 May	Balance	4,000

Sales

7 May	Balance	c/d	3,090	2 May	Cash		600
				3 May	Cash		550
				4 May	Cash		720
				5 May	Cash		680
				6 May	Cash		540
			3,090				3,090
				8 May	Balance	b/d	3,090

Purchases

3 May	PB Ltd		1,200	7 May	Balance	c/d	1,400
6 May	Greasoils		200				
			1,400				1,400
8 May	Balance	b/d	1,400				

PB Ltd

7 May	Bank		1,164	3 May	Purchases		1,200
7 May	Discount received		36				
			1,200				1,200

Rent

5 May	Bank		160				

Greasoils Ltd

				6 May	Purchases		200

Discount received

				7 May	PB Ltd		36

Trial Balance of Mike Bishop as at 7 May 1988

Accounts	Dr balances £	Cr balances £
Equipment and machinery	12,000	
Stock	8,000	
Bank	1,176	
Cash	1,790	
Capital		17,200
Petrofinance Ltd		4,000
Sales		3,090
Purchases	1,400	
Rent	160	
Greasoils		200
Discount received		36
	24,526	24,526

COMMENT I have balanced only those accounts which contain more than one entry. In the others the sole entry stands out clearly and this is the balance in that account. The following procedure is recommended if your trial balance fails to agree.

1 Make certain that you calculated the owner's capital correctly and that the balance sheet was the same as the example shown above.

2 Check that the opening assets and sources of finance were entered on the correct side of their accounts. The opening asset balances should equal the opening balances for capital and liabilities.

3 Go through each transaction following the rules on page 72. Make certain that for each debit entry there is a corresponding credit entry for the same amount.

4 Check that you have calculated the balances on each account accurately, paying particular attention to those accounts with most entries. Remember the balance of an account is a debit balance if the debit side is greater than the credit. If the credit side is greater it is a credit balance. It is the balance brought down, **not** the balance carried down that is the balance of the account.

5 Make certain you have put the balances in the right column of the trial balance.

IDENTIFYING THE TYPE OF ACCOUNT

One of the things you now ought to be able to do is to identify a type of account from the information given in the trial balance. Usually the name of the account is enough of a clue. For example, equipment and machinery is obviously a fixed asset; rent is an expense; and capital is a source of finance. When the name of the account is the name of a person or the name of another business it is not quite so easy. There are two possibilities. The other person or business could be a debtor or a creditor. In order to be certain with the identification you need to know something more than the name of the account. Of course if you have access to the account you can tell from the types of entries it contains whether it is the account of a customer who is a debtor or the account of a supplier who is a creditor. If you only know what kind of balance is in the account then you should still be able to identify it. **Assets** have debit balances and **liabilities** have credit balances. An account called FB Ltd which has a debit balance is therefore that of a debtor while an account called Percy Hodge with a credit balance is therefore that of a creditor.

4.4 ERRORS AND THE SUSPENSE ACCOUNT

When entering transactions it is likely that mistakes will be made occasionally. Practice helps to eliminate mistakes and experience assists in finding them when they do still happen. Preparing a trial balance regularly is one way of limiting the number of errors that may have to be dealt with. If a trial balance taken out one month ago showed everything was OK then any failure for the trial balance totals to agree now is good evidence that the mistake or mistakes are likely to have been made in the last month. If, however, a trial balance has not been prepared for a year then it does make a mistake more difficult to find.

Sometimes, though, finding why the trial balance does not agree proves to be very difficult, particularly in a large firm where hundreds of transactions are being recorded in a single day. There may not be enough time to look for the errors. What can be done? One temporary way around the problem is to invent an account and debit or credit it with the amount needed to make the trial balance agree. This account is called a suspense account. When the error is discovered the suspense account can be closed.

Example

On 30 April the debit balances in our firm's trial balance totalled £100 more than the credit balances and a suspense account is opened.

Suspense a/c

30 April	Difference in books	100

If this credit balance is now added to the other credit balances in the trial balance the debit total will now equal the credit total. They have been **made** to be equal.

Staff will now be alerted to look for any error or errors that might account for this. The larger the amount involved the greater will be the urgency! For a big firm £100 is not a large amount and it might not be worthwhile diverting staff to look for it. They will just be told to keep their eyes open. Frequently mistakes solve themselves.

Suppose that on 27 May Mrs Merry writes to complain that the statement we have sent her shows that she owes £450 when in fact she owes £350 because she paid £100 on 29 April. When this is checked we discover that a debit entry has been made in our bank account to record the money received but no entry has been made in Mrs Merry's account to reduce the amount she owes. We can put the matter right by debiting the suspense account and crediting the account of Mrs Merry. We should also apologise to her of course! The accounts will then look like this:

Suspense account

27 May	Merry		100	30 April	Difference in books	100

S. Merry

1 May	Balance	b/d	450	27 May	Suspense account	100

The suspensé account is now closed until it is needed again and Mrs Merry's account is reduced by £100 to a debit balance of £350. Provided no other errors have been made in the meantime the totals of a trial balance now extracted would agree.

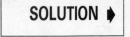
SELF-CHECK ▶
4.4

Suppose that your trial balance of 30 June shows that the credit balances are £25 greater than the debits. A discount received of £25 for promptly settling an amount owing to R. Stevens has been entered on the credit side of the discount received account but had not been debited to Stevens' account. This was discovered on 4 August.

First open a suspense account to record the difference in the books at 30 June and then show the entries in the ledger that would be needed to correct the error.

SOLUTION ▶

Suspense a/c

30 June	Difference in books		25	4 Aug	R. Stevens	25

R. Stevens

4 Aug	Suspense account	25	

COMMENT ▶ When asked to make entries to correct mistakes it is useful to picture what the correct entries should have been. In this case there should have been a debit entry in the account of Stevens and a credit entry in the account for discount received. As the entry in the discount received account was the one made and the entry in Stevens' account not made then after you have done the correction you should end up with the debit entry in the account of Stevens.

4.5 ERRORS NOT REVEALED BY A TRIAL BALANCE

Although useful as a means of checking the accuracy of transactions in the ledger, the trial balance is not foolproof. There are some errors it will not reveal. These are often grouped into five main types.

(a) Errors of omission
A transaction omitted from both the debit and credit sides of the account will leave the trial balance unaffected.

(b) Errors of commission
This means that something has been done but has been done incorrectly. A common example is when M. R. Smith's account is debited with £10 instead of, say, M. B. Smith's. As long as the credit entry has been made such an error will not show up in the trial balance.

(c) Errors of principle
These are errors that offend aginst a basic rule of book-keeping. For example the purchase of stock should be entered in the purchases account while the purchase of another asset should be entered in its own account. A garage which purchased a breakdown vehicle for £4,000 and records this in the purchases account containing vehicles bought for resale would be making an error of principle. Such an error would not affect the trial balance.

(d) Compensating errors
If the sales account is overcast (overadded) by, say, £100 and the wages account is overcast by the same amount the trial balance will not be affected. The extra £100 credit in the sales account will be compensated for by the extra £100 debit in the wages account.

(e) Original errors
These are made when copying figures from the documents from

which the entries are made. For example if an invoice for £110 received from T. Jones, a supplier, is entered in the supplier's account and the purchases account as £11, the trial balance will not show that an error has been made.

All such errors must be put right as soon as they are discovered. This is how the above errors should be corrected.

(a) Errors of commission
These can be put right by making the entries that have been omitted.

(b) Errors of commission

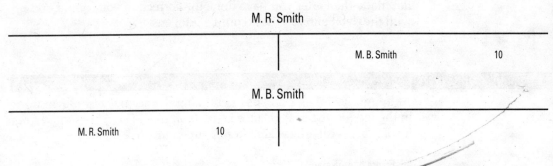

M. R. Smith

| | | M. B. Smith | 10 |

M. B. Smith

| M. R. Smith | 10 | | |

The credit entry in the account of M. R. Smith removes the mistake and the debit entry in M. B. Smith's account places the £10 where it really belongs.

(c) Errors of principle

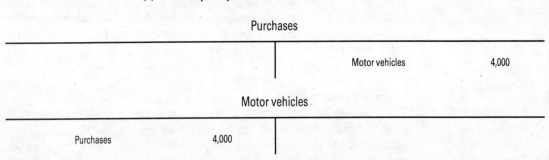

Purchases

| | | Motor vehicles | 4,000 |

Motor vehicles

| Purchases | 4,000 | | |

This is similar to Smith's case as it involves removing an amount from one account (purchases) where it had been placed incorrectly and entering it where it should have been (motor vehicles).

(d) Compensating errors
These can be corrected by repeating the addition of the sales and wages accounts and amending the totals.

(e) Original errors

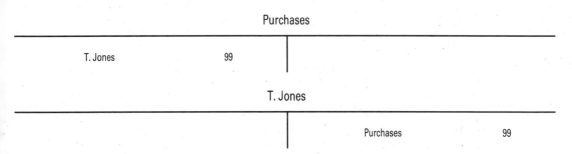

Purchases

| T. Jones | 99 | | |

T. Jones

| | | Purchases | 99 |

The £99 debited to purchases account and credited to Jones' account raises the £11 to £110.

SELF-CHECK ▶
4.5

Questions involving errors are often set in examinations at this level. Learn the types of error that do *not* affect the trial balance and make up some examples of your own to illustrate them.

COMMENT ▶

There is no way of checking this work. You will have to be honest with yourself! It is well worth learning these types of error and this is a topic you could also return to when you have completed the rest of the book.

EXERCISES

4.1

(*a*)   The following account appears in the ledger of H. Highgate & Co. Balance it at the close of business on 28 Feb and state what this balance means.

(*b*)   Describe the transaction that has resulted in each entry.

T. Smith & Co

1 Feb	Balance	b/d	350	7 Feb	Returns in	58
4 Feb	Sales		234	9 Feb	Bank	243
				9 Feb	Discount	7
					Balance	276
			584			584
			276			

4.2

Bryn Evans opened a shop on 1 August 1988. He had £1,350 in the bank, £253 in cash, £8,575 worth of stock and furniture and fittings worth £9,000. He had borrowed £5,000 from Busifinance for two years and provided the rest of the finance himself.

(a)   Draft a balance sheet to show Bryn's position on 1 August 1988.

(b)   Open a ledger account for each item and enter the opening balances.

(c)   Enter the following transactions in the ledger, opening new accounts when necessary.

(d)   Prepare a trial balance on 10 August.

2 Aug   Cash sales £400.

3 Aug   Cash sales £575; purchases £1,250 on credit.

4 Aug   Cash sales £356; paid £800 into the bank.

5 Aug   Paid rent £160 by cheque.

6 Aug   Credit sales £40; purchases £200 on credit.

7 Aug   Paid wages £90 by cheque.

8 Aug   Cash sales £450; cash purchases £94.

9 Aug   Paid insurance £45 in cash.

10 Aug Paid creditors £790 by cheque; received £20 from debtors.

4.3

John Henry's trial balance of 31 July shows that the debit balances are £124 less than the credits. Open a suspense account to record the difference.

On 19 August it was discovered that a cheque for this amount paid to Country Supplies on 5 July had been entered in the bank account but the other entry had not been made.

Make entries in the ledger to correct the error.

4.4

(a)   The following accounts appear in the books of Yvette Hughes. Explain the transactions that gave rise to the entries.

Not more than a single sentence is needed to explain each entry.

(i)   A Sowter a/c

16 Jan	Purchases returns	5	1 Jan	Balance	b/d	65
28 Jan	Bank	65	14 Jan	Purchases		90

(ii)   Purchases a/c

31 March	Sundries	724	30 March	Drawings		44

(iii)   Drawings a/c

28 Feb	Bank	96			
30 March	Purchases	44			

(b) (i) Calculate the balance of Sowter's account and state what it means.
(ii) Assume that the purchases account and drawings account are closed on 31 March. State precisely the entry which will be made in each case.

(MEG specimen paper)

4.5 Below are the ledger accounts as they appear in the books of R. Eastern, Butchers.

John Evans' account

1986								
1 April	Balance	b/d	600	12 April	Cheque			580
10 April	Goods		600	12 April	Discount			20
				16 April	Returns			10
				30 April	Balance	c/d		590
			1,200					1,200
1 May	Balance	b/d	690					

Welsh Meat Suppliers plc

18 April	Cheque		600	1 April	Balance	b/d	650
18 April	Discount		50	20 April	Goods		400
30 April	Balance	c/d	400				
			1,050				1,050
				1 May	Balance	b/d	400

Vehicles and equipment

1 April	Balance	b/d	10,000	10 April	Bank		2,000
28 April	Meat Trade Supply Association		5,000	30 April	Balance	c/d	13,000
			15,000				15,000
1 May	Balance	b/d	13,000				

You are required to take each ledger account in turn and briefly explain the meaning of each entry (taken in date order).
Answer in the manner set out overleaf:

John Evans a/c

1 April	John Evans owes R. Eastern £600
10 April	etc.

(WJEC specimen paper)

4.6

I. Whale commenced business on 1 December 1986 with £10,000 in a bank account. He purchased furniture and fittings for £2,000 and paid immediately by cheque.

His other transactions for the month of December were:

8 December	Bought goods for resale from T. Cod £800 plus £120 VAT on credit.
12 December	Sold goods on credit to R. Pike £1,200 plus £180 VAT.
19 December	Paid electricity by cheque £180.
29 December	R. Pike settled his account by cheque.
	I. Whale cashed a cheque for £400 private expenses.
	Cash sales during the month all paid into the bank totalled £900 plus £135 VAT.

Required

(a)   (i) Preparation of each of the following ledger accounts of I. Whale for the month of December 1986: Bank, Capital, Furniture and fittings, Purchases, T. Cod, VAT, Sales, R. Pike, Electricity, Drawings.

(ii) Preparation of I. Whale's trial balance as at 31 December 1986.

(b)   (i) **Two** types of error which would **not** prevent trial balance totals from being the same.

(ii) An explanation, using an example in each case, why the trial balance would still agree, even though such errors exist.

(SEG specimen paper)

ACCOUNTING FOR PROFIT

CONTENTS

In chapter two we defined profit as: total revenue for a period less total expenses for that period. If you are uncertain about what counts as revenue and expenses in this calculation read chapter two. In order to be able to show the calculation of profits in the accounts of a business, we need to distinguish between gross profit and net profit.

First refer back to the answer to self-check 2.4(b) on page 48. You will see that the total amount of profit earned by Liz Fry in 1988 was £15,800. This, in fact, is more correctly known as the net profit. Most businesses do not calculate this figure by deducting total revenue expenditure from total revenue in one single calculation as we did. They introduce a preliminary stage in which gross profit is calculated.

Gross profit may be defined as the difference between the revenue earned from sales and the cost of goods sold. If this definition is applied to the information on page 48 we can calculate Liz Fry's gross profit for the year 1988.

	£
Sales revenue	50,000
Less Cost of food and drink sold	12,000
Gross profit	38,000

In this case the cost of goods sold had been calculated. It is not always that easy! The following information relates to the business of Vic Sharpe who buys and sells motor vehicles in his spare time:

1988

1 Jan–31 Dec	Vehicles bought by Sharpe for £9,000.
1 Jan–31 Dec	Revenue earned from sales £14,000.
1 Jan	Sharpe's stock of vehicles: two Fords, cost price £500 each.
31 Dec	Sharpe's stock of vehicles remaining: two Renaults, cost price £750 each.

At first glance you might think that Sharpe's gross profit for 1988 was

£5,000. This is calculated as the difference between the revenue earned from sales (£14,000) and the cost of vehicles bought (£9,000). This is **not** correct. The total cost of cars bought in 1988 is not the same as the cost of the cars sold in 1988.

There are two reasons for this. First, some of the cars sold in 1988 had been bought the previous year and would have been part of his stock at the beginning of 1988. Second, some of the cars bought in 1988 had not been sold by the end of the year and form the closing stock on 31 December. A simple formula can be applied to work out the cost of the cars sold. Add the cost of the stock purchased to the value of the opening stock at cost price. This gives us the cost of the stock **available** for sale. If we deduct from this the cost of the stock not sold – i.e. the closing stock at cost price – we are left with the actual cost of the stock sold. This may be seen more easily in the following form:

	Opening stock at cost price
add	Cost of stock purchased during the year
=	Cost of stock available for sale
Less	Closing stock at cost price
=	Cost of stock sold

If this formula is applied to Sharpe's dealings we can calculate his cost of stock sold for 1988:

	£
Opening stock at cost price	1,000
add Cost of stock purchased during the year	9,000
Cost of stock available for sale	10,000
less Closing stock at cost price	1,500
Cost of stock sold 1988	8,500

It is then possible to put this figure from the sales revenue to find the gross profit:

	£
Revenue earned from sales in 1988	14,000
less Cost of stock sold in 1988	8,500
Gross profit for 1988	5,500

Sharpe's gross profit of £5,500 seems very good – especially as it is earned from an interest that only occupies his spare time. However, it is not the same as his true or **net profit**, which is the total revenue received from business operations less the total revenue expenditure incurred. So far we have only deducted one item of revenue expenditure – the actual cost of the cars sold. To calculate net profit we must deduct all the other items of revenue expenditure from gross profit. In 1988 Sharpe paid rent and rates on his workshop of £900 and purchased parts and lubricants costing £800. His net profit for 1988 is therefore £3,800.

	£	£
Gross profit 1988		5,500
less Rent and rates	900	
Lubricants and parts	800	
		1,700
Net profit		3,800

The account in which profit is measured is called the **trading and profit and loss account**. The example following contains the information relating to Sharpe's business for 1988.

Trading and profit and loss account of Vic Sharpe for the year ended 31 December 1988

	£	£
Sales		14,000
less Cost of goods sold:		
Opening stock	1,000	
Purchases	9,000	
	10,000	
less Closing stock	1,500	
		8,500
Gross profit		5,500
less Expenses:		
Rent and rates	900	
Lubrication and parts	800	
		1,700
Net profit		3,800

Notes

1　The heading contains the name of the account, the name of the business or owner and the period for which profit is being measured.

2　It is incorrect to date such an account 'as at 31 December' as you would a balance sheet, because it contains information relating to the measurement of profit over a particular period of time – usually a year.

3　The section of the account in which gross profit is calculated is known as the trading section, while that in which net profit is measured is known as the profit and loss section. Sometimes these sections are shown as separate accounts, in which case gross profit is measured in the trading account and net profit in the profit and loss account.

4　The earlier account is in vertical style. This is only one of a number of styles that can be used. At one time the trading and profit and loss account was prepared like other ledger accounts with debits (expenses) on the left and credits (revenue) on the right. It is important that whatever layout is used, the contents should be easily understood.

SELF-CHECK 5.1

Prepare a trading and profit and loss account from the following information relating to the business of Katie Shaw for the period 1 Jan 1988 to 30 June 1988.

	£
Sales of meals and drinks	20,000
Purchases of food and drinks	5,000
Stock of food and drink 1 January 1988	300
Stock of food and drink 30 June 1988	650
Rent and rates	360
Purchase of new equipment	1,575
Depreciation on fixed assets	375
Insurance	150
Staff salaries	9,000
Electricity	750

SOLUTION ▶

Trading and profit and loss account of Katie Shaw for the six months ended 30 June 1988

	£	£
Sales		20,000
less Cost of goods sold:		
Opening stock	300	
Purchases	5,000	
	5,300	
less Closing stock	650	
		4,650
Gross profit		15,350
less Expenses:		
Staff salaries	9,000	
Rent and rates	360	
Depreciation on fixed assets	375	
Insurance	150	
Electricity	750	
		10,635
Net profit		4,715

COMMENT ▶

One item included in the information was not needed – the new equipment purchased. This was included to reinforce the point that only revenue expenditure is deducted from revenue in order to calculate profit. Purchase of new equipment is capital expenditure and should not have been included.

Once you have grasped the basic layout of a trading and profit and loss account it is possible to extend it to enable other information to be included.

5.2 THE TRADING ACCOUNT

The additional items that appear most frequently in the measurement of gross profit in the trading account are **returns inward** and **returns outward**. The first of these is also known as sales returns and has the effect of reducing the value of the sales of a business. It is therefore essential to deduct the amount of returns inward from the figure for sales in order to find the true or net value of the sales. Similarly, returns outward or purchases returns must be deducted from the purchases to obtain the true or net purchases figure. Suppose that in self check 5.1 there had been returns inward of £2,000 and returns outward of £1,000. The trading section would have appeared like this:

Trading account of Katie Shaw for the six months ended 30 June 1988

	£	£	£
Sales		20,000	
less Returns inward		2,000	
Net sales			18,000
less Cost of goods sold:			
Opening stock		300	
Purchases	5,000		
less Returns outward	1,000		
Net purchases		4,000	
		4,300	
less Closing stock		650	
			3,650
Gross profit			14,350

You will see that I have added an extra column. The advice on the drafting of a balance sheet also applies to the trading and profit and loss account. Use the end column for the subtotal figures and work inwards when you need to make further calculations. Practice makes perfect when it comes to layout but remember there are other acceptable methods and the most important thing is that your account is easily read and understood.

EXPENSES INCURRED BEFORE THE GOODS ARE READY FOR SALE

Trading accounts are sometimes further complicated by the existence of expenses which are thought to be better placed there than in the profit and loss account. These are expenses incurred before the goods are ready for sale. There are two common examples.

1 Carriage inwards

The first of these is the transport cost of getting the goods into the firm. **Carriage inwards** is the term used to describe this expense. Suppliers who deliver goods may not make a separate charge for delivery. The charge may be included in the purchase price. If, however, a separate charge is made for transporting the goods this expense should be added to the purchases figure in the trading account as clearly it is part of the cost of obtaining the stock.

If the business also pays for transporting goods that have been sold this is known as **carriage outwards**. As this expense is one that is incurred *after* goods are ready for sale it takes its place with the other expenses in the profit and loss section.

2 Wages

The second example involves labour costs. In some businesses a distinction is made between employees who receive **wages** and those who receive **salaries**. There is no one set criterion for making this distinction. In some firms staff receiving their pay on a weekly basis may be said to be wage earning while those receiving their pay monthly are salaried. In other firms the production staff are the wage earners and all other staff are salaried. Clearly in this case production wages are related to the time before the goods are actually ready for sale and should be shown in the trading account. When doing examination exercises you will not be in a position to ask anyone what the firm's policy is regarding the distinction between wages and salaries. The best solution is therefore to regard wages as a production expense and enter it in the trading account leaving salaries to be included in the profit and loss account.

The following is an example of a trading account containing wages and carriage in addition to the other items we have covered.

Trading account of Katie Shaw for the six months ended 30 June 1988

	£	£	£
Sales		20,000	
less Returns inward		2,000	
Net sales			18,000
less Cost of goods sold:			
Opening stock		300	
Purchases	5,000		
less Returns outward	1,000		
	4,000		
Carriage inward	200		
Net purchases		4,200	
		4,500	
less Closing stock		650	
		3,850	
Wages		4,000	
			7,850
Gross profit			10,150

It is obviously a little more complicated, but do not worry, this is about as detailed as it can get! Attempt the following to see if you have mastered it.

SELF-CHECK ▶
5.2

The following information relates to Tom Brown's business for the year ended 31 December 1988:
Purchases £50,000; Sales £90,000; Opening stock £5,000; Closing stock £6,500; Returns inward £450; Returns outward £675; Carriage inwards £360; Carriage outwards £298; Salaries £17,000; Wages £23,560.

SOLUTION ▶

Trading account of Tom Brown for the year ended 31 December 1988

	£	£	£
Sales		90,000	
less Returns inward		450	
Net sales			89,550
less Cost of goods sold:			
Opening stock		5,000	
Purchases	50,000		
less Returns outward	675		
	49,325		
Carriage inward	360		
Net purchases		49,685	
		54,685	
less Closing stock		6,500	
		48,185	
Wages		23,560	
			71,745
Gross profit c/d			17,805

COMMENT ▶

It is important to remember that salaries and carriage outwards are both expenses which are incurred after the goods are ready for sale. They do not therefore appear in the trading section. Another thing to look out for in the trading account is the careless replacement of an addition by a deduction. This is most likely to occur with carriage inwards. Students get used to deducting returns inward from sales and returns outward from purchases and sometimes then make the mistake of deducting carriage inwards instead of adding it to the purchases figure. Gross profit is the final figure in the trading account but it is going to be needed again in the profit and loss account. Therefore many accountants show the gross profit being carried down (c/d) from the trading account and brought down (b/d) to the profit and loss account.

5.3 THE PROFIT AND LOSS ACCOUNT

The profit and loss account is used to obtain the net profit. This is normally much less complicated than the trading account. Usually all that has to be done is to total all revenue expenditure items that have not already been dealt with in the trading account and then deduct this total from the gross profit. This was demonstrated in section 5.1. Most businesses earn all their revenue from sales of a product or service but, as we have seen, sometimes revenue is earned from an extra activity such as letting out property. In this case the rent received has to be added to the gross profit. This is normally done before the total revenue expenditure is deducted. For example, suppose that the Tom Brown in the last self-check rented out some spare land to another business and received £3,500 for it in 1988. If his only expenses in addition to the ones mentioned in self-check 5.2 are insurance £460, depreciation £600, and bad debts £50, his profit and loss account would look like this:

Profit and loss account of Tom Brown for the year ended 31 December 1988

1988	£	£
Gross profit		17,805
Rent received		3,500
		21,305
Less expenses:		
Salaries	17,000	
Carriage outwards	298	
Insurance	460	
Depreciation	600	
Bad debts	50	
		18,408
Net profit		2,897

Another revenue that occurs quite frequently is that of discount received. As we know from section 3.6 this involves reducing the amount that has to be paid to creditors by making prompt payment. The effect is the same as if the cash was received. Discount received may be added to gross profit in the same way that rent received was added in the above example. Discount allowed, of course, is an expense and as such should be included in the profit and loss account with the other expenses.

SELF-CHECK ▶
5.3

The following trial balance has been extracted from the accounts of Ted Tucker on 31 December 1988.

	£	£
Sales		75,000
Purchases	35,000	
Returns inward and returns outward	1,650	2,650
Stock (1 Jan 1988)	4,670	
Carriage inward	276	
Discount allowed and received	360	179
Salaries	20,560	
Rates	786	
Insurance	465	
Depreciation on fixed assets	650	
Premises	21,000	
Equipment	7,000	
Debtors	1,235	
Trade creditors		3,452
Capital (1 Jan 1988)		20,000
Bank	7,629	
	101,281	101,281

The stock was valued at £6,500 on 31 December 1988. Prepare Tucker's trading and profit and loss account for the year ended 31 December 1988.

SOLUTION ▶

Trading and profit and loss account of T. Tucker for the year ended 31 December 1988

	£	£	£
Sales		75,000	
less Returns inward		1,650	
Net sales			73,350
Less Cost of sales:			
Opening stock		4,670	
Purchases	35,000		
less Returns outward	2,650		
	32,350		
Carriage inward	276		
Net purchases		32,626	
		37,296	
less Closing stock		6,500	
			30,796
Gross profit			42,554
Discount received			179
			42,733
Less expenses:			
Salaries		20,560	
Discount allowed		360	
Rates		786	
Insurance		465	
Depreciation		650	
			22,821
Net profit			19,912

COMMENT ▶

Questions requiring the preparation of a trading and profit and loss account from a trial balance are met frequently in examinations. It is worth getting into the habit of approaching such questions in a logical and careful manner.

You will probably have noticed that the information in this trial balance was displayed in groups. Trading account items came first followed by the profit and loss account items and then finally those that were not relevant to the calculation of profit. This was done to help you but it is not usually done by examiners. It is a good idea, therefore, to begin such a question by marking the trial balance. You may choose any method you wish but I always use T for a trading account item, P for a profit and loss account item and B for a balance sheet item. It seems the most logical.

The next thing to note is that some lines contained two items and two figures. I would not recommend that you did this if you were drawing up a trial balance, but examiners frequently do so as it is testing your knowledge as to which balance is which. If you did not remember that returns inward was the debit balance and returns outward the credit then I hope you looked it up and did not simply guess. If you understand the principles of book-keeping you should always be able to work out which figure refers to which item. Returns inward are a reduction of sales and therefore, as sales is a credit item, returns inward must be a debit in order to effect a reduction. Similarly returns outward must be a credit as purchases is a debit. Discount allowed is a debit because all expenses are debits, while discount received is the credit because it is a form of income.

5.4 TRANSFERS TO THE TRADING AND PROFIT AND LOSS ACCOUNT

It is a good idea to return briefly to the ledger to see how we show the transfer of an item into the profit and loss account. For example, the sales in the last self-check totalled £75,000. This figure would have been the total of all the credit entries in the sales account. To save space we will assume that the sales account would have been balanced correctly before preparing the trial balance. We can then show the sales account like this.

Sales

	1988			
	31 Dec	Balance	b/d	75,000

To transfer an amount from one account to another you must not break the rule that double entry book-keeping requires two entries. The first entry is in the account from which the figure is being transferred. It is made on the *opposite* side to which the amount is at present found. Thus in the sales account a debit entry is needed. The account will then be temporarily closed as there is now no balance in it and it will look like this.

Sales

1988				1988			
31 Dec	Transferred to Trading a/c	75,000		31 Dec	Balance	b/d	75,000

The second entry is then made in the trading account as we have already seen. Strictly following the rules of double entry book-keeping this second entry should be a credit entry. Today it is unusual to see a trading and profit and loss account prepared as a ledger account with debits on the left and credits on the right. Instead the calculation of gross and net profit is normally shown in vertical style and represents the equations on which the calculations are based. Provided that the rules of book-keeping are carefully followed the correct answer for gross and net profit may be obtained in the form of a ledger account. It is less likely, however, that there will be real understanding of how these figures have been obtained. For example, the following trading and profit and loss account uses the same figures as in self-check 5.3. It has been obtained by carefully transferring all the relevant figures to the correct side of a ledger style trading and profit and loss account:

Trading and profit and loss account of T. Tucker for the year ended 31 December 1988

Opening stock		4,670	Sales		75,000
Purchases		35,000	Returns outward		2,650
Returns inward		1,650	Closing stock		6,500
Carriage inward		276			
Gross profit	c/d	42,554			
		84,150			84,150
Salaries		20,560	Gross profit	b/d	42,554
Discount allowed		360	Discount received		179
Rates		786			
Insurance		465			
Depreciation		650			
Net profit		19,912			
		42,733			42,733

Compare this with the vertical layout of self-check 5.3 and note the following points.

1   The gross profit and net profit figures are the same.

2 Gross profit is the balance of the trading account and net profit is the balance of the profit and loss account.

3 All the items that were shown as balances in the trial balance are on the same of the trading and profit and loss account as they were in the trial balance.

4 In the vertical account returns inward were deducted from sales while returns outward and closing stock were deducted from purchases. The same effect is obtained in the ledger account version because returns outward and closing stock are on the opposite side to purchases while returns inward is on the opposite side to sales.

5 There is one entry that did not show in the trial balance. This is the figure for closing stock which was given to you as extra information below the trial balance. Because the trading account requires two stock figures it is important that you label or date them in order not to confuse the opening and closing stocks. This is what the stock account will look like after preparing the trading account.

Stock

1988				1988		
1 Jan	Balance	b/d	4,670	31 Dec	Transferred to trading a/c	4,670
31 Dec	Trading a/c		6,500			

The opening stock is transferred to the trading account at the end of the trading period for which profit is being measured. The account is temporarily closed as there is now no balance in it. When the closing stock entry is made in the trading account it is accompanied by an entry in the stock account. As stock is an asset this entry is, of course, a debit. The closing stock for 1988 will, of course, become the opening stock for 1989.

Which of the two styles of layout do you think is best for displaying clearly the calculations of gross and net profit? This question has been put to all the groups of students I have taught for a number of years. The vote is overwhelmingly in favour of the newer vertical layout. Examination questions, however, still sometimes make use of the horizontal ledger account format. It is therefore essential that you understand it.

SELF-CHECK ▶
5.4

The following information relates to the business of J. Spry for the six months ended 31 December 1988: Opening stock £4,000; purchases £14,000; sales £53,000; returns inward £1,300; returns outward £700; carriage inwards £450; carriage outwards £396; closing stock £5,000.
(a)   Prepare a vertical trading account.
(b)   Prepare a ledger-style horizontal trading account.

SOLUTION ▶

(a) Trading account of J. Spry for the half-year ended 31 December 1988

	£	£	£
Sales		53,000	
less Returns inward		1,300	
Net sales			51,700
less Cost of goods sold:			
Opening stock		4,000	
Purchases	14,000		
less Returns outward	700		
	13,300		
Carriage inwards	450		
Net purchases		13,750	
		17,750	
less Closing stock		5,000	
			12,750
Gross profit			38,950

(b) Trading account of J. Spry for the half-year ended 31 December 1988

1988	£		£
Opening stock	4,000	Sales	53,000
Purchases	14,000	Returns outward	700
Returns inward	1,300	Closing stock	5,000
Carriage inwards	450		
Gross profit	38,950		
	58,700		58,700

COMMENT ▶

I recommend that you use the vertical layout when requested to prepare a trading account. Knowledge of the ledger style layout is needed, however, when examiners choose to present their questions in that way. I hope you remember to exclude the carriage outwards from both your accounts as this expense is shown in the profit and loss account.

5.5 FINAL ACCOUNTS AND THE BALANCE SHEET

Questions requiring you to prepare a trading and profit and loss account for a period and a balance sheet at the end of that period are extremely common. Sometimes the question is shortened to state, for example: 'Prepare final accounts at 31 December'.

A balance sheet is not, strictly speaking, an account. It is a collection of the balances in the ledger that refer to assets and sources of finance. However, when a question requires you to prepare 'final accounts' you should take it to mean that a balance sheet as well as a trading and profit and loss account is required. The term 'final accounts' comes from the fact that they are prepared at the end of the financial period.

After the trading and profit and loss account has been prepared a large number of accounts in the ledger will be closed, albeit temporarily, by entries transferring these items into this account. The accounts that still have balances in them will be those accounts that were not needed to calculate gross and net profit. In other words they will be the accounts relating to assets and sources of finance – those that you need to prepare the balance sheet. If you look back to self-check 5.3 you will find the following accounts in T. Tucker's trial balance that were not used in preparing the trading and profit and loss account:

	Dr	Cr
Premises	21,000	
Equipment	7,000	
Debtors	1,235	
Trade creditors		3,452
Capital (1 Jan 1988)		20,000
Bank	7,629	

We can now use these to prepare a balance sheet at 31 December 1988. You will need to remember that since this trial balance was extracted from the books we have had a stock-take which resulted in the information that the stock is now valued at £6,500. We also know that the owner has made a net profit of £19,912. This profit belongs to the owner and therefore increases the owner's capital.

Balance Sheet of T. Tucker as at 31 December 1988

Fixed assets	£	£	£
Premises		21,000	
Equipment		7,000	
			28,000
Current assets			
Stock	6,500		
Debtors	1,235		
Bank	7,629		
		15,364	
Less **current liabilities**			
Trade creditors		3,452	
Working capital			11,912
Total assets less current liabilities			39,912
Financed by:			
Owner's capital (1 Jan 88)		20,000	
Add Net profit for year		19,912	
			39,912

You must not think that because we have been concentrating on the end of year accounts that the ledger accounts can be forgotten. Questions are asked frequently on matters to do with the ledger. Each item appearing in the balance sheet has one thing in common. They are the only accounts that at present have balances in the ledger. Two key ones are the accounts for stock and capital. This is because entries are made in both of these after preparing the trial balance. Look back at the stock account on page 125. You will see that the opening stock was transferred into the trading account at the end of the financial period and a new entry made for the closing stock. Before writing out the balance sheet this account will have been balanced and will now look like this.

Stock

1988				1988			
1 Jan	Balance	b/d	4,670	31 Dec	Transferred to trading a/c		4,670
31 Dec	Trading a/c		6,500	31 Dec	Balance	c/d	6,500
1989							
1 Jan	Balance	b/d	6,500				

The end of year (1988) stock is clearly shown as a debit balance which identifies it as an asset. It is also the opening stock for the next year (1989) and as such will eventually be transferred into the trading account for that period.

The capital account will need to show the increase in capital caused by the net profit made. This needs a credit entry and will look like this after it has been balanced.

Capital account

1988				1988			
31 Dec	Balance	c/d	39,912	1 Jan	Balance	b/d	20,000
				31 Dec	Net profit		19,912
			39,912				39,912
				1989			
				1 Jan	Balance	b/d	39,912

Analyse the following trial balance and then prepare final accounts for the financial year 1988.

Trial Balance of P. Reeve as at 31 December 1988

	£	£
Sales		99,000
Purchases	32,500	
Returns inward and returns outward	1,675	2,257
Stock (1 Jan 1988)	4,170	
Wages	15,000	
Salaries	10,500	
Discount allowed and received	260	149
Rent received		985
Rates	686	
Insurance	365	
Carriage outwards	850	
Premises	65,000	
Furniture and fittings	6,000	
Debtors	1,565	
Trade creditors		3,652
Drawings	4,000	
Capital (1 Jan 1988)		30,000
Bank		6,528
	142,571	142,571

Note: Stock at 31 December 1988 was valued at £6,876.

SOLUTION ▶

Trading and profit and loss account of P. Reeve for the year ended 31 December 1988

	£	£	£
Sales		99,000	
less Returns inward		1,675	
Net sales			97,325
less Cost of goods sold:			
Opening stock		4,170	
Purchases	32,500		
less Returns outward	2,257		
Net purchases		30,243	
		34,413	
less Closing stock		6,876	
		27,537	
Wages		15,000	
			42,537
Gross profit			54,788
add Discount received			149
Rent received			985
			55,922
less Expenses:			
Salaries		10,500	
Discount allowed		260	
Rates		686	
Insurance		365	
Carriage outwards		850	
			12,661
Net profit			43,261

Balance Sheet of P. Reeve as at 31 December 1988

Fixed assets	£	£	£
Premises		65,000	
Furniture and fittings		6,000	
			71,000
Current assets			
Stock	6,876		
Debtors	1,565		
		8,441	
less **Current liabilities**			
Trade creditors	3,652		
Bank overdraft	6,528		
		10,180	
Working capital			(1,739)
Total assets less current liabilities			69,261
Financed by:			
Owner's capital (1 Jan)		30,000	
add Net profit		43,261	
		73,261	
less Drawings		4,000	
			69,261

COMMENT ▶

This question illustrates nicely the advantage to be gained by analysing the trial balance before launching into the trading and profit and loss account. Such analysis would make it much more likely that you would remember that when a distinction is made between wages and salaries then the wages should be shown in the trading account. You will notice that in the balance sheet working capital is enclosed in brackets. This is done to show that it is a negative figure caused by the fact that the current liabilities are greater in total value than the current assets. Use of brackets to indicate a negative figure is standard practice.

We have now come in a full circle. We started out several chapters ago with the balance sheet. We saw how ledger accounts could be opened from the information contained in it and how to open new ledger accounts when needed. You then learnt how to select the relevant items for calculating gross and net profit. This left us with the items concerned with assets and finance and enabled us to prepare a new balance sheet which incorporated our calculation of net profit. Having done this the ledger accounts are then ready for the new entries that will be needed in the new financial year. Understanding this cycle is very important, indeed it is essential. If you have any doubts after completing the following exercises I advise you to reread the preceding chapters.

EXERCISES

5.1

Select the information that is relevant and prepare a trading and profit and loss account for the period 1 July 1988 to 31 December 1988. The accounts are those of Tim Sharpe, grocer.

	£
Sales	34,000
Purchases	10,560
Stock at 1 July	2,300
Stock at 31 December	3,540
Rent and rates	750
Purchase of delivery vehicle	2,595
Depreciation on fixed assets	375
Insurance	250
Drawings	9,000
Electricity	950

5.2

The following information relates to Tom Brown's business for the year ended 31 March 1989:
Purchases £48,700; sales £96,470; opening stock £8,560; closing stock £9,573; returns inward £356; returns outward £534; carriage inwards £464; carriage outwards £798; salaries £27,000; wages £13,660.

Select the items that are relevant and prepare a trading account.

5.3

The following trial balance has been extracted from the accounts of S. Strong on 31 May 1989.

	£	£
Sales		85,453
Purchases	35,654	
Returns inward and returns outward	1,754	2,352
Stock (1 June 1988)	6,750	
Carriage inward	292	
Discount allowed and received	163	279
Salaries	22,456	
Rates	386	
Insurance	263	
Depreciation on fixed assets	545	
Premises	34,000	
Furniture and fittings	6,000	
Debtors and creditors	1,655	876
Drawings	6,500	
Capital (1 June 1988)		28,000
Bank	542	
	116,960	116,960

The stock was valued at £8,560 on 31 May 1989.

Prepare Strong's trading and profit and loss account for the year ended 31 May 1989 and a balance sheet as at that date.

5.4 The following information relates to the business of F. Green for the six months ended 31 October 1989: opening stock £4,870; purchases £23,450; sales £46,920; returns inward £980; returns outward £689; carriage inwards £667; closing stock £6,870.

(a) Prepare a vertical trading account.
(b) Prepare a ledger-style horizontal trading account.
(c) Show the stock account as it would appear after a balance sheet had been prepared on 31 October.

5.5 Analyse the following trial balance and then prepare final accounts for the financial year ended 31 May 1989.

Trial balance of T. Leaf as at 31 May 1989

	£	£
Sales		79,700
Purchases	30,780	
Returns inward and returns outward	797	1,457
Stock (1 June 1988)	4,680	
Wages	14,700	
Salaries	12,500	
Discount allowed and received	426	349
Rent received		655
Rates	526	
Insurance	315	
Carriage outwards	350	
Carriage inwards	198	
Premises	55,500	
Furniture and fittings	7,000	
Debtors and creditors	1,565	4,765
Drawings	7,000	
Capital (1 June 1988)		51,000
Bank	1,589	
	137,926	137,926

Note: Stock at 31 May 1988 was valued at £9,185.

5.6   Certain mistakes have been made in drawing up the trading and profit and loss account and the balance sheet of J. Tomlison, a sole trader.

Trading and profit and loss account of J. Tomlison for the year ended 31 December 1985

	£		£
Purchases	10,200	Sales	11,860
Sales returns	70	Discounts received	100
General expenses	500	Closing stock	2,970
Opening stock	3,160		
Profit (net)	1,000		
	14,930		14,930

Balance Sheet of J. Tomlison as at 31 December 1985

	£	£		£
Capital at 1 Jan 1985	3,300		Trade debtors	1,840
add Long term loan	1,200			
		4,500	Trade creditors	2,465
Drawings		300	Bank overdraft	415
Fixtures & fittings		610	Motor vehicles	2,660
Stock (31 Dec 1985)		2,970	Net profit	1,000
		8,380		8,380

You are required to:

(a)   draw up the Trading and profit and loss account in correct form clearly showing, within the trading and profit and loss account:

(i) the cost of goods sold;

(ii) the net sales;

(iii) the gross profit;

(iv) the net profit;

(b)   draw up the balance sheet in correct form clearly showing within the balance sheet:

(i) the total of the capital account on 31 December 1985;

(ii) the total of the current liabilities;

(iii) the total of the fixed assets;

(iv) the total of the current assets.

(WJEC specimen paper)

PREPAYMENTS AND ACCRUALS

CONTENTS

The next few chapters are going to deal with adjustments that may have to be made to entries in the ledger and the reasons for them. This is an area in which examiners set many questions. It is important, therefore, that you master it.

Until now all the expenses and revenues in the accounts have been assumed to belong to the period for which we have been preparing the trading and profit and loss account. This is a reasonable assumption. However if we have information that tells us that this is **not** the case then we must do something about it. This is because accounting does not take a cash view of receipts and payments but a real view. In other words, what matters when measuring profit is not the date that the cash was received and paid but the date the expense was incurred or the revenue earned.

6.1 EXPENSES PREPAID

A prepaid expense is not just one that has been paid for in advance. It is an expense that has been paid for in a financial period **prior** to the one in which the benefit of the expense is received. For example, a trader's financial year ends on 31 December and he pays his insurance broker by four quarterly instalments on the first day of January, April, July and October. For the year ended 31 December 1988 the total insurance bill was £400. You would expect therefore to find debit entries totalling £400 in his insurance account at the end of that year. It is possible, however, that towards the end of the year he might make a payment for insurance that relates to the next financial period. If this was done it would have to be recorded in the books and the total payments would now be £500. Care would have to be taken not to transfer this amount to the profit and loss account for the year 1988 because the real amount of the expense is only £400 which is £100 less than the cash amount. To do this we have to make an adjustment to the books. To see how that is done look first at the insurance account as it would appear in the ledger immediately before the trading and profit and loss account was prepared.

Insurance a/c

1988			£	
1 Jan	Bank		100	
1 April	Bank		100	
1 July	Bank		100	
1 Oct	Bank		100	
9 Dec	Bank		100	

As you can see, the four instalments for 1988 were all paid on the due date and an extra payment made on 9 December. As we know that the correct amount of insurance for 1988 is £400, the additional £100 must be an early payment for the next financial period. It is correct to make the entries in the bank account and the insurance account for this, but it would not be correct to transfer the whole of the £500 to the profit and loss account for 1988. We make an entry to transfer the **real** amount of the insurance to the profit and loss account leaving the remainder as a balance in the account.

Insurance a/c

1988		£	1988		£
1 Jan	Bank	100	31 Dec	Transfer to profit and loss a/c	400
1 April	Bank	100	31 Dec	Balance prepaid c/d	100
1 July	Bank	100			
1 Oct	Bank	100			
9 Dec	Bank	100			
		500			500
1988					
1 Jan	Balance prepaid b/d	100			

Like all accounts that have balances in them at the end of the financial period, the amount of the balance is entered in the balance sheet. All such debit balances are assets. The trader has the advantage of knowing that he is due to receive the benefit of £100 worth of insurance in 1989 for which he has already paid in 1988. As this asset will be used up very early in 1989 it will be shown as a current asset. The relevant entries in the final accounts follow:

Profit and loss account for year ended 31 December 1988

Expenses:	£
Insurance	400

Balance Sheet as at 31 December 1988

Current assets	£
Stock	—
Debtors	—
Bank	—
Prepaid insurance	100

Some textbooks advise placing prepayments with, or next to, the debtors. This is acceptable as logically the benefit of the insurance which is to be received is owed by the insurance company to the trader who has paid for it in advance. Others prefer to place it last on the grounds that it is even more liquid than cash as the money has already been spent. I leave the choice to you but stress the value of consistency.

SELF-CHECK ▶
6.1(a)

Mary Wilson's financial year ends on 30 June. She rents her premises at £200 per quarter which is payable on 1 July, 1 October, 1 January and 1 April. In the year ended 30 June 1988, which is her first year of trading, she made the following payments by cheque: 1 July 1987, £200; 3 October 1987, £200; 1 January 1988, £200; 2 April 1988, £200; 4 June 1988, £200.

Write up Mary's ledger account for rent and show all relevant entries in the final accounts at the end of the year.

SOLUTION ▶

Rent a/c

1987		£	1988		£
1 July	Bank	200	30 June	Transferred to profit & loss a/c	800
3 Oct	Bank	200	30 June	Balance prepaid c/d	200
1988					
1 Jan	Bank	200			
2 April	Bank	200			
4 June	Bank	200			
		1,000			1,000
1 July	Balance prepaid b/d	200			

Profit and loss account of Mary Wilson for the year ended 30 June 1988

Expenses	£
Rent	800

Balance Sheet of Mary Wilson as at 30 June 1988

Current assets	£
Prepaid rent	200

COMMENT ▶

As it has been stated that the premises were rented for £200 per quarter, and as there are four quarters in a year, it is clear that £800 must be the **real** expense of rent incurred in the year ended 30 June 1988. The additional £200 must therefore relate to the next financial year and be brought forward as a debit balance in the rent account. It thus represents an asset to Mary at the end of June 1988. In the first quarter of 1988 she will enjoy the use of premises for which she has already paid. You will notice that when balancing the rent account the word 'prepaid' has been inserted in the balances. While this is not absolutely necessary it is a useful reminder of the fact that an expense account has in it a balance which belongs in the balance sheet at the end of the financial year.

In both the example and the self-check the true expense for the year is known. Very often, however, only how much has been paid for an expense and how much of that amount is a prepayment is known. The correct amount to be transferred to the profit and loss account then has to be calculated. This often happens in an examination when a trial balance entry is given and you are told by how much it should be adjusted. For example the following appeared in Mary's trial balance at 30 June 1988.

Accounts	dr	cr
Rates	350	

You are then told that on 30 June £50 of rates had been paid in advance. Deducting this from the amount paid gives you the true value of rates for the year ended 30 June 1988, that is, £300. The final accounts would include the following entries:

Profit and loss account of M. Wilson for the year ended 30 June 1988

Expenses	£
Rates	300

Balance Sheet of M. Wilson as at 30 June 1988

Current assets	£
Prepaid rates	50

If a question only asks you to show the entries in the final accounts it is not essential that you show the rates account – though if the figures are complicated you might find it useful to get the answer right. You do need to be able to make the correct entries in the ledger, however, because sometimes you are asked to do so.

Rates

1987/8		£	1988		£
—	Bank (total)	350	30 June	Profit and loss a/c	300
			30 June	Balance prepaid c/d	50
		350			350
1988					
1 July	Balance prepaid b/d	50			

If you are not required to make the ledger account entries you could show the calculation in the profit and loss account like this:

Profit and loss account

Expenses	£	£
Rates	350	
less Prepaid	50	
		300

The advantage of doing this rather than just making an entry for £300 is that you are demonstrating to the examiner that you know how to deal with the matter of a £50 prepayment. While it might be unlikely that you will make an arithmetical error in a simple calculation there are times when the figures are not so easy. A mistake will always cost you marks but if you demonstrate the correct method you will not normally lose as much as if you did not.

SELF-CHECK ▶ 6.1(b)

Complete the following table in which (*a*) has been done for you.

	A/c	Trial balance 31.12.88 dr	Prepaid at 31.12.88 £	Profit & loss a/c 1988 £	Current asset in balance sheet 31.12.88 £
(a)	Rent	900	100	800	100
(b)	Rates	750	150		
(c)	Insurance	620		480	
(d)	Salaries		640	4,320	
(e)	Fuel			1,600	300
(f)	wages	490			120

SOLUTION ▶		
	(b)	Profit and loss a/c £600, current asset £150.
	(c)	Prepaid at 31.12.88 £140, current asset £140.
	(d)	Trial balance £4,960, current asset £640.
	(e)	Trial balance £1,900, prepaid at 31.12.88 £300.
	(f)	Prepaid at 31.12.88 £120, profit and loss a/c £370.

6.2 EXPENSES ACCRUED

The word 'accrued' here means outstanding or owing. Thus an accrued expense is one which is owing for a financial period but which is not paid until a subsequent financial period. The same rule applies in this case as it did to prepayments. The profit and loss account must show the **real** expense of the period and not just the amount paid. For example, suppose that a business rents property for £1,200 per annum and that this sum is payable in four quarterly instalments on the first day of January, April, July and October. In 1988 the rent account looked like this when the firm's financial year ended on 31 December.

Rent a/c

1988		£	
1 Jan	Bank	300	
1 April	Bank	300	
1 Sept	Bank	300	

Although the account contains £900 it would not be correct to transfer this amount to the profit and loss account for the year ended 31 December 1988 because the real expense of rent for the year is £1,200. In order to transfer this amount the amount outstanding is entered on the debit side as a balance accrued to carry down at the end of the year. It is then possible to transfer £1,200 to the profit and loss account. This amount is made up of £900 actually paid and £300 owing. Of course it is necessary that any balance carried down is then brought down to the other side of the account. The credit balance indicates that it is a liability and as such will appear in the balance sheet at the end of the year. Because payment will have to be made very soon, it will be placed next to the creditors in the current liabilities.

When completed, the rent account and the relevant entries in the final accounts will be as follows.

Rent

1988		£	1988		£
1 Jan	Bank	300	31 Dec	Profit & loss a/c	1,200
1 April	Bank	300			
1 Sept	Bank	300			
31 Dec	Balance accrued c/d	300			
		1,200			1,200
			1989		
			1 Jan	Balance accrued b/d	300

Profit and loss account for year ended 31 December 1988

Expenses	£
Rent	1,200

Balance Sheet as at 31 December 1988

Current liabilities	£
Accrued rent	300

SELF-CHECK ▶ 6.2(a)

The trial balance of a firm whose financial year ends on 31 March 1988 contains the following item.

A/cs	dr	cr
Wages	30,000	

Because the weekly wages were last made up on 26 March the amount of £350 has accrued by 31 March. Make the necessary adjustments to the wages account and show the relevant entries in the final accounts at the end of the year.

SOLUTION ▶

Wages a/c

1987/8		£	1988		£
—	Bank (total)	30,000	31 March	Profit & loss a/c	30,350
31 March	Balance accrued c/d	350			
		30,350			30,350
			1 April	Balance accrued b/d	350

Profit and loss account for year ended 31 March 1988

Expenses	£
Wages	30,350

Balance Sheet as at 31 March 1988

Current liabilities	£
Accrued wages	350

 **COMMENT ▶**

Many examination questions require only the final accounts to be shown. While you may decide to complete the ledger account adjustment as an aid to obtaining the correct answer, it is not absolutely necessary. The adjustment could be shown in the profit and loss account like this:

Profit and loss account for year ended 31 March 1988

Expenses	£	£
Wages	30,000	
add Accrual	350	
		30,350

The key point to keep in mind when deciding the amount of an expense to be included in the profit and loss account is the date it is incurred. If the expense refers to, say 1988, it must be included in that year's profit and loss account. If the full amount has not been paid in 1988 then the expense account must be adjusted to show the real expense for the period. Remember, however, to include the amount of any such adjustment for an expense outstanding in the balance sheet under the heading of current liabilities.

SELF-CHECK
6.2(b)

Complete the following table in which (a) has been done for you.

	A/c	cr	Accrued at 31.12.88 £	Profit & loss a/c 1988 £	Current liability in balance sheet 31.12.88 £
(a)	Rent	600	200	800	200
(b)	Rates	400	300		
(c)	Insurance	750		820	
(d)	Wages		100	800	
(e)	Salaries			900	300
(f)	Fuel	420			90

SOLUTION ▶

(b) Profit and loss a/c £700, current liability £300.
(c) Accrued at 31.12.88 £70, current liability £70.
(d) Trial balance £700, current liability £100.
(e) Trial balance £600, accrued at 31.12.88 £300.
(f) Accrued at 31.12.88 £90, profit and loss account £510.

6.3 INCOME IN ADVANCE

The rule to follow when allocating income to the correct accounting period is the same as the one applied to costs. Income or revenue is counted when goods are sold or services provided, not when the money is received. We have dealt already with the sale of goods on credit. The amount of the sale is credited to the sales account and a debit entry made in the account of the customer who is a debtor. The total sales will be transferred to the trading account at the end of the period whether or not the customer has paid for them. Similarly all other income must be shown in its correct period.

Example

Suppose a restaurant owner rents out the flat above his business to earn extra profit. He charges £100 per month and his financial year ends on 31 December. In the year ended 31 December 1988 the tenant paid the amount due on the first of each month and in December he made an additional payment of £100 for January 1989. The rent received account will have been credited with a total of £1,300 and the trial balance will like like this.

A/cs	dr	cr
Rent received		1,300

It would be wrong, however, to show the whole amount in the profit and loss account for 1988. Clearly £100 is income for 1989. This amount must therefore be deducted from the £1,300 to show the correct income relating to 1988 as £1,200. The ledger account and final accounts' entries will look like this.

Rent received a/c

1988			£	1988			£
31 Dec	Profit & loss a/c		1,200	1 Jan–31 Dec	Bank (total)		1,300
31 Dec	Balance in advance	c/d	100				
			1,300				1,300
				1989			
				1 Jan	Balance in advance	b/d	100

Profit and loss account for year ended 31 December 1988

	£
Gross profit	–
add Rent received	1,200

Balance Sheet as at 31 December 1988

	£
Current liabilities	
Rent received in advance	100

As it is an income the £1,200 rent received is added to the gross profit. The £100 rent received in advance represents a liability of the owner of the restaurant. He owes this sum, or rather the use of the flat which is worth this amount, to his tenant. It therefore appears in the balance sheet as a current liability. Note that this is the exact opposite to an expense which is paid in advance and which counts as a current asset in the balance sheet.

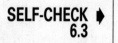

SELF-CHECK ▶ 6.3

An hotel allows local firms to advertise in the foyer for which it makes a charge. During the year ended 30 June 1988 it has received £250 income for this. However, one firm has paid £20 in June for an advertisement to be displayed in July 1988. Show relevant entries in the final accounts.

SOLUTION

Profit and loss account, year ended 30 June 1988

Gross profit	£	£
Advertising received	250	
less Received in advance	20	
		230

Balance Sheet as at 30 June 1988

Current liabilities	£
Advertising received in advance	20

6.4 INCOME OUTSTANDING

Sometimes a business will not have received all the income to which it is entitled by the end of its financial year. When this happens, the amount owing or accrued must be added to what has been received to show the real income for the year. For example, a retailer rents part of his store room to another firm and charges £50 per month. On 31 December 1988, when his financial year ends, only eleven months rent has been received. The rent received account will appear in the trial balance like this:

A/cs	dr	cr
Rent received		550

It is necessary to adjust the rent received account so that the correct amount of £600 can be transferred to the profit and loss account. The ledger account and final accounts' entries will then look like this:

Rent received a/c

1988		£	1988		£
31 Dec	Profit & loss a/c	600	1 Jan–31 Dec	Bank (total)	550
			31 Dec	Balance accrued c/d	50
		600			600
1989					
1 Jan	Balance accrued b/d	50			

Profit and loss account, year ended 31 December 1988

	£
Gross profit	–
add Rent received	600

Balance Sheet as at 31 December 1988

Current assets	£
Rent due	50

The £50 due from the tenant is a debt which the retailer will count as a current asset. In practice it will probably be included with sundry debtors.

SELF-CHECK ▶ 6.4

In the year ended 31 October 1988 an hotel received £160 for allowing firms to advertise in its reception area. One firm, however, had not paid a bill of £40 for an advertisement displayed in September. Show the relevant entries in the final accounts.

SOLUTION ▶

Profit and loss account, year ended 31 October 1988

	£	£
Gross profit	–	–
Advertising received	160	
add Amount due	40	
		200

Balance Sheet as at 31 October 1988

Current assets	£
Advertising due	40

6.5 OPENING AND CLOSING ADJUSTMENTS

Sometimes you may need to calculate the amount of an expense or income to be included in the profit and loss account from information that includes an opening as well as a closing adjustment. For example, the following information relates to a firm whose financial year ends on 31 December:

		£
31 December 1987	Rent prepaid	400
Jan–Dec 1988	Rent paid	2,300
31 December 1988	Rent prepaid	500

To calculate the amount of rent to be shown in the profit and loss account for 1988 two adjustments have to be made.

	£
Rent paid in 1988	2,300
add Rent paid in 1987 for 1988	400
	2,700
less Rent paid in 1988 for 1989	500
Real amount of rent for 1988	2,200

The closing prepayment is deducted from the amount paid because it has been paid for 1989. The opening prepayment is added because although it was money that was paid in 1987, it had been paid for 1988.

The rent account would look like this:

Rent a/c

1988			£	1988		£
1 Jan	Balance prepaid	b/d	400	31 Dec	Profit & loss a/c	2,200
....	Cash/bank (total)		2,300	31 Dec	Balance prepaid c/d	500
			2,700			2,700
1989						
1 Jan	Balance prepaid	b/d	500			

A similar calculation is needed if the information involves amounts outstanding:

		£
31 December 1987	Insurance accrued	500
Jan–Dec 1988	Insurance paid	1,300
31 December 1988	Insurance accrued	300

		£
Insurance paid in 1988		1,300
less Insurance paid in 1988 for 1987		500
		800
add Insurance owing for 1988 at 31 December		300
Real amount of insurance for 1988		1,100

The closing accrual is added because this amount belongs to 1988, while the opening accrual is deducted because this belongs to 1987. The insurance account would look like this:

Insurance a/c

1988		£	1988			£
....	Cash/bank (total)	1,300	1 Jan	Balance acrrued b/d		500
31 Dec	Balance accrued c/d	300	31 Dec	Profit & loss a/c		1,100
		1,600				1,600
			1989			
			1 Jan	Balance accrued b/d		300

If you are given figures which involve a mixture of prepayments and accruals you need to remember when to add and when to subtract. You should **add** opening prepayments and closing accruals but **deduct** opening accruals and closing prepayments. For example:

		£
31 December 1987	Rates accrued	100
Jan–Dec 1988	Rates paid	900
31 December 1988	Rates prepaid	200

	£
Rates paid in 1988	900
less Rates paid in 1988 for 1987	100
	800
less Rates paid in 1988 for 1989	200
Real amount of rates for 1988	600

The rates account would look like this:

Rates a/c

1988		£	1988			£
....	Cash/bank (total)	900	1 Jan	Balance accrued b/d		100
			31 Dec	Profit & loss a/c		600
			31 Dec	Balance prepaid c/d		200
		900				900
1989						
1 Jan	Balance prepaid b/d	200				

SELF-CHECK 6.5 ▶

Calculate the amount of rates to be shown in the profit and loss account of 1988 from the following information:

		£
31 December 1987	Rates prepaid	250
Jan–Dec 1988	Rates paid	650
31 December 1988	Rates accrued	150

SOLUTION ▶

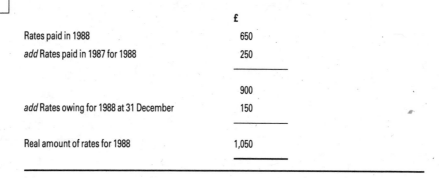

	£
Rates paid in 1988	650
add Rates paid in 1987 for 1988	250
	900
add Rates owing for 1988 at 31 December	150
Real amount of rates for 1988	1,050

COMMENT ▶ When a question asks only for a calculation it is not essential that a
ledger account is completed. The rates account would look like this:

Rates a/c

1988			£	1988		£
1 Jan	Balance prepaid	b/d	250	31 Dec	Profit & Loss a/c	1,050
....	Cash/bank (total)		650			
31 Dec	Balance accrued	c/d	150			
			1,050			1,050
				1989		
				1 Jan	Balance accrued b/d	150

EXERCISES

6.1   M. White's financial year ends on 30 June. He rents his premises at
£300 per quarter which is payable on 1 July, 1 October, 1 January and
1 April. In the year ended 30 June 1988, which is his first year of
trading, he made the following payments by cheque: 1 July 1987,
£300; 5 October 1987, £300; 4 January 1988, £300; 4 April 1988, £300; 6
June 1988, £300.

Write up White's ledger account for rent and show all relevant
entries in the final accounts at the end of the year.

6.2   Complete the following table, in which (a) has been done for you.

	A/c	Trial balance 31.12.88 dr	£	Prepaid at 31.12.88 £	Profit & loss a/c 1988 £	Current asset in balance sheet 31.12.88 £
(a)	Rent	800		100	700	100
(b)	Rates	450		165		
(c)	Insurance	267			196	
(d)	Salaries			264	9,832	
(e)	Fuel				1,256	300
(f)	Wages	996				125

6.3

The trial balance of a firm whose financial year ends on 30 November 1988 contains the following item.

A/cs	dr	cr
Wages	53,456	

Because the weekly wages were last made up on 27 November, £735 has accrued by 30 November. Make the necessary adjustments to the wages account and show the relevant entries in the final accounts at the end of the year.

6.4

Complete the following table, in which (a) has been done for you.

	Trial balance 31.12.88		Accrued at 31.12.88	Profit & loss a/c 1988	Current liability in balance sheet 31.12.88
	A/c	cr	£	£	£
(a)	Rent	900	· 100	1,000	100
(b)	Rates	496	232		
(c)	Insurance	457		682	
(d)	Wages		156	9,457	
(e)	Salaries			19,568	830
(f)	Fuel	563			129

6.5

A service station allows a car dealer to use the forecourt to display his cars for sale. During the year ended 30 June 1988 it has received £1,250 income for this. This includes a payment in advance for July 1988 of £200. Show relevant entries in the final accounts of the service station.

6.6

Calculate the amount of rent to be shown in the profit and loss account of 1988 from the following information:

		£
31 December 1987	Rent prepaid	178
Jan–Dec 1988	Rent paid	654
31 December 1988	Rent accrued	57

6.7 Prepare final accounts from the following information.

Trial balance of The White Hart Hotel as at 31 October 1988

	£	£
Capital		85,800
Stocks (1 Nov 1987)	2,250	
Loan from Busifinance		15,000
Premises	97,500	
Furniture and equipment	22,500	
Debtors and Creditors	900	750
Advertising and Insurance	1,905	
Salaries and Wages	16,500	
Rates	1,350	
Discounts allowed and received	300	105
Purchases and Sales	37,500	84,000
Rent received		1,800
Heat and light	825	
Sundry expenses	675	
Bank	1,500	
Cash	150	
Drawings	3,600	
	187,455	187,455

Additional information at 31 October 1988:
(a)   Stocks were now valued at £3,000.
(b)   Wages outstanding amounted to £200.
(c)   Insurance paid in advance was £30.
(d)   The loan from Busifinance had been made on 31 July at an agreed interest of 12% flat rate per annum. None of this had yet been paid.
(e)   The rent received includes £200 in advance for November 1988.

PROVISION FOR BAD DEBTS

CONTENTS

In this chapter we are going to look at an adjustment involving debtors. It will enable the true amount of bad debts for a period to be entered in the profit and loss account. In addition the asset debtors will be shown at its proper value in the balance sheet. There are two methods of book-keeping that can be used and both will be illustrated. Make certain you understand the process of writing off a bad debt (Section 3.7) before continuing.

7.1 CREATING A PROVISION FOR BAD AND DOUBTFUL DEBTS

At the end of his first year of trading R. Bowe had written off a total of £300 worth of bad debts. **After** doing so his bad debts account and debtors' account looked like this:

Bad debts a/c

1986		£	1986		£
1 Jan–31 Dec	Sundry debtors	300	31 Dec	Transferred to profit & loss a/c	300

Sundry debtors a/c

1986		£		
31 Dec	Balance	4,000		

Two thoughts occurred to him: first, that it was likely that some of this £4,000 would not be paid. In other words it included some debts that would also prove to be bad. The figure in the profit and loss account was thus likely to be an understatement of the **real** amount of the bad debts for the year. Second, if he showed the £4,000 in the balance sheet as an asset at 31 December he would be overstating the value of this asset. These problems may be overcome by creating a provision for bad and doubtful debts. It is done in three steps:

1 Estimate the amount of remaining debts that are likely to be bad or doubtful. We will assume that Bowe thought that £200 was the right amount to allow.

2 The amount of the estimate is then entered in the profit and loss account as an expense, thus reducing net profit by a further £200. The

profit and loss account will now contain two amounts as an expense for bad debts: the actual amount written off for the year and an estimate of those likely to be written off – the provision.

3   The double entry corresponding to this entry in the profit and loss account is made in a provision for bad and doubtful debts account. As this is rather a long title we will refer to it as the provision for bad debts account.

Provision for bad debts

		1986		£
		31 Dec	Profit and loss a/c	200

This is a credit balance at the end of the financial year and as such appears in the balance sheet. As a credit balance it is technically a source of finance, i.e. finance taken out of profits to be used for writing off bad debts when they occur. Instead of showing this with the other finance, however, it is usual practice to show it as a deduction from the asset debtors.

Balance Sheet of R. Bowe as at 31 December 1986

Current assets	£	£
Debtors	4,000	
less Provision for bad debts	200	
		3,800

Thus the balance sheet now shows debtors at a more realistic valuation. The question arises as to how much should be provided for bad debts. Greatest accuracy would be achieved if all the debts in the accounts were analysed at the end of the year to decide which ones were likely to prove uncollectable. In practice those debts which have been due longest will probably be the most suspect. This, however, is a time-consuming process and it is much simpler to allow a certain percentage for probable bad debts. Bowe allowed five per cent. Experience will show how accurate this figure is and, if necessary, it can be adjusted upwards or downwards.

SELF-CHECK ▶
7.1

R. Simons began trading as a retailer on 1 January 1986. By the end of his first year of trading he had written off a total of £140 worth of debts as irrecoverable. On 31 December 1986 his debts were valued in the books at £2,500. He decided to create a provision for bad debts that would allow for five per cent of that amount to be irrecoverable. Show the bad debts account, the provision for bad debts account and relevant entries in the final accounts.

SOLUTION ▶

Bad debts

1986		£	1986		£
1 Jan–31 Dec	Sundry debtors	140	31 Dec	Transferred to profit & loss a/c	140

Provision for bad debts

1986			£	1986			£
31 Dec	Balance	c/d	125	31 Dec	Profit & loss a/c		125
				1987			
				1 Jan	Balance	b/d	125

Profit and loss account of R. Simons, year ended 31 December 1986

Expenses	£
Bad debts	140
Provision for bad debts	125

Balance Sheet of R. Simons as at 31 December 1986

Current assets	£	£
Debtors	2,500	
less Provision for bad debts	125	
		2,375

COMMENT ▶ It is very important to read the instructions of a question carefully. Sometimes you may be asked to write off the actual debts before creating a provision based on the figure remaining in the debtors' account. In this self-check the actual bad debts had already been written off. The provision therefore had to be based on the £2,500 actually in the account on 31 December. Note that in both the bad debts account and the provision for bad debts account there is an entry relating to the profit and loss account. However, there is a difference. The entry in the bad debts account is made to transfer that debit balance to the profit and loss account. The entry in the provision account is a credit entry made to correspond to the debit entry in the profit and loss account that is made first. In effect £125 of finance is being taken from the profits and specifically earmarked to cover future bad debts. It is very important that you realise that this adjustment does not actually involve the movement of any cash.

Once a provision for bad debts has been created there are two methods by which you can proceed:

1 All entries relating to bad debts from now on can be made in the provision account.
2 Separate accounts are maintained for actual bad debts and the provision for bad debts.

We will consider each in turn, using the business of R. Bowe as an illustration.

7.2 PROVISION FOR BAD DEBTS: METHOD ONE

Remind yourself of the position of R. Bowe on 31 December 1986. The two accounts with balances in them on that date were debtors (debit balance £4,000) and provision for bad debts (credit balance £200). The debtors' account will be changing frequently during 1987. Whenever Bowe sells goods on credit he will debit it and whenever the retailers pay him he will credit it with the money received and any discount allowed. Also, at various dates during the year he may have to write off some of the debts as irrecoverable. This will require a credit entry in the debtors' account. The corresponding entry can now be made in the provision for bad debts account because it contains an amount specifically earmarked for this purpose.

Suppose that in 1987 Bowe wrote off £250 of debts as being irrecoverable. Before preparing the final accounts, the provision account will look like this:

Provision for bad debts

1987		£	1987			£
....	Sundry debtors	250	1 Jan	Balance	b/d	200

Clearly the provision made at the end of 1986 is a slight underestimate. All the £200 has been used and an extra £50 is needed to make up the deficiency. In addition it will be necessary to provide for the fact that some of the debtors at the end of 1987 will probably fail to pay.

Assume that Bowe's debtors are valued at £6,000 on 31 December 1987 and that he decides that a provision of five per cent for likely bad debts is still about right. He will need a provision balance of £300 to meet this requirement (5% × £6,000). In order to achieve this he will need to make a credit entry for £350. This is made up of the £300 needed **plus** the £50 required to make up the deficiency from last year. After the final accounts have been prepared the situation will be as follows:

Provision for bad debts

1987			£	1987			£
....	Sundry debtors		250	1 Jan	Balance	b/d	200
				31 Dec	Profit & loss a/c		350
31 Dec	Balance	c/d	300				
			550				550
				1988			
				1 Jan	Balance	b/d	300

Profit and loss account of R. Bowe for the year ended 31 December 1987

Expenses	£
Provision for bad debts	350

Balance Sheet of R. Bowe as at 31 December 1987

Current assets	£	£
Debtors	6,000	
less Provision for bad debts	300	
		5,700

Note that the balance sheet entry consists of the two balances in the relevant accounts at 31 December. The profit and loss account entry is the amount needed to be withdrawn from profit in order to provide the balance of £300.

SELF-CHECK 7.2

Remind yourself of R. Simon's position at 31 December 1986 in the last self-check.

During 1987, his second year of trading, he wrote off debts to the value of £110 and at the end of the year the debtors amounted to £1,500. He decided to retain a provision of five per cent of outstanding debtors to allow for bad debts. Show his provision for bad debts account and the relevant entries on the final accounts at the end of 1987.

SOLUTION ▶

Provision for bad debts account

1987			£	1987			£
1 Jan–31 Dec	Debtors		110	1 Jan	Balance	b/d	125
31 Dec	Balance	c/d	75	31 Dec	Profit & loss a/c		60
			185				185
				1988			
				1 Jan	balance	b/d	75

Profit and loss account of R. Simon, year ended 31 December 1987

Expenses	£
Provision for bad debts	60

Balance Sheet of R. Simon as at 31 December 1987

Current assets	£	£
Debtors	1,500	
less Provision for bad debts	75	
		1,425

COMMENT ▶

Many students find provision for bad debts the most difficult of the adjustments so let us repeat the explanation. At the beginning of 1987 the credit balance of £125 in the provision for bad debts account represented five per cent of the debtors figure at 31 December 1986. During 1987 bad debts actually written off against this provision amounted to £110, thus £15 of the provision was unused. At the end of 1987 you were told that the debtors amounted to £1,500 and that the provision was to be maintained at five per cent. Thus the provision balance needed is £75, i.e. 5% × £1,500. As there is still a £15 balance in the provision account it requires only £60 from this year's profits to obtain the balance needed. Note that the balance sheet entry uses the two balances in the ledger accounts after the profit and loss account has been prepared, i.e. £1,500 and provision £75.

7.3 PROVISION FOR BAD DEBTS: METHOD TWO

This involves keeping separate accounts for bad debts and the provision. We will use the information relating to Bowe's accounts for 1987 so that we can compare the results with those obtained by using method one.

Bad debts a/c

1987		£	1987		£
1 Jan–31 Dec	Sundry debtors	250	31 Dec	Transferred to profit & loss a/c	250

Provision for bad debts a/c

1987			£	1987			£
31 Dec	Balance	c/d	300	1 Jan	Balance	b/d	200
				31 Dec	Profit & loss a/c		100
			300				300
				1988			
				1 Jan	Balance	b/d	300

Profit and loss account of R. Bowe, year ended 31 December 1987

Expenses	£
Bad debts	250
Provision for bad debts	100

Balance Sheet of R. Bowe as at 31 December 1987

Current assets	£
Debtors	6,000
less Provision for bad debts	300
	5,700

Let us summarise what has happened:
1   The actual bad debts for 1987 have been written off the debtors as they occurred and then transferred to the profit and loss account at the end of the year.
2   It is calculated that a provision balance of £300 is needed at the end of the year, i.e. 5% × £6,000.

3   The balance in the provision account will not have altered since last year. A credit entry of £100 is made to adjust this balance to the £300 needed and the double-entry completed in the profit and loss account.

4   The balance sheet contains the £6,000 balance for debtors and the £300 provision balance. As before, the provision balance is deducted from outstanding debtors so that a true value can be placed on the asset (i.e. debtors).

In comparing this with method one you will notice that the real difference concerns the profit and loss account. Instead of one entry for £350 we now have two entries – £250 for actual bad debts and £100 adjustment to the provision. The net result is, of course, the same; i.e. £350 is being counted as the expense relating to bad debts. While the entry in the provision account at the end of the year differs, the final balance is exactly the same as with method one. A final difference concerns the number of accounts used. Method two required an account for bad debts whereas in method one the bad debts were written off in the provision account and no bad debts account was needed.

SELF-CHECK ▶ 7.3

Rewrite the relevant accounts of R. Simon at the end of 1987 using method two.

SOLUTION ▶

Bad debts a/c

1987		£	1987		£
1 Jan–31 Dec	Sundry debtors	110	31 Dec	Transferred to profit & loss a/c	110

Provision for bad debts a/c

1987			£	1987			£
31 Dec	Profit & loss a/c		50	1 Jan	Balance	b/d	125
31 Dec	Balance	c/d	75				
			125				125
				1988			
				1 Jan	Balance	b/d	75

Profit and loss account of R. Simon, year end 31 December 1987

Expenses	£
Bad debts	110
Reduction in provision for bad debts	(50)

Balance Sheet of R. Simon as at 31 December 1987

Current assets	£	£
Debtors	1,500	
less Provision for bad debts	75	
		1,425

The figure of £50 in the profit and loss account for the provision is placed in brackets to indicate that it is a deduction from the expenses. As you can see, the two entries combined; i.e. the actual bad debts of £110 and the provision adjustment of −£50 give the same final result as obtained by method one – a net £60 is being deducted from profits to cover bad debts. As an alternative to deducting the provision adjustment from expenses you could add the £50 back into profits. In effect what has happened is that the amount of the debtors is less than last year. To retain a five per cent provision therefore needs less finance than we already have in the provision account. A debit entry in the provision account for £50 reduces the credit balance to the sum that we require. Thus with the method you must be prepared to make adjustments on either side of the provision account as needed. A credit entry will increase the provision and a debit entry will reduce it.

7.4 BAD DEBTS RECOVERED

Sometimes businessmen receive a pleasant surprise in connection with bad debts. A bad debt that has been written off as irrecoverable is paid by a debtor. Suppose that on 7 May 1988 the wholesaler Bowe recovers a debt that he had written off in 1987. The cash or bank account will be debited with the money received. The credit entry to be made varies according to which of the two methods of dealing with bad debts is used.

Method one The recovered debt will be credited to the provision for bad debts account where it will help to offset the bad debts written off in 1987.

Provision for bad debts

1988				
1 Jan	Balance	b/d		300
7 May	Bank			45

Method two A separate account for bad debts recovered will be credited with the £45. This amount wil be transferred to the profit and loss account at the end of the year along with any other recovered debts. For the sake of simplicity we will assume that this was the only such recovery in 1988.

Bad debts recovered account

1988		£	**1988**		£
31 Dec	Transferred to profit & loss a/c	45	7 May	Bank	45

Profit and loss account, year ended 31 December 1988

Expenses	£
Bad debt recovered	(45)

The £45 is shown in brackets to indicate that it will be deducted from the expenses for 1988. Alternatively the sum could be added to the gross profit along with other incomes such as rent received.

SELF-CHECK ▶ 7.4

During 1988, R. Simon's third year of trading, he wrote off debts to the value of £130 and on 8 June recovered one debt of £30 which he had written off in 1987. At the end of 1988 his debtors amounted to £1,600 and he decided to retain a provision of five per cent of outstanding debtors to allow for bad debts. Show his accounts as they would appear using method one and method two. (Reminder – he starts 1988 with an opening provision of £75.)

SOLUTION ▶	Method one

Provision for bad debts

1988			£	1988			£
1 Jan–31 Dec	Bad debts		130	1 Jan	Balance	b/d	75
31 Dec	Balance	c/d	80	8 June	Bank		30
				31 Dec	Profit & loss a/c		105
			210				210
				1989			
				1 Jan	Balance	b/d	80

Profit and loss account of R. Simon for the year ended 31 December 1988

Expenses	£
Provision for bad debts	105

Balance Sheet of R. Simon as at 31 December 1988

Current assets	£
Debtors	1,600
less Provision for bad debts	80
	1,520

Method two

Bad debts a/c

1988		£	1988		£
1 Jan–31 Dec	Sundry debtors	130	31 Dec	Transferred to profit & loss a/c	130

Bad debts recovered a/c

1988		£	1988		£
31 Dec	Transferred to profit & loss a/c	30	8 June	Bank	30

Provision for bad debts a/c

1988			£	1988			£
31 Dec	Balance	c/d	80	1 Jan	Balance	b/d	75
				31 Dec	Profit & loss a/c		5
			80				80
				1989			
				1 Jan	Balance	b/d	80

Profit and loss account of R. Simon, year ended 31 December 1988

Expenses	£
Bad debts	130
Bad debts recovered	(30)
Provision for bad debts	5

Balance Sheet of R. Simon as at 31 December 1988

Current assets	£
Debtors	1,600
less Provision for bad debts	80
	1,520

COMMENT ▶

As you can see, the balance sheet is identical whichever method is used. The entries in the profit and loss account differ in form but the effect is the same, i.e. a 'net' effect of reducing profits by £105 in 1988. You can decide for yourself which method you prefer. In examinations, however, you may not be given a choice. The way the question is worded may indicate that you have to follow one particular method.

EXERCISES

7.1

T. Brown began trading on 1 January 1987. By the end of his first year of trading he had written off a total of £165 worth of debts as irrecoverable. On 31 December 1987 his debts were valued in the books at £2,760. He decided to create a provision for bad debts that would allow for five per cent of that amount to be irrecoverable. Show the bad debts account, the provision for bad debts account and relevant entries in the final accounts.

7.2 G. Read began 1987 with a provision for bad debts balance of £145. During 1987 he wrote off debts to tbe value of £110 and at the end of the year his debtors amounted to £4,500. He decided to maintain a provision of five per cent of outstanding debtors to allow for bad debts. Show his provision for bad debts account and the relevant entries on the final accounts at the end of 1987.

7.3 S. Wilkins began 1987 with a provision for bad debts balance of £450. During 1987 he wrote off debts to the value of £540 and recovered debts of £70 which he had written off in 1986. At the end of 1987 his debtors amounted to £9,600 and he decided to retain a provision of four per cent of outstanding debtors to allow for bad debts. Show all relevant accounts including entries in the profit and loss account and balance sheet.

7.4 The following list of balances was extracted from the books of Ian Brown on 31 March 1986.

	£
Premises	36,230
Stock, 1 April 1985	5,500
Drawings	2,224
Provision for doubtful debts	100
Returns outward	350
Carriage outwards	85
Purchases	62,000
Sales	72,350
Sundry creditors	3,834
Bank	1,930
Discount received	25
Insurance	940
Sundry debtors	3,250
Rent and rates	2,500
Salaries and wages	7,000
Mortgage on premises	15,000
Capital	??

Prepare a trial balance for Ian Brown.

(MEG specimen paper)

ESTIMATING AND RECORDING DEPRECIATION

CONTENTS

This chapter looks at the way in which capital expenditure can be spread over the life of an asset. This is done so that a fair amount of the expenditure can be shown in the profit and loss account and an up-to-date valuation shown in the balance sheet. Three methods of estimating depreciation and two methods of book-keeping will be considered because they are all encountered in examination questions.

8.1 ESTIMATING DEPRECIATION

The process by which an asset decreases in value over time is known as depreciation. There are three main ways of estimating the amount by which a fixed asset has decreased in value by any particular date.

REVALUATION METHOD

A qualified person is given the task of valuing the fixed assets at the end of a trading period. Thus if a motor vehicle is valued at £2,000 on 31 December 1988, having previously been valued at £2,800 on 31 December 1987, we can assume that £800 would be a reasonable estimate of the depreciation for the year ended 31 December 1988. On a regular basis this method is only really suitable for relatively small businesses with comparatively few fixed assets. Accountants prefer to use one of the following methods under normal circumstances.

EQUAL INSTALMENT METHOD

This involves depreciating an asset by an equal amount each year of its life. For example, machinery purchased for £20,000 on 1 January 1985 might be expected to last for ten years. To depreciate this in equal instalments would require an amount of £2,000 to be written off the value of the asset each year. A simple formula can be applied:

$$\frac{\text{Cost of asset}}{\text{Estimated life in years}} = \frac{£20,000}{10} = £2,000 \text{ depreciation per annum}$$

Many fixed assets will have some value when their working life is over. This is known as their scrap value. The above formula can be adapted to allow for an asset having some value as scrap:

$$\frac{\text{Cost of asset less estimated scrap value}}{\text{estimated life in years}}$$

If the machinery in the above example had an estimated scrap value of £1,000 the amount of depreciation to be written off each year for the next ten years would be:

$$\frac{£20,000 \text{ less } £1,000}{10 \text{ years}} = \frac{£19,000}{10} = £1,900 \text{ per annum}$$

It is possible to obtain a valuation of an asset at any stage of its life by referring to a schedule like the following example.

Machinery X   Purchase date: 1 Jan 1985; estimated life 10 years;
Purchase price: £20,000; estimated scrap value £1,000

Year	Depn for the year ended 31 Dec	Accumulated depn to year ended 31 Dec	Asset value at 31 Dec
	£	£	£
1985	1,900	1,900	18,100
1986	1,900	3,800	16,200
1987	1,900	5,700	14,300
1988	1,900	7,600	12,400
1989	1,900	9,500	10,500

Each year the same amount of depreciation is being written off the asset value. The column for the accumulated depreciation enables you to see at a glance the total amount of depreciation that has been written off to date. Deducting this figure from the cost of the machinery provides the value at the end of any year in the schedule. Thus by the end of December 1989 five years' depreciation, i.e. £9,500, will have been written off and the machinery will be worth £10,500.

This method is also known as **straight-line depreciation** because the amount is the same each year. If the depreciation was plotted on one axis of a graph and the years on the other axis it would give you a straight line graph.

REDUCING INSTALMENT METHOD

This involves depreciating the asset by a fixed percentage each year based on the value of the asset at the *beginning* of that year. Suppose, for example, the company that purchased machinery X for £20,000 on 1 January 1985 decided to depreciate it by ten per cent per annum by this method. At the end of 1985 the depreciation to be written off will be

$$\frac{10}{100} \times 20,000 = £2,000$$

At the beginning of 1986 the machinery will be valued at £18,000, i.e. its cost less depreciation to date (£20,000 less £2,000). The rate of depreciation will remain at ten per cent but the actual amount written off for 1986 will be

$$\frac{10}{100} \times 18,000 = £1,800$$

You can see why this method is known as the reducing instalment method. Although the percentage rate of depreciation stays the same it is being calculated on the diminishing asset value. Thus each year the actual amount of depreciation written off will be less. This method of calculating depreciation is also known as the diminishing balance method. There is no need to allow for a scrap value with this method.

SELF-CHECK ▶
8.1

Prepare a five year depreciation schedule for the machinery in the above example using the reducing instalment with a fixed rate of ten per cent. Depreciation should be calculated to the nearest £.

SOLUTION ▶

Machinery X Purchase date: 1 Jan 1985; purchase price: £20,000; depreciation rate – ten per cent on reducing balance.

Year	Depn for the year ended 31 Dec	Accumulated depn to year ended 31 Dec	Asset value at 31 Dec
	£	£	£
1985	2,000	2,000	18,000
1986	1,800	3,800	16,200
1987	1,620	5,420	14,580
1988	1,458	6,878	13,122
1989	1,312	8,190	11,810

Comment
The only occasion when it was necessary to round the depreciation to the nearest £ was in 1989 when 10% × £13,122 would have given a precise answer of £1,312.20p.

8.2 RECORDING DEPRECIATION: THE SIMPLE METHOD

Each asset which is to be depreciated is given its own depreciation account. At the end of each financial year the asset account is credited with the amount of depreciation for that year and the depreciation account is debited. The entry in the depreciation account is then transferred to the profit and loss account as an expense for that period. Finally the asset account is balanced to reveal the value of the asset at the end of the year.

Example
We will use the information provided in the last self-check using the reducing instalment method.

Machinery a/c

1985			£	1985			£
1 Jan	Bank		20,000	31 Dec	Depreciation		2,000
				31 Dec	Balance	c/d	18,000
			20,000				20,000
1986				1986			
1 Jan	Balance	b/d	18,000	31 Dec	Depreciation		1,800
				31 Dec	Balance	c/d	16,200
			18,000				18,000
1987							
1 Jan	Balance	b/d	16,200				

Depreciation on machinery a/c

1985		£	1985		£
31 Dec	Machinery	2,000	31 Dec	Profit & loss a/c	2,000
1986			1986		
31 Dec	Machinery	1,800	31 Dec	Profit & loss a/c	1,800

Profit and loss account, year ended 31 December 1985

Expenses	£
Depreciation on machinery	2,000

Balance Sheet as at 31 December 1985

Fixed assets	£	£
Machinery	20,000	
less Depreciation for year	2,000	
	————	
		18,000

Profit and loss account, year end 31 December 1986

Expenses	£
Depreciation on machinery	1,800

Balance Sheet as at 31 December 1986

Fixed assets	£	£
Machinery	18,000	
less Depreciation for year	1,800	
	————	
		16,200

It is normal practice to repeat the calculation of the asset value in the balance sheet rather than simply entering the balance from the account.

SELF-CHECK 8.2

Complete the accounts relating to the machinery and its depreciation, together with relevant final account entries, up to the end of 1987.

SOLUTION

Machinery a/c

1987			£	1987			£
1 Jan	Balance	b/d	16,200	31 Dec	Depreciation		1,620
				31 Dec	Balance	c/d	14,580
			————				————
			16,200				16,200
			————				————
1988							
1 Jan	Balance	b/d	14,580				

Depreciation on machinery a/c

1987		£	1987		£
31 Dec	Machinery	1,620	31 Dec	Profit & loss a/c	1,620

Profit and loss account, year ended 31 December 1987

Expenses	£
Depreciation on machinery	1,620

Balance Sheet as at 31 December 1987

Fixed assets	£	£
Machinery	16,200	
less Depreciation for year	1,620	
		14,580

8.3 RECORDING DEPRECIATION: THE ACCUMULATION METHOD

Compared with the method just discussed, this method requires one additional account which is used to record the depreciation accumulated to date. This account is usually called the provision for depreciation account, though a more accurate title would be accumulated depreciation account. This method is also known as the provision for depreciation method.

The main difference is that no credit entry for depreciation is made in the asset account. Instead it is made in the provision for depreciation account. Using the example of the machinery being depreciated by reducing instalments the ledger accounts for the first two years will look like this:

Machinery a/c

1985			£	1985			£
1 Jan	Bank		20,000	31 Dec	Balance	c/d	20,000
1986				1986			
1 Jan	Balance	b/d	20,000	31 Dec	Balance	c/d	20,000
1987							
1 Jan	Balance	b/d	20,000				

Provision for depreciation on machinery a/c

1985			£	1985			£
31 Dec	Balance	c/d	2,000	31 Dec	Depreciation		2,000
1986				1986			
31 Dec	Balance	c/d	3,800	1 Jan	Balance	b/d	2,000
				31 Dec	Depreciation		1,800
			3,800				3,800
				1987			
				1 Jan	Balance	b/d	3,800

Depreciation on machinery a/c

1985		£	1985		£
31 Dec	Provision for depreciation	2,000	31 Dec	Transferred to profit & loss a/c	2,000
1986			1986		
31 Dec	Provision for depreciation	1,800	31 Dec	Transferred to profit & loss a/c	1,800

As you can see the depreciation account is substantially the same as in the simpler method – only the description has changed slightly. The asset account is much different. This now shows the asset at cost with no depreciation being deducted from it within the account. You might argue that it is not worth balancing this account each year. Doing so does, however, indicate that the account has been looked at each year and it is probably a good thing to keep all the accounts up to date.

The new account – provision for depreciation – has a credit entry each year for the amount of that year's depreciation. It is then balanced so that the amount of the depreciation accumulates as a new balance each year. In order to obtain the value of the asset at any date it is now necessary to combine the asset balance with the accumulated depreciation from the provision account. Thus the value of the machinery at 31 December 1986 will be £16,200, i.e.

Cost of asset	£20,000	(from the asset account)
less Depn to date	3,800	(from the provision account)
	16,200	

The profit and loss account entries will be exactly the same as they were using the other method. The balance sheet entries will differ because we will be showing the current value of the asset by deducting the accumulated depreciation from the cost of the asset. This difference will not be apparent in the first year's balance sheet because the first year's depreciation will be identical to the accumulated depreciation. From the second year, however, you will notice the difference. It must be emphasised that the actual final value of the asset shown in the balance sheet will be the same whichever book-keeping method is used. This can be seen by comparing the extracts below with those on page 179.

Balance Sheet as at 31 December 1985

Fixed assets	£	£
Machinery at cost	20,000	
less Depreciation to date	2,000	
		18,000

Balance Sheet as at 31 December 1986

Fixed assets	£	£
Machinery at cost	20,000	
less Depreciation to date	3,800	
		16,200

SELF-CHECK ▶
8.3

Complete the accounts relating to the machinery and its depreciation, together with the relevant entries in the final accounts, up to the end of 1987. This time use the provision for depreciation method.

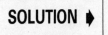
SOLUTION ▶

Machinery a/c

1987			£	1987			£
1 Jan	Balance	b/d	20,000	31 Dec	Balance	c/d	20,000
1988							
1 Jan	Balance	b/d	20,000				

Provision for depreciation on machinery a/c

1987			£	1987			£
31 Dec	Balance	c/d	5,420	1 Jan	Balance	b/d	3,800
				31 Dec	Depreciation		1,620
			5,420				5,420
				1988			
				1 Jan	Balance	b/d	5,420

Depreciation on machinery a/c

1987		£	1987		£
31 Dec	Provision for depreciation	1,620	31 Dec	Transferred to profit & loss a/c	1,620

Profit and loss account, year ended 31 December 1987

Expenses	£
Depreciation on machinery	1,620

Balance Sheet as at 31 December 1987

Fixed assets	£	£
Machinery at cost	20,000	
less Depreciation to date	5,420	
		14,580

COMMENT ▶ Compare this solution with that of self-check 8.2 on pages 179–80. You will see that the net result is exactly the same as far as the entries in the final accounts are concerned. One problem that arises from the use of the provision for depreciation method is that the title gives the impression that finance has actually been set aside which can be used to purchase a replacement for the fixed asset when its working life is over. This is a false impression. The provision for depreciation account is simply an account in which the aggregate or total depreciation is accumulated each year. For this reason the term 'aggregate' or 'accumulated depreciation account' would be a more accurate title. There is, of course, nothing to prevent a businessman from keeping back a greater amount of the net profit for use within the business to replace worn-out assets. This, however, is not automatic on creating a provision for depreciation account – a conscious policy decision would have to be made to retain or 'plough back' profits for this use.

8.4 PROFITS AND LOSSES ON SALE OF FIXED ASSETS

When a fixed asset is sold it is unlikely that the amount received for it will be exactly the same as its value in the books. For this to happen the depreciation estimate would have to be 100 per cent accurate.

If the asset sells for less than its book value we might say that we have made a loss on its sale, whereas in fact we have probably underestimated the depreciation to be written off against that asset. Similarly, if the asset sells for more than its book value we might say that we have made a profit on the sale when, in reality, we have probably overestimated the depreciation that has occurred. When either of these eventualities occurs, an entry must be made in the profit and loss account for the year in which the asset is sold.

Example
A motor vehicle which has a book value of £2,000 is sold for £1,800 on 6 October. Assuming that the simple method of depreciation is used and that this is the only motor vehicle in the account, the relevant entries will look like this.

Motor vehicle a/c

			£			£
1 Jan	Balance	b/d	2,000	6 Oct	Bank	1,800
				31 Dec	Loss on sale	200
			2,000			2,000

Profit and loss account, year ended 31 December 19—

Expenses	£
Loss on sale of motor vehicle	200

The entry in the profit and loss account could also have been labelled 'under-estimate of depreciation on motor vehicle'.

It is not quite so straightforward if the provision for depreciation account method has been used. This is because the current book value of the asset cannot be found by simply looking at the account for that asset. It is necessary to bring together the cost of the asset, which will be found in the asset account, and the aggregate depreciation written off to date, which will be found in the provision for depreciation account. This is done in an account called 'disposal of (name of fixed asset) account'.

Example

Suppose equipment which cost £5,000 in 1985 and had been depreciated by a total of £2,000 by the end of 1987 was sold on 5 May 1988 for £3,400. This is £400 more than the accounts suggest that the asset is worth. The sale would be recorded as follows.

Equipment a/c

			£			£
1 Jan	Balance	b/d	5,000	5 May	Transferred to disposal a/c	5,000

Provision for depreciation on equipment a/c

		£				£
5 May	Transferred to disposal a/c	2,000	1 Jan	Balance	b/d	2,000

Disposal of equipment a/c

		£			£
5 May	Equipment at cost	5,000	5 May	Total depreciation to date	2,000
31 Dec	Profit on sale	400	5 May	Bank	3,400
		5,400			5,400

Profit and loss account, year ended 31 December 1988

	£
Gross profit	—
Profit on sale of equipment	400

Transferring the cost of the equipment and the aggregate depreciation into the disposal of equipment account reveals that the current book value of the equipment at the time of sale is £3,000. When this account is then credited with the amount received, £3,400 (the bank account will be debited) it shows that the amount received is £400 more than the book value. This £400 is then transferred into the profit and loss account where it has been added to the gross profit. The profit and loss account entry could alternatively have been labelled 'overestimate of depreciation'.

A motor vehicle which cost £6,000 in 1984 and which had been depreciated by £3,500 by 31 December 1987 was sold on 8 June 1988 for £1,900. Show the motor vehicle disposal account and the relevant entry in the profit and loss account.

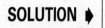

Motor vehicle disposal account

		£			£
8 June	Vehicle at cost	6,000	8 June	Total depreciation to date	3,500
			31 Dec	Bank	1,900
			31 Dec	Loss on sale	600
		6,000			6,000

Profit and loss account, year ended 31 December 1988

Expenses	£
Loss on sale of vehicle	600

It is important to remember that once it is sold the asset will no longer appear in the balance sheet.

EXERCISES

8.1

Complete the following depreciation schedule, calculating depreciation to the nearest £.
Motor vehicle Z   Purchase date: 1 Jan 1985; purchase price: £10,000; depreciation rate – twenty-five per cent on reducing balance.

Year	Depn for the year ended 31 Dec	Accumulated depn to year ended 31 Dec	Asset value at 31 Dec
	£	£	£
1985			
1986			
1987			

8.2 Repeat 8.1 using the equal instalment method. Compare your answers.

8.3 Prepare ledger accounts and show relevant final account entries for the information in 8.1 using the simple method of depreciation.

8.4 Prepare ledger accounts and show relevant final account entries for the information in 8.1 using the provision for depreciation method.

8.5 A motor vehicle which cost £9,000 in 1985 and which had been depreciated by £4,750 by 31 December 1987 was sold on 5 May 1988.

Show the motor vehicle disposal account and the relevant entry in the profit and loss account if the vehicle was sold for:
(a)   £4,000
(b)   £5,000.

8.6   (a)   Explain the meaning of
(i) depreciation
(ii) bad debts.
(b)   Explain, using your own figures, how depreciation on motor vehicles may be calculated over a two year period by:
(i) the diminishing balance method
(ii) the equal instalment method.
(c)   (i) Give the double entry needed to write off a bad debt of £200
(ii) Explain the effect of each part of the double entry on the balance sheet.
(d)   Explain the significance of accounting for depreciation on the balance sheet.

(SEG specimen paper)

8.7

The following trial balance was extracted from the books of J. Robinson, a retailer, on 31 May 1986.

Trial Balance as at 31 May 1986

	£ dr	£ cr
Fixtures and fittings	5,000	
Motor van	2,000	
Stock (1 Jan 1985)	6,520	
Debtors	1,140	
Cash in hand	80	
Cash at bank	2,040	
Creditors		3,050
Capital		14,000
Purchases	26,320	
Sales		44,400
Motor running expenses	510	
Wages and salaries	3,100	
Light, heat and power	850	
Rent and rates	4,200	
Advertising	940	
Drawings	9,000	
Rent received		860
Sundry expenses	610	
	62,310	62,310

You are required to prepare Robinson's trading and profit and loss account for the financial year ended 31 May 1986 together with a balance sheet at that date, taking into account the following adjustments:

(i) The closing stock was valued at £7,450.

(ii) There was an unpaid electricity account amounting to £120.

(iii) There was a prepayment on the rates to the value of £90.

(iv) Allow for depreciation on the motor van at the rate of 20% per annum.

THE CASH BOOK AND OTHER DIVISIONS OF THE LEDGER

CONTENTS

9.1 SUBDIVIDING THE LEDGER

Until now the ledger has been mentioned as if it was a single book containing all the ledger accounts. It is often known as the general ledger. This has one obvious disadvantage. Only one person may use it at a time. A large business having more than one accounts clerk would not be able to operate efficiently. Subdividing the ledger to enable the work of recording transactions to be shared and carried out more efficiently is one obvious solution. Figure 9.1 summarises a way in which this is often done.

Figure 9.1 Divisions of the ledger

		General Ledger			
1		General Ledger			Cash book
2	General Ledger		Debtors Ledger	Creditors Ledger	Cash book
3	General Ledger	Private Ledger	Debtors Ledger	Creditors Ledger	Cash book

The first stage is to take out the two accounts which are most used – the cash account and bank account – and place them in a separate book which is known as the cash book. A business which only went as far as this would then keep all other accounts in the general ledger. The second stage involves extracting debtors and creditors accounts from the general ledger and placing them in their own separate books. Note that the terms 'purchases ledger' and 'bought ledger' are sometimes used instead of creditors' ledger – goods purchased on credit are bought from creditors. Similarly the debtors' ledger might be called the 'sales ledger' or 'sold ledger' because sales of goods on credit are made to debtors.

When the terms debtors' ledger and creditors' ledger are used the names are a good indication of the accounts contained within them. If the terms purchases ledger and sales ledger are used it is perhaps less obvious what they contain. It would be a mistake to think that they contain the purchases and sales accounts respectively. They contain the accounts of the people and other businesses from whom you purchase goods on credit or to whom you sell on credit.

If the owner wishes to extract some accounts which he has a particular wish to keep private they could be placed in a private ledger. The sort of accounts to which this might apply are the owner's capital account and his drawings account.

These stages do not have to occur in any particular order. Nor is it necessary for all to be used. A business with a large number of credit customers will probably find it advantageous to have a debtors' ledger to contain them. If, however, it purchases stock on credit from only a few suppliers it might not be worth taking these accounts out of the general ledger. It is also possible that some businesses will want to subdivide the accounts to an even greater extent. For example, a business with a large number of debtors might have these accounts entered on cards and filed alphabetically with A–D kept separately from E–J etc.

SELF-CHECK
9.1

A business has a cash book, sales ledger and a general ledger. In which of these would you find the following accounts:

(a)   T. Evans, a customer
(b)   bank account
(c)   wages account
(d)   E. Smith, a supplier
(e)   sales account.

SOLUTION ▶

(a)   sales ledger
(b)   cash book
(c)   general ledger
(d)   general ledger
(e)   general ledger.

COMMENT ▶

It is important to remember that if there is no division of the ledger for a particular account it remains in the general ledger. If the business had kept a purchases ledger or creditors ledger Smith's account would have been in it. The sales account will not be in the sales ledger (which contains only the accounts of *people* to whom the business has sold on credit).

9.2 TYPES OF ACCOUNT

It is also possible to classify ledger accounts into personal and impersonal accounts. The former comprises the accounts of people and other firms with which a business deals and the latter all other accounts. The impersonal accounts can then be further divided into real accounts and nominal accounts. Real accounts are those in which a record is kept of the assets of the business. They are real in the sense that it is possible to touch them – for example, buildings, equipment and cash. Nominal accounts contain the records of incomes and expenses. Nominal means 'in name only'. The rent account may have a balance of £800 but the money will not really be there. It represents the amount that has been paid out to rent the property. Figure 9.2 summarises this classification.

Figure 9.2 Types of account

Personal (Debtors and creditors)	Impersonal (All other accounts)	
Personal (Debtors and creditors)	Real Accounts (Assets)	Nominal Accounts (Incomes and expenses)

SELF-CHECK ▶
9.2

Classify the following accounts as real, nominal or personal:
(a)   C. Pinch, supplier   *Personal*
(b)   rates   *nominal*
(c)   stock   *Asset Real*
(d)   machinery   *As Real.*
(e)   T. Wills, customer   *Personal.*
(f)   cash   *Real.*
(g)   discount received   *nominal*
(h)   capital.   *Personal*

SOLUTION ▶

(c), (d) and (f) are real accounts because they are assets. (b) and (g) are nominal accounts. (a), (e) and (h) are personal accounts.

COMMENT ▶

There are two interesting classification points here. First, it might be argued that as a debtor is an asset the account of T. Wills could be classified as real rather than personal. The personal aspect takes priority, however, because the division between personal and impersonal comes before the further subdivision of impersonal accounts into real and nominal. Second, the classification of capital. This is regarded as a special kind of personal account recording the relationship of the business with a person – the owner. The owner's capital can be regarded as the amount owing to him by the business.

9.3 THE TWO COLUMN CASH BOOK

In the cash book it is usual not just to keep the cash and bank records separate from the rest of the ledger accounts but also to combine the accounts together to form one unit. Figure 9.3 shows an example of a two column cash book. Although the accounts for cash and bank are put together they are still in reality separate. The debit entries for cash must be kept apart from the debit entries for bank and the credit entries must also be kept apart. It is a convention that the cash column always appears to the left of the bank column.

Dr								Cr	
Date	Details	F	Cash	Bank	Date	Details	F	Cash	Bank
1 Feb.	Balances	b/d	100.20	700.60	2 Feb.	Postage	GL 4	12.15	
3 Feb.	Sales	GL 6	220.60		3 Feb.	N. Keegan	CL 9		150.00
4 Feb.	C. Winston	DL 41		320.50	4 Feb.	Purchases	GL 12		260.00
5 Feb.	N. Jones	DL 20		110.90	6 Feb.	Rates	GL 15		79.00
8 Feb.	Sales	GL 6	600.20		7 Feb.	Wages	GL 19	60.00	
9 Feb.	Cash	c		750.00	9 Feb.	Bank	c	750.00	
11 Feb.	R. Starr	DL 31		140.30	10 Feb.	R. Willis	CL 10	60.00	
13 Feb.	Bank	c	150.00		12 Feb.	Insurance	GL 6	20.00	
					13 Feb.	Cash	c		150.00
					14 Feb.	Balances	c/d	168.85	1,383.30
			1,071.00	2,022.30				1,071.00	2,022.30
15 Feb.	Balances	b/d	168.85	1,383.30					

Figure 9.3 The two column cash book

The rules regarding the entries are the same as before, i.e. debit entries are used to record increases of cash or bank and credit entries are used to record decreases. Remembering this should enable you to explain any of the entries recorded. For example, on 4 Feb £320.50 was received by cheque from C. Winston while on 10 Feb £60 was paid to R. Willis in cash.

Full use has been made of the folio column for the first time. It is used as a reference to make it easy to locate the other entry in the ledger. GL is short for general ledger, CL for creditors ledger and DL for debtors ledger. Thus, Winston's account will be found on page number 41 of the debtors ledger and the account for Willis on page 10 of the creditors ledger. Sometimes the number refers to the account number rather than the page number (but the principle is the same). As these entries are on page 6 of the cash book you would expect to see the reference CB6 in the folio column in the accounts of Winston and Willis.

Two of the above transactions that require special care are those of 9 and 13 February. On 9 February £750 of the cash of the business has been paid into the bank. This is evidenced by the credit entry in the cash column, used to reduce the asset cash, and the debit entry in the bank column, used to increase the asset bank. There will be no other entries elsewhere because both are in the cash book. The 'c' in the folio column is short for 'contra', a Latin term for opposite or against.

It is used here to indicate that the double entry is on the same page of the same book. The description is the name of the other account affected. If you ever make a credit entry in the bank column and enter the description 'bank' you will have made a mistake.

SELF-CHECK ▶ 9.3	Explain the transaction that has taken place on 13 February in Figure 9.3.
SOLUTION ▶	£150 was withdrawn from the bank for use as cash.
COMMENT ▶	Note this is the reverse of the transaction dated 9 February. The debit entry in the cash column shows this asset increasing and the credit entry in the bank column shows that asset decreasing. This transaction must not be confused with money withdrawn from the business for the owner's private use, termed **drawings**. In this case the debit entry would be in the drawings account.

DISHONOURED CHEQUES

A dishonoured cheque is one which the bank of the person issuing the cheque refuses to honour (usually because there are not enough funds in the account). On receiving the cheque a trader will have credited the debtor's account and debited the bank account. When he learns that the cheque has been dishonoured it is necessary to reverse these entries. This will be done by crediting the bank account and debiting the account of the debtor. Thus the debt is restored to the debtor. As this is another tricky transaction it is often included in examination questions.

9.4 THE THREE COLUMN CASH BOOK

Combining the cash and bank accounts together in one book can be taken a step further. In many businesses payments to suppliers are timed to enable the business to receive a discount. At the same time money will be received from customers who will have deducted discount allowed in return for prompt settlement. A simple way of recording these discounts in the cash book at the same time as the money is recorded will increase efficiency. This can be done by extending the cash book into three columns on each side. Figure 9.4 is an example of a three column cash book.

The only additions to the two column cash book are the columns for discount allowed to customers on the debit side and discount received from suppliers on the credit side. Only the transactions involving these new columns require further comment.

On 3 May B. Thomas was paid £206.29 by cheque and £4.21

Dr   Cash book   Cr

Date	Details	Fol.	Discount allowed	Cash	Bank	Date	Details	Fol.	Discount received	Cash	Bank
1 May	Balances	b/d		115.20	760.50	2 May	Wages			80.00	
2 May	Sales			120.80		3 May	B. Thomas		4.21		206.29
3 May	Sales			109.55		4 May	J. Rees		2.00		98.00
4 May	R. Evans		12.00		388.00	5 May	W. Jones			88.47	
5 May	Sales			96.47		6 May	B. Robson		3.01		147.49
6 May	Sales			80.21		7 May	Bank	c		190.00	
7 May	Cash	c			190.00	7 May	Rent				45.00
8 May	J. Morris		1.77		86.73	9 May	C. Blimp		5.00		205.00
9 May	Sales			95.60		9 May	Wages			80.00	
10 May	N. Smith		4.15		220.50	10 May	A. Hazel		1.50		75.50
11 May	D. Baker		1.87		84.62	11 May	Rates				86.25
12 May	Sales			221.40		12 May	Insurance				42.60
13 May	W. Bolton		4.20		195.80	14 May	Postage			20.14	
14 May	Sales			262.30		14 May	Balances	c/d		642.92	1,020.02
			23.99	1,101.53	1,926.15				15.72	1,101.53	1,926.15
15 May	Balances	b/d	GL 21	642.92	1,020.02				GL 27		

Figure 9.4 The three column cash book

discount received for prompt payment. The debit entries relating to both the cheque and the discount received will be in the account of Thomas. There are three other similar transactions on the credit side of the cash book.

On 4 May a cheque for £388 has been received from R. Evans, who has paid promptly enough to have deducted a discount of £12. The credit entries for both the cheque and the discount allowed will be in the account of Evans. There are four other similar transactions on the debit side of the cash book.

Note the balancing of the three column cash book. The cash and bank columns are balanced as usual and the balances carried down to begin the next period. The column discount allowed and discount received, however, are not balanced. This is because they are not proper ledger accounts. They are merely supplementary or memorandum records. There will still be an account in the ledger for both discount allowed and discount received. The totals of the cash book columns are transferred into these ledger accounts at regular intervals. The references tell you that the discount received account is on page 27 and the discount allowed account page 21 of the general ledger. The entries in these accounts will look like this:

Discount received   GL 27

		1–14 May	Sundry creditors		£15.72

Discount allowed   GL 21

1–14 May	Sundry debtors	£23.99	

The debits corresponding to the one credit in the discount received account will be in the accounts of the various suppliers from whom discount was received during this period. Similarly, the credits corresponding to the one debit in the discount allowed account will be in the accounts of the customers or debtors who have been allowed discounts. Hence the descriptions 'sundry creditors' and 'sundry debtors'.

SELF-CHECK ▶
9.4

Enter the following transactions in the three column cash book of P. Broad and balance it on 14 April.

1 April	Cash balance £67.23; bank balance £191.20.
2 April	Cash sales £138.00.
3 April	Paid £100 cash into the bank.
4 April	Paid Bentley £120 by cheque, receiving discount of £3.
5 April	Paid Royce £94 by cheque in full settlement of an amount owing of £100 (balance is discount).
6 April	Cash sales £97.24.
7 April	Received a cheque from W. Barnes for £169.50 to settle an amount due of £178.50.
8 April	Paid wages in cash £120.80.
9 April	Paid T. Ford £98.00 in cash, having deducted a discount of £4.
10 April	Withdrew £75 from the bank for use as cash.
11 April	R. Hewitt paid £95 in cash, having deducted a discount of £5.
12 April	Paid insurance on car by cheque £78.90.
13 April	Cash sales £120.62.

SOLUTION ▶

Dr   Cash book   Cr

Date	Details	Folio	Discount allowed	Cash	Bank	Date	Details	Folio	Discount received	Cash	Bank
1 April	Balances	b/d		67.23	191.20	3 April	Bank	c		100.00	
2 April	Sales			138.00		4 April	Bentley		3.00		120.00
3 April	Cash	c			100.00	5 April	Royce		6.00		94.00
6 April	Sales			97.24		8 April	Wages			120.80	
7 April	W. Barnes		9.00		169.50	9 April	T. Ford		4.00	98.00	
10 April	Bank	c		75.00		10 April	Cash	c			75.00
11 April	R. Hewitt		5.00	95.00		12 April	Car insurance				78.90
13 April	Sales			120.62		14 April	Balances	c/d		274.29	92.80
			14.00	593.09	460.70				13.00	593.09	460.70
15 April	Balances	b/d		274.29	92.80						

9.5 THE PETTY CASH BOOK

This is used for recording small (petty comes from the French 'petit') payments for such items as postage, taxi fares and window cleaning. It may also include receipts for cash – for example when someone uses the business telephone and pays for it. The rules for entering transactions are the same as for any other cash account, i.e. debit receipts of cash and credit payments.

The petty cash book is usually operated on the **imprest** system. An imprest is a sum of money advanced to the cashier or clerk in charge of the petty cash. This is used to make payments for those items mentioned above. It is often called a float. At the end of a short period a senior clerk will check that the amount of the cash left is in agreement with the amount shown in the book. As with all transactions involving cash it is necessary to obtain a receipt. Such receipts for items in the petty cash book are known as vouchers. They are a means of checking that the cashier has indeed spent the money in the manner described in the book. The imprest will then be restored to its starting level. Figure 9.5 shows a typical example of a petty cash book.

Figure 9.5 The petty cash book

Dr	Date	Details	PCV	Total	Postage	Canteen	Travel	Stationery
30.00	1 May	Imprest	CB 6					
	2 May	Stamps	1	4.50	4.50			
	3 May	Teas	2	1.05		1.05		
	4 May	Taxi	3	2.25			2.25	
	4 May	Envelopes	4	1.50				1.50
	5 May	Coffees	5	0.75		0.75		
	6 May	Stamps	6	3.75	3.75			
	6 May	Bus fares	7	0.95			0.95	
	9 May	Lunch	8	1.20		1.20		
	10 May	A4 Paper	9	2.54				2.54
	11 May	Taxi	10	1.35			1.35	
	12 May	Petrol	11	1.95			1.95	
	13 May	Stamps	12	2.50	2.50			
				24.29	10.75	3.00	6.50	4.04
	14 May	Balance c/d		5.71	GL 27	GL 41	GL 29	GL 30
30.00				30.00				
5.71	15 May	Balance b/d						
24.29	15 May	Imprest						

SELF-CHECK 9.5

(a) Explain the entry 15 May for £24.29.
(b) For what is PCV an abbreviation?

SOLUTION

(a) This entry restores the float or imprest to £30.
(b) Petty cash voucher.

9.6 SINGLE ENTRY CASH BOOK

So far it has been assumed that businesses will have their accounts kept on a double entry basis. This is not usually done by small businesses if it is felt that the effort involved is not worthwhile. Such businesses will normally keep only a record of money received and paid in a cash book of one kind or another. Such a system is known as single entry because only one entry is made for each transaction. Where this is done, the cash book becomes of even greater importance because it contains the only record of a transaction. It is possible to gain some of the advantages of a double entry system while keeping only a cash book if the number of columns are expanded and the receipts and payments of money analysed.

The cash book on page 200 is used by a trader who makes all his payments by cheque and who banks all receipts of cash each day. As he is liable to the government for VAT he uses two columns for this. The debit column contains the amounts of VAT he has charged his customers and the credit column the amount of VAT he has paid to his suppliers. Apart from purchases, wages are the only other expense regular enough to need its own column so all the other expenses are classified as sundries. A larger number of columns could be used if there were sufficient items regular enough to make it worthwhile.

Figure 9.6 Single entry cash book

Cash book

Receipts	Sales	VAT	Date	Details	Payments	Purchases	Wages	Sundries	VAT
500.00			1 Mar.	Balance b/d					
151.80	132.00	19.80	1 Mar.	J. Smith					
			2 Mar.	B. Jones	115.00	100.00			15.00
			3 Mar.	R. Evans	75.50		75.50		
			4 Mar.	British Rail	24.00			24.00	
193.20	168.00	25.20	4 Mar.	W. Toms					
			5 Mar.	M. Morgan	312.80	272.00			40.80
103.73	90.20	13.53	6 Mar.	T. Lewis					
			7 Mar.	Balance c/d	421.43				
					948.73	372.00	75.50	24.00	55.80
948.73	390.20	58.53							
421.43			8 Mar.	Balance b/d					

SELF-CHECK ▶ 9.6 What is the main difference between double entry and single entry book-keeping?

SOLUTION ▶ In single entry, only transactions involving the receipt or payment of money are recorded. There will therefore be only one entry for each transaction.

9.7 BANK RECONCILIATION STATEMENTS

Businesses are not the only organisations that keep records of the money they have paid in to or out of their bank account. The bank will also keep a record. A copy of this record will be sent to each client at agreed intervals – often monthly. It is known as a bank statement. A typical example is shown opposite:

Royal Bank
Tavy Branch
A/c R. Drew
A/c No 45678
Statement date: 31 May 1988

Description of entries
BGC: Bank giro credit
Div: Dividend
D/D: Direct debit
S/O: Standing order

Date	Particulars	Cheque No	Payments	Receipts	Balance
			£	£	£
1 May	Balance				130.65
4 May	Sundry credit			250.45	381.10
7 May		3961	19.67		361.43
		3962	132.45		228.98
10 May	Sundry credit			350.60	579.58
		3964	49.90		
		3965	20.65		509.03
17 May	BGC			43.60	552.63
24 May		3963	68.50		
		3966	140.00		344.13
25 May	SO		250.00		94.13
27 May	Div			75.25	169.38

Balance marked O/D when overdrawn

In whatever kind of cash book a trader keeps a record of his bank account, it is likely that the balance recorded will not agree with the balance shown in the bank's own records. On the date that Drew received the above statement the bank columns of his cash book looked like this.

Dr				Cash Book			Cr
			£				£
1 May	Balance	b/d	130.65	3 May	Insurance		19.67
4 May	Sales		250.45	5 May	T. Smith		132.45
10 May	B. Timms		350.60	7 May	R. Brian		49.90
17 May	D. Wills		43.60	8 May	T. Evans		20.65
31 May	Cash		100.00	18 May	Rates		68.50
				19 May	W. Trott		140.00
				27 May	Rent		75.50
				28 May	I. Bright		36.40
				31 May	Balance	c/d	332.23
			875.30				875.30
1 June	Balance	b/d	332.23				

When Drew looks at his bank statement he will immediately notice that the balance shown at the end of the month is different to the balance shown in his cash book. There is one other major difference that should be noted:

In the bank statement the receipts column is the credit column while in the cash book it is the debit column. Payments are debited by the bank whereas Drew makes a credit entry in the cash book to record payments. This is because, from the bank's point of view, money in the bank represents a liability to Drew. Therefore payments into the bank by Drew increase the liability and are credited while payments made by Drew reduce the liability and are debited. From Drew's viewpoint money in the bank is an asset and represented by a debit balance. Consequently amounts of money paid into the bank are debited by Drew to increase his asset while payments made by Drew are credited to show a reduction in the value of the asset.

It is essential that you understand this reversal of entries. A debit balance in the cash book is equivalent to a credit balance in the bank statement, while a credit balance in the cash book is the same as a debit or overdraft balance in the bank statement.

The cash book extract and bank statement above are fairly normal in that the amount of the balances recorded in them differ. There are two main reasons why this may have happened.

First, and most likely, one party may not know what the other party has done (or perhaps it was known but has been forgotten). The most common example of this surrounds the writing of cheques. The account holder is able to record a payment by cheque in the cash book on the day he writes the cheque. His bank will learn of this only when the cheque is presented for payment. This will take a few days even when the receiver pays it into his own bank immediately. It is also possible that the account holder will lack knowledge of a transaction completed by his bank. For example, it is normal practice not to invoice clients for the charges due for operating the account. A deduction is made from the account and the client learns of this only when he receives his next statement. In addition many people forget they have completed a form permitting their bank to make payments for them by standing order or direct debit. The arrival of the statement serves as a timely reminder.

The second reason for a discrepancy in the balances is that an error has been made by either the client or the bank. The sooner errors are discovered the sooner they can be corrected. This is why explaining the differences between the cash book balance and the balance in the statement is so important. The process of explaining the differences is known as reconciliation. There are three main steps:

1 Compare the cash book entries with those of the bank statement

It is useful to tick each entry in the cash book that is also in the statement and each entry that is in the statement that is also in the cash book. The entries not ticked will help to explain why the balances are different. It is useful to write them down, stating clearly which ones are in the cash book but not in the statement and which are in the statement but not in the cash book.

If you do this for Drew, in the cash book the payments of 27 May and 28 May will not be ticked nor will the amount of cash banked on 31 May. The items not ticked in the bank statement will be the payment by standing order on 25 May and the dividends received on 27 May. These could be written down as follows:

In the cash book but not in the statement:

27 May	Paid rent by cheque £75.50
28 May	paid I. Bright by cheque £36.40
31 May	Cash paid into bank £100

In the statement but not in the cash book:

| 25 May | Payment by standing order £250 |
| 27 May | Dividends received £75.25 |

2 Bring the cash book up to date

This is done by entering any items which are not yet included but which are in the statement. If the cash book has already been balanced at the end of the month then the late entries can be dated on the first day of the new month.

Cash Book

1 June	Balance	b/d	£ 332.23	1 June	Smith SO		£ 250.00
1 June	Share dividend		75.25	1 June	Balance	c/d	157.48
			407.48				407.48
2 June	Balance	b/d	157.48				

The bank statement will have reminded Drew about the dividends he was expecting and the payment by standing order he had forgotten. He could enter more detail about them if he wished. If these were the only differences noted between cash and statement the new balance should be the same in both. There would be no need to take the reconciliation process any further. In this case other differences have been noted so there is a need for further work to reconcile the two balances.

3 Draft a bank reconciliation statement

The remaining differences are ones which have arisen because the bank is not up to date. It is not within Drew's power to bring the bank up to date so what he does is to draw up a brief statement using the remaining differences to reconcile the newly amended balance in the cash book with the balance in the statement.

Bank reconciliation statement 1 June 1988

	£	£
Balance (amended) as per the cash book		157.48
Add Cheques not presented:		
	75.50	
	36.40	
		111.90
		269.38
Less Lodgement not credited by bank		100.00
Balance as per bank statement		169.38

The cheques are added back to the cash book balance because the bank statement will be that much **greater** because the bank has not yet deducted them from Drew's account. The money lodged (paid into) the bank by Drew is deducted because the bank statement will be that much **less** because the bank has not yet recorded it.

The above statement achieves its purpose in that it successfully explains the differences between the cash book balance and the bank statement balance. If the two balances had not been reconciled by this process, it suggests that there is an error in either the bank statement or cash book. This error would then have to be located and corrected. Bank reconciliation statements are usually filed with bank statements for future reference.

SELF-CHECK ▶ 9.7

A trader checked his cash book against the bank statement dated 31 July and noted the following discrepancies:

1 Balance as per cash book £456.71; balance as per statement £182.78
2 Cheques written by him but not yet presented for payment: No. 2179 £20.50; No. 2181 £5.32; No. 2184 £65.74
3 His takings of £300 on 31 July had been banked late in the day and were not shown in the statement.
4 Payment had been made to Grampian Insurance for £48.25 by direct debit.
5 Bank charges £17.24

First bring the cash book up to date by entering those transactions that would be in the statement but not yet included in the cash book. Then draft a bank reconciliation statement to explain the remaining differences between the bank statement balance and the amended cash book balance.

SOLUTION ▶

Cash Book

			£					£
31 July	Balance	b/d	456.71	31 July	Bank charges		17.24
				31 July	Grampian	SO	48.25
				31 July	Balance	c/d	391.22
			456.71				456.71
1 Aug	Balance	b/d	391.22				

Bank reconciliation statement 31 July 1988

		£	£
Balance (amended) as per cash book			391.22
add Cheques not presented:	2179	20.50	
	2181	5.32	
	2184	65.74	
			91.56
			482.78
less Cash lodgement not entered by bank			300.00
Balance as per bank statement			182.78

It is important to sort out the differences that have arisen because an entry is in the cash book and not in the statement from those that are in the statement and not in the cash book. The trader would not have known the amount of the bank charges until he received his statement. He should have known that he had completed a direct debit form for payments to be made to Grampian Insurance but it is the type of transaction often overlooked when making up the cash book. These items must therefore be inserted in the cash book. The other items would be known by the trader before the bank and therefore would be in the cash book and not the statement. It is these items, therefore, which must be shown in the bank reconciliation statement. This kind of question is very popular and great care should be taken over it.

EXERCISES

9.1

A business has a cash book, purchases ledger and a general ledger. In which of these would you find the following accounts:
(a)   T. Smith, a customer   G. L.
(b)   cash account   C.B.
(c)   motor expenses account   G. L.
(d)   R. Willis, a supplier   P. L.
(e)   purchases account   G. L.

9.2

Classify the following accounts as real, nominal or personal:
(a)   W. Rade, customer   P
(b)   rent   N.
(c)   bank   R.

(d)   motor vehicle
(e)   motor expenses
(f)   T. White, supplier
(g)   discount allowed
(h)   capital

9.3

Enter the following transactions in the three column cash book of T. Sawyer and balance it on 14 May.

1 May	Cash balance £47.53; bank balance £449.52
2 May	Cash sales £313.56
3 May	Paid £250 cash into the bank
4 May	Paid Bennett £152 by cheque, receiving discount of £13.
5 May	Paid Johns £47 by cheque in full settlement of an amount owing of £50 (balance is discount)
6 May	Cash sales £297.54
7 May	Received a cheque from R. Robbins for £369.50 in full settlement of an amount due of £378.50 (balance is discount)
8 May	Paid wages in cash £92.80
9 May	Paid G. Edwards £132.00 by cheque, having deducted a discount of £14
10 May	Withdrew £75 from the bank for use as cash
11 May	R. Hewitt paid Sawyer £105 in cash, having deducted a discount of £5
12 May	Paid insurance on car by cheque £97.39
14 May	Sawyer withdrew £100 cash and £200 by cheque for private use

9.4

A sole trader L. Bright receives a statement of his current account at his bank and finds that the figure for the balance does not equal that in the cash book.

> Bank statement balance £7,000
> Cash book balance £2,800

It appears that several matters mentioned in the cash book have not been taken into account by the bank:

(i) cheques for £1,000, £500 and £2,000 have been issued and not cleared;

(ii) a direct debit in the cash book for £50 and a standing order for £75 have not yet appeared in the bank statement.

Certain entries in the bank statement do not appear in the cash book:

(i) the bank has entered charges for £25;

(ii) a payment by a debtor £500 appears in the bank statement and not in the cash book;

(iii) a dividend paid on shares for £100 has been sent direct to the bank and is in the statement.

(*a*)   What is a bank statement?

(*b*)   In what ways are standing orders and direct debits similar and in what ways are they dissimilar?

(*c*)   Why do cash books and their related bank statements differ in content?

(*d*)   Why are bank reconciliation statements prepared?

(*e*)   Prepare a bank reconciliation statement to reconcile the cash book and the bank statement.

(NISEC specimen paper)

9.5

(*a*)   Prepare Clive Allen's three column cash book from the folowing information.

1986

1 April	Balance **cash** £30.00 and **bank** £10.00
13 April	Cash sales paid into bank, £600.00
19 April	Received cheque from D. Smithies for £98.00 in settlement of his balance outstanding of £100.00
20 April	Paid wages in cash, £10.00
21 April	Paid insurance premiums by cheque, £31.00
29 April	Cash sales, £350.00
29 April	Paid G. Gutteridge by cheque the balance due to him, £120.00 less 2½% cash discount
30 April	Received cheque from A. Blyth for £147.00 in settlement of his debt of £150.00
30 April	Deposited all cash except £25 in the bank, together with Blyth's cheque

(*b*)   Clive received the following bank statement on 3 May 1986:

Bank Statement

Date	Particulars	Payments	Receipts	Balance
1 April	Balance			10.00
3 April	Sundry credits		600.00	610.00
19 April	Sundry credits		98.00	708.00
24 April	107651	31.00		677.00
30 April	D.D. Newton B.C.	60.00		617.00
30 April	Charges	17.00		600.00
1 May	Sundry credits		492.00	1,092.00

(i) Bring Clive's cash book up to date.

(ii) Prepare a statement reconciling the revised cash book balance with the balance on the bank statement.

(MEG specimen paper)

9.6

(*a*)   As the clerk in charge of petty cash you are required to enter the following transactions into a petty cash book, which should have four analysis columns headed as follows:

(i) canteen (ii) travelling (iii) postage (iv) cleaning

The petty cash book is to be kept on the imprest system, the amount spent to be reimbursed at the end of each week. The opening cash float is £45.

1986			£ p
1 April	Voucher no. 123	Postage stamps	6.00
1 April	Voucher no. 124	Milk	4.30
2 April	Voucher no. 125	Bus fare	52
2 April	Voucher no. 126	Window cleaner	3.00
2 April	Voucher no. 127	Tea	1.10
3 April	Voucher no. 128	Registered letter	60
3 April	Voucher no. 129	Sugar	2.12
3 April	Voucher no. 130	Train ticket	4.19
4 April	Voucher no. 131	Broom	2.40
4 April	Voucher no. 132	Bus fare	80
4 April	Voucher no. 133	Polish	2.14
5 April	Voucher no. 134	Coffee	3.82
5 April	Voucher no. 135	Postage stamps	5.00
5 April	Voucher no. 136	Car expenses	4.84

(*b*)   If the balance in the petty cash book at 5 April failed to agree with the money in the cash box, what steps would you take to find the error(s)?

(WJEC specimen paper)

9.7

State the entries needed in a trader's accounts if a debtor's cheque is returned from the bank marked 'dishonoured cheque refer to drawer'.

9.8

(*a*)   Why do businesses keep a cash book **and** a petty cash book?

(*b*)   Explain clearly the meaning of the imprest system of petty cash.

(*c*)   Record the following transactions in the cash book and petty cash book of A. Milne. The petty cash book should have three analysis columns: Postages, Stationery, Office Expenses.

On 1 January 1986 A. Milne's books showed the following balances.

Cash...........................	69.70
Bank overdraft..............	201.10
Petty cash (imprest)	50.00

1 Jan	Bought stamps: 20 at 17p each and 50 at 13p each Sent cheque to G. Hammond £41 in full settlement of a debt of £42.80 Paid wages in cash £68.70. Cash sales £110.40
2 Jan	Paid for shop cleaning £5.60 Bought goods and paid by cheque £21.20
3 Jan	Postage on parcels £4.40
4 Jan	Bought stationery for office £5.30 Received cheque from W. May £96
6 Jan	Paid rent by cheque £28.40. Cash sales banked £90.65
7 Jan	Paid for milk £2.36. Bought envelopes £1.20
8 Jan	The cheque received from W. May on 4 January was returned by the bank dishonoured Paid all cash into bank except £30.00 The petty cashier was reimbursed in cash to restore the imprest

(d)   Balance the cash book and the petty cash book.
                                        (NEA specimen paper)

9.9   (a)   Briefly explain the difference between a bank statement and a bank reconciliation statement.

(b)

Cash Book (Bank columns only)

		£			£
1 Jan	Balance	600	18 Jan	D. Anderson	145
13 Jan	T. Francis	224	28 Jan	R. Patrick	72
31 Jan	L. Bond	186	30 Jan	B. Thompson	109

Bank Statement

		Debit	Credit	Balance
1 Jan	Balance			635
3 Jan	H. Turner	35		600
13 Jan	T. Francis		224	824
23 Jan	D. Anderson	145		679
31 Jan	Standing order	30		649

Using the information given opposite:
      (i) prepare a corrected cash book;
      (ii) draw up a bank reconciliation statement.

                                      (NEA specimen paper)

9.10

The cashier of your firm has been absent owing to illness and no entries have been made in the cash book for the period 24–30 November. The cash book has three columns, for discounts, cash and bank. On 23 November the balances on the cash book were: cash in hand £86 and cash at bank £420. There were no cash discount items in the cash book at that date. The following additional information is available:

24 November   Paid cash for stationery £8 and stamps £11
25 November   Sent S. Davis a cheque for £280 and took £20 cash discount
26 November   Received and paid bank a cheque from T. Griffiths £432 accepted in full settlement of his debt of £470
28 November   Banked a cheque from K. Stephens £506 on account
29 November   Cashed a cheque £42 for office use
30 November   Cash sales for the period 24–30 November, £544, paid direct to bank

Required

(a)   Preparation of the cash book for the period 24–30 November, bringing down the balances to 1 December.
(b)   An explanation of why you may be dissatisfied with the correctness of the cash balance.
(c)   An explanation of where discount allowed and discount received will be posted from the cash book and how each of them will affect the net profit calculation.

On 3 December the bank supplies you with a statement, from which you extract the following items relating to the period 24–30 November but omitted from the bank columns of your cash book.

Cheque received from K. Stephens has been dishonoured by his bank; your bank has made a charge of £4 for its services; credit transfers by customers, totalling £480, have been paid direct to your bank.

Required

(d)   A statement showing the calculation of the actual bank balance at 30 November.   (SEG specimen paper)

OURNALS AND LEDGER
CONTROL ACCOUNTS

CONTENTS

The term **journal** means daily record (from the French 'jour'). It is possible to have a full system of double entry book-keeping without making use of journals at all – this book has done so until now. However, they are useful in certain situations and it is necessary to know how to operate a journal system.

Journals are also known as the books of original entry because transactions are entered in them before they are entered in the ledger. The process of making the entries in the ledger from the journals is called 'posting to the ledger'. Journals are also known as subsidiary books because they are regarded as subsidiary or secondary to the main ledger system. In other words they supplement the ledger. They are not part of the ledger system itself but relieve it of much unnecessary detail.

The three column cash book has already been used to reduce the amount of detail appearing in two ledger accounts. The columns for discount allowed and received were used as memorandum records and were not in themselves part of the double entry system. At the end of a regular period the columns were added and the totals entered in their respective ledger accounts. This considerably reduced the information contained in the ledger accounts for discount allowed and received. There are five main journals:

1 The sales journal.
2 The sales returns or returns inward journal.
3 The purchases journal.
4 The purchases returns or returns outward journal.
5 The journal.

The first four are kept for **credit** transactions involving sales, purchases and returns. The term 'day book' or 'book' often replaces 'journal' so do not be confused if you encounter a sales day book or returns outward book. The fifth – **the** journal is often pronounced with emphasis on the first word to distinguish it from the other journals. It is sometimes referred to as 'the journal proper' for the same reason. It is used for a number of different transactions when it is felt that extra detail needs to be recorded.

Ledger control accounts These help to provide a check on the accuracy of certain ledger accounts. They make use of information obtained in the journals.

10.1 THE SALES AND PURCHASES JOURNALS

The sales journal This is used to enter details of all credit sales of stoc
The information will be obtained from duplicate copies of the invoic
sent to customers by the trader.

Sales Journal

Date	Customer	Invoice	Folio	£ p
1 July	Robinsons	1690	DL 147	77.50
4 July	Carter & Sons	1691	DL 12	31.20
5 July	Allens DIY	1692	DL 6	80.80
6 July	RKL Electrics	1693	DL 152	388.00
7 July	Electroshop	1694	DL 21	163.12
7 July	Transferred to sales a/c		GL 21	740.62

Each customer to whom the trader sells will have his own person
account in the debtors' ledger. This assumes that the trader su
divides his ledger as in section 9.1. If not, the folio reference of D
will be replaced by GL for general ledger or just L for ledger. Th
debit entries will be made in each customer's personal account fro
the duplicate of the invoice as soon as the invoice is sent. Instead
making a credit entry in the sales account for each sale, the entries ar
saved up and **one** entry made at a convenient time to correspond t
the total number of debits made in the customer's accounts. In th
above example one credit entry of £740.62 on 7 July will be the doubl
entry corresponding to the five separate debits from 1 July to 7 July i
the customer's accounts. The sales account will look like this:

Sales a/c GL 21

7 July	Sundry debtors	SJ 28	740.62

Note the cross reference to the sales journal and the description tha
indicates that several debtors' accounts are involved. The delay ir
posting the credit entry to the sales account means that a trial balanc
extracted between 1 July and 6 July will not agree. This is because
debit entries have been without a corresponding credit entry.

The purchases journal This will contain all purchases of stock on credit. I
will be made up from the invoices received from suppliers. The
suppliers accounts affected will be in the creditors' ledger and the
other ledger account involved will be the purchases account. Apart
from these obvious differences the procedure is the same as with the

sales journal. You should, therefore, be able to complete the following:

SELF-CHECK ▶
10.1

A trader received the following invoices for purchases of stock during July:

Date	Supplier	£ p
3 July	Wireplies	289.50
16 July	UVC	341.38
17 July	Plugplies	429.17
24 July	Jones	121.12
29 July	Electose	321.03

Enter them in a purchases journal and show all relevant ledger account entries. Invent suitable folio and invoice numbers.

SOLUTION ▶

Purchases Journal   8

Date	Supplier	Invoice	Folio	£ p
3 July	Wireplies	7/1	CL 29	289.50
16 July	UVC	7/2	CL 17	341.38
17 July	Plugplies	7/3	CL 22	429.17
24 July	Jones	7/4	CL 14	121.12
29 July	Electose	7/5	CL 7	321.03
31 July	Transferred to purchases account		GL 16	1,502.20

Creditors Ledger

Wireplies a/c   CL 29

	3 July	Purchases	PJ8	289.50

UVC a/c   CL 17

	16 July	Purchases	PJ8	341.38

Plugplies a/c   CL 22

	17 July	Purchases	PJ8	429.17

Jones a/c   CL 14

	24 July	Purchases	PJ8	121.12

Electose a/c   CL 7

	29 July	Purchases	PJ8	321.03

General Ledger

Purchases a/c   GL 16

31 July	Sundry creditors	PJ8	1,502.20	

COMMENT ▶

Each of the trader's suppliers will have a personal account in th creditors ledger. The credit entries are made in each of these account from an invoice as soon as it is received. **One** debit entry of £1,502.2 is made in the purchases account to correspond to the total number o credits that have been made in the suppliers' accounts. Invoice received from suppliers will have a variety of different reference numbers. To aid filing the trader will probably stamp each one with his own reference number.

10.2 RETURNS JOURNALS

These take the same form as the above. They will be used for returns of stock purchased or sold on credit. The document from which they will be entered will be the credit note. This is sent by the firm which receives the goods to the firm that has returned them. A credit note is literally a note telling the customer that you have accepted the returned goods and have accordingly credited his account.

The returns inward journal is used to list all sales returns.

Returns inward journal 3

Date	Supplier	Cr/Note	Folio	£ p
6 July	Robinsons	217	DL 147	50.12
15 July	RKL	218	DL 152	48.00
24 July	Evans DIY	219	DL 24	6.54
31 July	Walters	220	DL 189	22.12
31 July	Transferred to returns inward a/c		GL 22	126.78

A credit entry will be made in each customer's account in the debtors ledger as the returns are accepted and the credit note sent. A copy of the credit note will be kept for the trader's own records. **One** debit entry will be made in the returns inward account in the general ledger at a convenient time to correspond to the total credit entries made in the customers' accounts.

Returns inward a/c GL 22

July	Sundry debtors	RIJ 3	126.78	

The returns outward journal This will contain a list of all the returns of goods purchased on credit. It will be made up from the credit notes received from suppliers to whom the returned goods have been sent. The suppliers accounts affected will be in the creditors' ledger and the other ledger account involved will be the returns outward account. Apart from these obvious differences, the procedure is the same as with the returns inward journal. You should, therefore, be able to complete the following:

SELF-CHECK ▶ 10.2

A trader received the following credit notes for returns of stock during July:

Date	Supplier	£ p
8 July	EQP Ltd	38.29
10 July	Electose	49.54
23 July	Plugplies	56.20
28 July	Jones	17.47
29 July	Wilsons	38.25

Enter them in a purchases returns journal and show all relevant ledger account entries. Invent suitable folio and credit note numbers.

SOLUTION ▶

Returns outward journal   6

Date	Supplier	Cr/Note	Folio	£ p
8 July	EQP Ltd	1/7	CL 9	38.29
10 July	Electose	2/7	CL 7	49.54
23 July	Plugplies	3/7	CL 22	56.20
28 July	Jones	4/7	CL 14	17.47
29 July	Wilsons	5/7	CL 27	38.25
31 July	Transferred to returns outward a/c		GL 17	199.75

General Ledger

Returns outward a/c

	31 July	Sundry creditors ROJ 6	199.75

Creditors Ledger

EQP Ltd

8 July	Returns out	ROJ 6	38.29	

Electose

10 July	Returns out	ROJ 6	49.54	

Plugplies

23 July	Returns out	ROJ 6	56.20	

Jones

28 July	Returns out	ROJ 6	17.47	

Wilsons

29 July	Returns out	ROJ 6	38.25	

COMMENT ▶ It is important to remember that all the journals we have dealt with so far are used only for the purchase and sales of stock on **credit**. Transactions involving money used to be recorded in a cash receipts journal or cash payments journal before being entered in the ledger accounts for cash and bank. These two journals are not often seen today. Most businesses consider their various cash books as books of original entry. Thus the cashbook can be seen as both a part of the ledger system containing the ledger accounts for cash and bank and the day book system.

10.3 THE JOURNAL

At one time this was used as a residual day book. In other words, it was used to record any transaction that did not have its own book of original entry. Today the journal is often reserved for those transactions that need extra explanation. There is much more space in the journal to enter details of transaction than there is in the ledger, where normally there is only sufficient space to enter the name of the other ledger account involved. If the journal is used it does not mean that no entries need be made in the ledger. These have to be made as normal. The format of the journal is the same as the day books above but the columns are used differently. The standard layout is like this:

Journal

Date	Details	Folio	£ dr	£ cr
	Name of the a/c to be debited			
	Name of the a/c to be credited			
	The narrative or explanation			

A few examples of how transactions could be entered in the journal should aid understanding:

THE PURCHASE OR SALE OF A FIXED ASSET ON CREDIT

On 21 May a trader purchased a motor van on credit from Newton Motors for £1,995.

Journal

Date	Description	Folio	£ dr	£ cr
21 May	Motor vehicle a/c	GL 6	1,995	
	Newton Motors a/c	GL 9		1,995
	Purchase of BL van registration No. YKK 345Y			

OPENING A SET OF LEDGER ACCOUNTS

On 1 April S. Thomas started in business with capital of £5,000 consisting of stock £1,000, bank £2,500 and cash £1,500.

Journal

Date	Description	Folio	£ dr	£ cr
1 April	Cash a/c	CB 1	1,500	
	Bank a/c	CB 1	2,500	
	Stock a/c	GL 1	1,000	
	Capital	GL 2		5,000
	Assets and capital at the start of business		5,000	5,000

In this case, because there is more than one debit the entries have been totalled. This was not done in the first example because it could be seen immediately that the value of the one debit equalled the value of the other credit entry. Entries in the journal cover a variety of transactions and it is necessary only to draw a line beneath one before writing the next.

WRITING OFF A BAD DEBT

On 12 May R. Bolt died owing a trader £34. The trader wrote off the debt when it was discovered that he died penniless.

Journal

Date	Description	Folio	£ dr	£ cr
12 May	Bad debts a/c	GL 37	34.00	
	R. Bolt	DL 4		34.00
	Debt written off owing to Bolt's death			

There is nothing to prevent any transaction being journalised before being entered in the ledger. It is most usual with difficult transactions that require extra information. For example, in examination questions transactions involving the correction of errors (see section 4.5) are frequently asked for in journal form.

SELF-CHECK ◗
10.3

On 15 June a trader sold a typewriter (serial number 87/234) valued in the books at £150 to Northern Electrical Factors for £90 on credit. Show the journal entries needed to record this transaction.

SOLUTION ◗

Journal

Date	Details	Folio	£ dr	£ cr
15 June	Northern Electrical Factors		90	
	Profit and loss a/c		60	
	Office equipment a/c			150
	Sale of typewriter serial no. 87/1234		150	150

COMMENT ▶	In examination questions it is not necessary to make up folio numbers but it is very important that you get the debits and credits right. Knowledge of the rules of double entry book-keeping is essential.

10.4 SALES LEDGER CONTROL ACCOUNTS

In chapter four a trial balance was used to check the accuracy of transactions in the ledger. This process can be extended to check individual sections of the ledger such as the sales ledger which is also known as the debtors' ledger. It is especially useful for firms with large numbers of debtors. In such a firm it is likely that a sectional system will be in operation.

As an illustration assume that Sheila is responsible for a firm's sales ledger containing the accounts of customers with names in the range A–E. She will have to make a large number of debit entries for sales and credits for money received, discounts allowed, returns accepted, and perhaps bad debts written off. Suppose that at the end of May the debit balances in her customers' accounts totalled £12,984. This could be checked by obtaining all the information referring to her customers and entering it into one account like this:

Dr   Sales ledger (A–E) control account   Cr

1 May	Balances	b/d	13,621	1–31 May	Cash		465
1–31 May	Sales		16,200	1–31 May	Bank		15,000
				1–31 May	Discount allowed		324
				1–31 May	Returns in		944
				1–31 May	Bad debts		104
				31 May	Balances	c/d	12,984
			29,821				29,821
1 June	Balances	b/d	12,984				

This account is also sometimes known as the total debtors (A–E) control account. This is because it contains as totals all the entries referring to debtors (A–E). It is not part of the double entry system but is kept outside as a memorandum account. You can see that when Sheila's balances from her section of the sales ledger are inserted on the credit side (ready to be brought down to the debit side where they belong), the totals of the account (£29,821) agree. This would be accepted as sufficient proof that there are no errors in this section of the sales ledger. To understand fully how this system works it is useful to see it when an error is revealed. For example, suppose the balances in Sheila's section totalled £12,274 on 31 May. The control account with this inserted would look like this:

Dr				Sales ledger (A–E) control account				Cr
1 May	Balances	b/d	13,621	1–31 May	Cash		465	
1–31 May	Sales		16,200	1–31 May	Bank		15,000	
				1–31 May	Discount allowed		324	
				1–31 May	Returns in		944	
				1–31 May	Bad debts		104	
				31 May	Balances	c/d	12,274	
			29,821				29,111	

Clearly something is wrong in this section of the sales ledger. The error or errors will have to be traced and corrected as soon as possible. If this control account had not been kept the error would not have been revealed until the trial balance was prepared. This would give no guidance as to which accounts in it were at fault.

The person responsible for preparing the sales ledger control account should obtain the figures from original entries. (There would be little point in simply taking the figures from the debtors' accounts themselves as this is where Sheila has already obtained her figure for the value of total debtors.) To do this easily the sales journal and returns inward journal should have analysis columns to match the sections of the ledger covered by the individual clerks. It will help also if the cash book is analysed in this way as the entries for cash and cheques received as well as discounts allowed will be obtained from that source. Entries for bad debts will be obtained from the journal which is not analysed. However, as such entries are comparatively few, it should not take too long to go through this book and extract the entries relevant to each of the sections of the sales ledger.

SELF-CHECK ▶ 10.4

From the following information about the sales ledger (F–J) prepare a control account on 31 May and state whether it reveals any errors.

1 May	Debit balances	£15,321
1–31 May	Total credit sales	20,640
1–31 May	Total cash received	1,220
1–31 May	Total cheques received	13,930
1–31 May	Total discounts allowed	480
1–31 May	Bad debts	306

1–31 May	Total returns inward		721				
31 May	Debit balances in sales ledger		19,304				

SOLUTION ▶

Sales ledger (F–J) control account

1 May	Balances	b/d	15,321	1–31 May	Cash		1,220
1–31 May	Sales		20,640	1–31 May	Bank		13,930
				1–31 May	Discounts allowed		480
				1–31 May	Returns inward		721
				1–31 May	Bad debts		306
				31 May	Balances	c/d	19,304
			35,961				35,961
1 June	Balances	b/d	19,304				

As the totals agree, no error is revealed.

10.5 PURCHASES LEDGER CONTROL ACCOUNTS

The purchases ledger can be controlled in a similar manner to the sales ledger. It will, of course, differ because it contains the accounts of suppliers. In these accounts the balances will be credit balances and there will be credit entries for goods bought on credit. The debit entries in these accounts will be for amounts paid by cash or cheque, discounts received and returns outward. The purchases ledger control account is also known as the total creditors control account. To obtain information easily the books of original entry should be analysed in the same manner in which the purchases ledger is subdivided.

SELF-CHECK ▶
10.5(a)

Prepare a control account from the following information which refers to the purchases ledger (A–L).

1 May	Credit balances	£27,431
1–31 May	Total credit purchases	88,500
1–31 May	Total cash paid	1,462
1–31 May	Total cheques paid	87,160
1–31 May	Total discounts received	2,605
1–31 May	Total goods returned	468
31 May	Credit balances in purchases ledger	24,236

SOLUTION ➡

Purchases ledger (A–L) control account

1–31 May	Cash		1,462	1 May	Balances	b/d	27,431
1–31 May	Bank		87,160	1–31 May	Purchases		88,500
1–31 May	Discounts received		2,605				
1–31 May	Returns out		468				
31 May	Balances	c/d	24,236				
			115,931				115,931
				1 June	Balances	b/d	24,236

As the totals agree, no errors are revealed.

As the purchases ledger control account contains total figures covering all the accounts in the purchases ledger it is possible that there will be some **debit** balances included. This is obviously unusual because a ledger containing the accounts of suppliers would naturally be expected to show credit balances. This situation can arise because sometimes returns are made **after** goods have been paid for. Thus, for a short time, the suppliers will owe the purchaser for the amount of the returns. Such accounts wil be relatively small, as can be seen from the following example.

Purchases ledger control account

1 June	Balances	b/d	200	1 June	Balances	b/d	20,600
1–30 June	Bank		68,720	1–30 June	Purchases		72,000
1–30 June	Discounts received		14,830	1–30 June	Balances	c/d	180
1–30 June	Returns outward		642				
30 June	Balances	c/d	8,388				
			92,780				92,780
1 July	Balances	b/d	180	1 July	Balances	b/d	8,389

At both the beginning and end of the month the credit balances are much bigger than the debit balances, as you would expect in a ledger containing the accounts of suppliers.

It is also possible for the sales ledger to have a number of accounts with temporary **credit** balances. These will probably be the accounts of customers who have returned goods after having paid for them.

Eventually they will purchase more goods and the credit balances will be set off against these purchases. The majority of the accounts in the sales ledger will, of course, have debit balances.

SELF-CHECK ▶
10.5(b)

Write up a sales ledger control account from the following information.

1 May	Debit balances in sales ledger	£25,860
1 May	Credit balances in sales ledger	690
1–31 May	Total credit sales	93,840
1–31 May	Total cheques received	88,420
1–31 May	Total discounts allowed	1,930
31 May	Total returns inward	975
31 May	Debit balances in sales ledger	28,185
31 May	Credit balances in sales ledger	500

SOLUTION ▶

Sales ledger control account

1 May	Balances	b/d	25,860	1 May	Balances	b/d		690
1–31 May	Sales		93,840	1–31 May	Bank			88,420
31 May	Balances	c/d	500	1–31 May	Discounts allowed			1,930
				1–31 May	Returns inward			975
				31 May	Balances	c/d		28,185
			120,200					120,200
1 June	Balances	b/d	28,185	1 June	Balances	b/d		500

In this explanation it has been assumed that the sales ledger and purchases ledger control accounts have been kept as memorandum accounts outside the double entry system. It is possible for them to become an integral part of that system. However, if this is done the personal accounts of the debtors and creditors must be regarded as outside the system otherwise some entries would be appearing twice.

EXERCISES

10.1   State the daybook associated with the following business documents:
(a)   invoice received
(b)   credit note received
(c)   copy of invoice sent
(d)   copy of credit note sent.

10.2   A trader sent the following invoices during July:

		£ p
4 July	Baxter	218.35
14 July	Carter	134.43
16 July	Davies	223.26
24 July	Evans	212.52
27 July	Fearns	132.73

Enter them in the relevant journal and show all relevant ledger account entries.

10.3   A trader sent the following credit notes during July:

		£ p
6 July	Gregg	28.79
14 July	Hector	79.78
21 July	Inder	59.86
26 July	Jones	16.97
29 July	Kelly	76.85

Enter them in the relevant journal and show all relevant ledger account entries.

10.4   State the journal entries needed in the following cases:
(a)   Purchase of motor vehicle on credit from Abbot Motors for £5,000.
(b)   Transfer sales total of £30,000 to the trading account.
(c)   Sale of delivery vehicle, book value £1,000, on credit to T. Hall for £1,200.
(d)   Bad debts of £58 written off sundry debtors.
(e)   Sale of equipment, book value £450, on credit to R. Bly for £390.

10.5

From the following information about the sales ledger (K–R) prepare a control account on 31 May and state whether it reveals any errors.

		£
1 May	Debit balances	14,000
1–31 May	Total credit sales	19,364
1–31 May	Total cash received	1,326
1–31 May	Total cheques received	17,693
1–31 May	Total discounts allowed	648
1–31 May	Bad debts	396
1–31 May	Total returns inward	672
31 May	Debit balances in sales ledger	12,629

10.6

From the following information about the purchases ledger prepare a control account on 31 May and state whether it reveals any errors.

		£
1 Jan	Debit balances	234
1 Jan	Credit balances	18,657
1–31 Jan	Total cheques paid	55,876
1–31 Jan	Returns outward	1,378
1–31 Jan	Discounts received	6,876
1–31 Jan	Purchases	63,143
31 Jan	Debit balances in purchases ledger	235
31 Jan	Credit balances in purchases ledger	15,671

10.7

Your firm trades in office machinery and on 1 March 1981 its financial position was as follows:

			£
Freehold land and buildings	25,000	Cash at bank	2,000
Fixtures and fittings	6,000	Trade debtors	250
Stock on hand	15,000	Trade creditors	200

(*a*)   Enter the above in the journal showing the capital at that date.

(*b*)   Enter the following transactions for the month of March in the appropriate day books.

1 March   Sold four typewriters to Office Services, list price £80 each, allowing them ten per cent trade discount.

4 March   Bought six calculators from Webb & Co. at £12 each net.

12 March   Sold duplicating machine to J. Hoy for £350.

16 March	Sold four calculators to E. Mark, list price £20 each, allowing them ten per cent trade discount.
17 March	Office Services returned one damaged typewriter.
20 March	Bought six typewriters from Ace Co., list price £40. Allowed 15% trade discount.
25 March	Sold two duplicating machines to Mills & Co., list price £350, allowing them ten per cent trade discount.

NB Entries in the ledger accounts are not required.

(LEAG specimen paper)

10.8

(*a*)   On 31 March 1985 Dermod Ruddock's debtors totalled £3,250. It was decided to write off the balance of A. Kitchen, £130, included in that total.

It was decided also to create a provision for doubtful debts equal to $2\frac{1}{2}$ per cent of the remaining debtors.

Show how these matters would be dealt with in Dermod Ruddock's journal. (Narratives need not be given.)

(*b*)   During the next financial year, a payment of £50 was received on 30 September from the accountants of A. Kitchen following the latter's bankruptcy.

The following decisions were also made on 31 March 1986:

A to write off debtors' balances totalling £182;

B to adjust the provision for doubtful debts to £90.

Show how these matters would be recorded in the following accounts in Dermod Ruddock's books:

(i) A. Kitchen's account.

(ii) Bad debts account.

(iii) Provision for bad debts account.

(iv) Profit and loss account for the year ended 31 March 1986.

Candidates who are unable to deal with the payment received on 30 September should attempt the rest of part (*b*), i.e. **A** and **B**.

(MEG specimen paper)

10.9

(*a*)   What is the purpose of a trial balance?

(*b*)   Name and give examples of **four** types of errors which may be in a trial balance even though the totals are equal.

(c)   The following trial balance was extracted from the books of Jane Smith on 31 March 1986:

	Dr £	Cr £
Premises	50,000	
Motor vans	7,400	
Sundry debtors	1,680	
Sundry creditors		2,385
Purchases	160,260	
Sales		200,490
Wages	12,000	
Drawings	1,600	
Capital		30,000
	232,940	232,875

As the trial balance totals did not agree, the difference was posted to a suspense account. The following errors were discovered.

1   The purchase of a motor van had been entered in the motor van account as £3,860 instead of £3,680.
2   The total of the purchases book, £32,543, had been posted to the purchases account as £32,453.
3   The proprietress had withdrawn £140 for private use during March which had been debited to the wages account.
4   A cash discount of £25 allowed by Diane Jones, a creditor, had not been entered in Diane Jones's account.

You are required to take the above information into account and show:

(i) journal entries to correct the errors;
(ii) the suspense account written up and balanced;
(iii) the corrected trial balance.

(NEA specimen paper)

PARTNERSHIP ACCOUNTS

CONTENTS

A partnership This is a business owned by at least two people who provide the owners' capital and are usually equally liable for the debts of the business.

For most businesses the maximum number of partners permitted is twenty. In fact the majority of such businesses usually comprise only two or three partners. The concept of equal liability does not apply if one partner is a limited partner. This means that his liability for any business debts is limited to the amount he agreed to contribute to the capital of the business. If he has already contributed this amount then he cannot be forced to make any further contributions, however great the debts of the business. In return for this benefit of limited liability the partner must agree to take no part in the management of the business. He is normally known as a dormant or sleeping partner. It is also necessary for at least one other partner to accept unlimited liability. This means that if business debts cannot be settled from assets within the business, the private assets of the unlimited partner may be used to settle business debts. This is the same legal position as that of the sole owner of a business. The vast majority of partnerships are ordinary partnerships where all the partners have unlimited liability and they share responsibility for the debts of the business.

Provided that you have mastered the concepts encountered so far, you should not have too much difficulty adapting your accounting knowledge to meet the requirements of keeping the accounts of a partnership.

11.1 LEGAL ASPECTS

A partnership can be created by an oral agreement between the partners. The way in which they decide to divide the work and its rewards is entirely up to them. As with all such legal agreements, however, it is advisable to put them in writing. A deed of partnership prepared by a solicitor is not an expensive document and it might save a great deal of argument later.

There are two basic points concerning the agreement that affect the accounts:

1 The amount of fixed capital to be contributed by each partner. This means the amount they invest and agree to leave in the business as permanent capital.

2   The way in which profits and losses should be shared. The simplest way of doing this is to agree to a profit sharing proportion. For example, if there are two partners they might agree to share the profits equally or perhaps in the ratio of 2:1. In the latter case one partner will be receiving two thirds of the profit while the other receives one third.

In many partnership questions the way in which the profits are divided are a little more complex than simply applying an agreed profit sharing proportion. It may be agreed that a partner who has contributed a greater amount of the capital of the business should receive extra profits as compensation. This can be done by giving all the partners interest on the fixed capital they have contributed. A partner contributing a greater amount of capital will thus gain more interest. The interest paid on capital is not a reduction of profits as in the case of interest paid to an outsider for a loan. It is part of the division of the profits. It is also likely that one partner may work longer hours than another. This effort may be rewarded by paying a salary to the partner working hardest. Again such a payment is a division of profits and not a reduction of profits as would be the case if a manager was employed to work in the business.

If partners have not agreed how they should conduct their affairs, the Partnership Act of 1890 is applied. Relevant rules contained in it are:

1   Profits and losses should be shared equally.
2   No salary or interest on capital should be paid to partners.
3   A partner lending money to the partnership in excess of his agreed capital contribution should receive interest of five per cent per annum.
4   No interest should be charged against drawings.

SELF-CHECK ▶
11.1

Learn the above rules contained in the Partnership Act of 1890 and test yourself.

11.2 PROFIT AND LOSS APPROPRIATION ACCOUNT

As far as the trading and profit and loss account of a partnership is concerned, there is no difference to that of a sole trader until net profit is known. At that point it becomes necessary to share out the profit. This is done in the appropriation account or appropriation section of the trading and profit and loss account.

Example

Smith and Jones formed a partnership on 1 January 1987. They agreed that Smith would contribute £20,000 and Jones £15,000 of fixed capital. They would each receive interest on capital of ten per cent and Jones was to receive a salary of £1,500. Profits or losses were to be shared in the proportion of two-thirds to Smith and one-third to Jones. At the end of their first year of trading the business made a net profit of £23,000. The appropriation account would look like this:

Profit and loss appropriation account

		£	£
Net profit	b/d		23,000
Salary – Jones		1,500	
Interest on capital:			
Smith (10% × £20,000)		2,000	
Jones (10% × £15,000)		1,500	
			5,000
Remaining profit available to be shared			18,000
Smith $\frac{(2 \times 18,000)}{3}$		12,000	
Jones $\frac{(1 \times 18,000)}{3}$		6,000	
			18,000

It is important that any salaries or interest on capital due to partners is deducted from the net profit *before* the profit sharing ratio is applied. There are various styles of layout – the above follows the vertical pattern we have used for earlier profit and loss accounts.

SELF-CHECK ▶ 11.2

Ash and Fox began trading as a partnership on 1 April 1987. Ash contributed fixed capital of £30,000 and Fox £50,000. It was agreed that interest on capital of fifteen per cent should be paid; Ash would have a salary of £8,000 and Fox a salary of £5,000. Any remaining profits would be shared equally. At the end of their first year of trading, a net profit of £49,000 was earned. Show the appropriation section of the profit and loss account.

SOLUTION ▶

Profit and loss appropriation section

	£	£
Net profit		49,000
Salaries:		
Ash	8,000	
Fox	5,000	
Interest on capital:		
Ash (15% × £30,000)	4,500	
Fox (15% × £50,000)	7,500	
		25,000
Remaining profit to be shared		24,000
Ash (50% × £24,000)	12,000	
Fox (50% × £24,000)	12,000	
		24,000

COMMENT ▶

It does not matter whether salaries or interest on capital is shown first, as long as both these items are calculated and deducted before applying the profit sharing proportions.

11.3 LEDGER ACCOUNT ENTRIES

Although it is rare for a profit and loss account to be displayed in the style of a ledger account it is technically part of the double entry system. The salaries, interest on capital and remaining shares of profit are regarded as debit entries and if a horizontal account was used they would appear on the debit side. Clearly, therefore, corresponding credit entries must be made.

In a sole trader's accounts the capital account of the owner was credited with the whole of the net profit earned. This account was also debited with any drawings made. In partnerships it is necessary for each partner to have his own capital account so that the correct amounts may be credited to each partner. Also, if the partners have agreed to contribute fixed amounts of capital then it is advantageous to have an extra capital account for each partner in which changes in capital may be recorded without disturbing the fixed capital. The name given to this account is the current capital account. It is usually abbreviated to current account but, of course, it has no connections with the current bank account.

Using the example of Smith and Jones in 11.2 and assuming that Smith withdrew £13,000 and Jones £8,500 their capital and current accounts would look like this:

Capital a/c Smith

				1987		
				1 Jan	Bank	20,000

Capital a/c Jones

				1 Jan	Bank	15,000

Current a/c Smith

1987				1987		
31 Dec	Drawings		13,000	31 Dec	Interest on capital	2,000
31 Dec	Balance	c/d	1,000	31 Dec	Share of profit	12,000
			14,000			14,000
				1988		
				1 Jan	Balance b/d	1,000

Current a/c Jones

1987				1987		
31 Dec	Drawings		8,500	31 Dec	Interest on capital	1,500
				31 Dec	Salary	1,500
31 Dec	Balance	c/d	500	31 Dec	Share of profit	6,000
			9,000			9,000
				1988		
				1 Jan	Balance b/d	500

The current accounts show that both Smith and Jones could have withdrawn more assets from the business without breaking their agreement with regard to the fixed capital amounts they contributed. The £1,000 that Smith did not draw and the £500 that Jones left in the business are extra finance for the business. We will see how to show these amounts in the balance sheet in the next section.

SELF-CHECK 11.3

Using the information in self-check 11.2, together with the additional information that Ash withdrew £24,000 and Fox £26,000 from the business during the financial year ended 31 March 1988, prepare current accounts for the partners and balance them at the end of the year.

SOLUTION

Current a/c Ash

1988				1988			
31 March	Drawings		24,000	31 March	Salaries		8,000
31 March	Balance	c/d	500	31 March	Interest on capital		4,500
				31 March	Share of profit		12,000
			24,500				24,500
				1988			
				1 April	Balance	b/d	500

Current a/c Fox

1988				1988			
31 March	Drawings		26,000	31 March	Salary		5,000
				31 March	Interest on capital		7,500
				31 March	Share of profit		12,000
				31 March	Balance	c/d	1,500
			26,000				26,000
1 April	Balance	b/d	1,500				

COMMENT

The account of Ash probably caused no bother because it fits the pattern of the accounts of Smith and Jones. The credit balance in his account means that he is still entitled to withdraw £500 from the business if he wishes. He might prefer to leave this amount in the business for the time being, in which case it will be added on to next year's earnings and thus still be available to be withdrawn. Fox's account is not so straightforward. In withdrawing £26,000 during the year he has taken out of the business £1,500 more than he has available to him in his current account. This is shown by the debit balance brought down in this account. A debit balance in a personal account is an asset to the business because the person to whom the account relates owes the business that amount. In other words, Fox is a debtor to the business of Ash and Fox. He would normally be expected to pay the amount due fairly quickly but might be allowed some grace if his partner agreed.

11.4 PARTNERSHIP BALANCE SHEETS

The only place in which the balance sheet of a partnership will differ from that of a sole trader is in the area of finance. There will be a capital item for each partner showing the fixed capitals they have contributed and a current item for each partner showing how many earnings they have left in the business after allowing for drawings. Taking the example of Smith and Jones the finance details of their balance sheet would look like this:

Balance Sheet (extract) of Smith and Jones as at 31 December 1987

	£	£
Financed by		
Capital – Smith	20,000	
Capital – Jones	15,000	
		35,000
Current account – Smith		
Interest on capital	2,000	
Share of profit	12,000	
	14,000	
less Drawings	13,000	
		1,000
Current account – Jones		
Interest on capital	1,500	
Salary	1,500	
Share of profit	6,000	
	9,000	
less Drawings	8,500	
		500
		36,500

It is usual practice to show for each partner how the present balance in the current account has been created. This involves repeating the current account in the form of a calculation in the same manner in which the sole trader's capital account was shown. It does mean that the balance sheet of a partnership is usually much longer than that of a sole trader. In examination conditions, if time is short, you might be well advised to merely write in the balances for the current accounts rather than showing the whole calculation.

Two other points are worth making. First, if the partnership was not a new one, partners might have credit balances in their current accounts from last year. These amounts should be added to their earnings for this year and thus increase the amount they are entitled to withdraw. Second, if a partner has a debit balance in his current account the amount of this balance could be shown in the current assets as it is an amount due to the business. The partner with the debit balance is in debt to the business.

SELF-CHECK ▶ 11.4

At the end of 1988 Smith was entitled to £10,000 as a share of the profits and Jones £5,000. Each was also entitled to the same interest on capital and salary as the previous year. During the year Smith withdrew £11,500 from the business and Jones £7,500. Show the finance section of their balance sheet at 31 December 1988. (Note: do not forget they will each have an opening balance in their current account from the previous year.)

SOLUTION ▶	Balance Sheet extract of Smith and Jones as at 31 December 1988

Financed by	£	£
Capital – Smith	20,000	
Capital – Jones	15,000	
		35,000
Current account – Smith		
Balance at 1 January 1988	1,000	
Interest on capital	2,000	
Share of profit	10,000	
	13,000	
less Drawings	11,500	
		1,500
Current account – Jones		
Balance at 1 January 1988	500	
Interest on capital	1,500	
Salary	1,500	
Share of profit	5,000	
	8,500	
less Drawings	7,500	
		1,000
		37,500

EXERCISES

11.1

D. Robinson in business as a sole trader was having a cash flow problem during a period of recession. He decided to enter into partnership with Brown and Green on 1 January 1985.

Robinson, Brown and Green are to share profits and losses in ratio 3:2:1. The partners are entitled to partnership salaries as follows: Robinson £1,000, Brown £800, Green £500.

Throughout the year their capital accounts have remained fixed at the following amounts: Robinson £12,000, Brown £9,000, Green £7,000.

The partners are entitled to interest on their capital accounts at the rate of five per cent per annum; the net profit of the partnership for the year amounted to £12,700.

(a)   Prepare the profit and loss appropriation account for the year ended 31 December 1985.

(b)   Show also the partners' current accounts as they would appear at 31 December 1985.

(c)   In the absence of an agreement how are profits or losses shared?

(d)   State one advantage and one disadvantage to Robinson in forming a partnership.   (NISEC specimen paper)

11.2

The following balances stood in the books of A. Brown, T. Lloyd and C. Williams at the end of trading on 31 March 1986.

	Brown	Lloyd	Williams
Capital	£40,000	£30,000	£20,000
Current a/c balances	7,500 (cr)	4,040 (cr)	1,000 (cr)
Drawings	9,200	8,750	5,900
Loan from A. Brown	15,000	—	—

The partnership agreement allows for interest on capital of five per cent, and on loans ten per cent.

A salary is payable to Lloyd of £5,000 and Williams £3,000. The profit before charging any of the above was £32,000. Partners share profits in accordance to their capitals.

Required

(a)   Prepare the appropriation section of the profit and loss account and the partners current accounts for Brown, Lloyd and Williams for the year ended 31 March 1986.

(b)   What is a partnership agreement? What sort of items would be contained in this agreement? If trading partners had no formal agreement, and a dispute arose over profit sharing, what would be the possible outcome?   (WJEC specimen paper)

11.3

The following balances remain in the books after completion of the trading and profit and loss accounts on 31 December 1980.

	£		£
xed assets at cost	70,000	Capital: A. Exworth	50,000
urrent assets	40,060	B. Young	40,000
rawings: A. Exworth	13,000	Current a/c: A. Exworth	420
B. Young	7,000	B. Young	640
		Net profit for year	25,000
		Creditors	4,000
		Provision for depreciation of fixed assets	10,000
	130,060		130,060

(a) (i) List *four* current assets.
(ii) To what kind of business unit do the above figures relate?
(iii) Why does this business keep current accounts as well as capital accounts?
(iv) Explain the importance of working capital.

(b) Prepare an account to show the division of profit between A. Exworth and B. Young, Profits and losses are shared equally after allowing A. Exworth a salary of £7,000 and interest on capital to both of ten per cent.

(c) Prepare the current accounts of A. Exworth and B. Young for the year.

(d) Set out a balance sheet as at 31 December 1980. Current account closing balances only need be shown.

(LEAG specimen paper)

LIMITED COMPANY ACCOUNTS

CONTENTS

12.1 DEFINITIONS AND TERMS

Limited companies are simply another form of business ownership. They are created by registration under the rules of the various Company Acts. In law they are recognised as having a separate legal existence from their owners who are known as shareholders. There are two types of limited company: **public limited companies** and **private limited companies**. Both of these provide their owners with the benefit of limited liability. This means that the amount of money that they risk is limited to the amount that they have agreed to pay for their shares. Their private wealth can not be taken to pay for the debts of the business.

Public limited companies must have the words 'public limited company' or the letters 'plc' ('ccc' in Welsh) after their name.

Private limited companies are followed by the word 'limited' or 'ltd'. The major difference between them is that public companies are able to have their shares quoted on the stock exchange and sell their shares to the general public; private companies cannot. Consequently public companies are likely to be much bigger than the private ones.

To register a company it is necessary to complete certain documents. The main ones are the memorandum of association and the articles of association. One of the clauses concerns the amount of capital that the company should be allowed to raise. This is known as the **authorised share capital** and it must be distinguished from the **issued share capital**, which is the amount actually raised. Clearly this amount is not allowed to exceed the authorised amount.

SHARES

There are two main types of share. **Ordinary shares** earn a dividend from profits which fluctuates according to how successful the company has been and how much of this profit the directors of the company wish to retain within the company as internal finance. **Preference shares** earn a dividend from profits that is fixed, irrespective of the amount of profit that the company has made. Preference shares are a safer investment from an investor's viewpoint because their dividends have to be paid *before* those paid to ordinary shareholders. When profits are low there might be enough to pay the preference shareholders their fixed dividend but not enough to pay any ordinary dividend. In return for the greater risk associated wit ordinary shares it is usually only these shares that carry the right t vote at the company's annual general meeting. Some preferenc shares are safer than others. The owners of **cumulative preferenc shares** may, like the other shareholders, receive no profit in a bad yea However, the first year that profits are sufficient to pay a dividend wi see the profits they have missed accumulate and be paid in full befor any other shareholders are able to receive any dividend.

All shares have a **nominal value**. This is the monetary value of th share on which dividends are calculated. Small denominations ar usual in the UK for example, 25p, 50p or £1. If a shareholder possesse 100 £1 ordinary shares and a dividend of twelve per cent is declared h will receive 12% × £100 = £12. The amount paid for the shares may b much greater or less than this nominal value. The price of shares wil vary according to factors such as the company's success and con fidence in the general business world. Many shareholders do no purchase shares for the dividend they might get. Their main aim is t choose a share that increases in price and enables them to sell at a profit; such a gain is known as a capital gain. Nominal value is also known as par value.

Most shares are not **redeemable** by the company that issued them. This means that a shareholder wishing to sell his shares in a company cannot sell them back to the company. They may be sold on the stock exchange if it is a public company. It is important to realise that the only time a company receives money from the sale of its shares is when it sells the shares for the *first* time. Subsequent sales involve a transfer of the shares and money between other individuals. The company will have to be told, of course, so that it is able to pay any dividends due to the new holder. But it will not raise any finance from such sales.

DEBENTURES

These often cause confusion in company accounts because of the similarities they possess with preference shares. It is important to stress from the outset, therefore, that a debenture is *not* a type of share. A debenture is a loan certificate issued in return for money loaned to a company. Such debentures are usually issued in units of £100. They carry a fixed rate of interest and it is this that often causes them to be confused with preference shares. The word interest is the significant one here. As creditors of the company they are entitled to this interest whether or not the company makes a profit. Interest is thus one of the business expenses that has to be paid and not, like share dividends, a distribution of the profits. Debentures are usually secured on the assets of the company. This means that if a company is wound up or liquidated the holders receive their money from the sale of the assets *before* any payment is made to the shareholders. Debentures are usually also redeemable by the company at a specified date or between two specified dates in the future. For example, twelve per cent debentures 96/98 will be bought back by the company during the years 1996 and 1998. Debentures are therefore safer investments than preference shares though, of course, if a company is in a very bad way it is possible that even debenture holders will lose their money invested in the business.

SELF-CHECK ▶
12.1

Learn the meaning of the terms in bold and test yourself until you know them.

12.2 TRADING, PROFIT AND LOSS AND APPROPRIATION ACCOUNTS

The trading and profit and loss account of a company

This is basically no different to that of a sole trader or partnership. It may contain some items of expenditure and income that you are less likely to find in the other types of businesses but as long as you identify them correctly you should have little trouble dealing with them:

Directors' salaries (or remuneration), auditor's fees and debenture interest are the additional expenses which you will most often meet. Unlike sole traders and partnerships limited companies have to have their accounts audited by a qualified person from outside the company. All three items must be included with the other expenses of the business. Of these, the one that causes most problems is that of interest on debentures. As explained in the last section, debentures are loans and the interest on them is an expense in the same way that interest on a bank loan would be an expense.

The appropriation account

This is where the main differences occur. Profits made by the company may be distributed to the shareholders by way of dividends or retained in the company. Generally speaking some will be retained and some distributed. Retained profits are known as revenue reserves. These reserves may be of two types:

1   Specific reserves to be kept permanently within the business and not used for the payment of dividends. Reserves for the replacement of fixed assets and general reserve are the examples you are most likely to meet.

2   Profits retained in the business which may be used in future years to pay dividends to shareholders. This is often called undistributed profits or the profit and loss account balance. The following example will help to make things clear:

Trading and profit and loss account of XYZ Ltd for the year ended 31 December 1988

Net profit is calculated as usual but look out for 'new expenses', especially interest on debentures, auditor's fees and directors' salaries: net profit is then carried down to the appropriation account.

Appropriation account of XYZ Ltd for the year ended 31 December 1988

	£	£
Net profit b/d (from above profit and loss a/c)	60,000	
Profit and loss a/c balance b/d (from last year)	5,000	
Profit available for distribution		65,000
General reserve	4,000	
Proposed dividends:		
Preference	15,000	
Ordinary	40,000	
		59,000
Profit and loss account balance c/d (to next year)		6,000

Comments in brackets have been added to help your understanding but some additional explanation is still needed.

As well as the net profit earned this year it is likely that there will be a reserve balance in the profit and loss account from last year. This has to be added to this year's profit as it is available for dividends. The directors have decided to place £4,000 into general reserve. This keeps that amount of the profit within the company for its use. As the general reserve is a form of finance it will have a credit balance in its own account. A credit entry will be made in the general reserve account for £4,000 to increase the amount of this finance. If we assume that the amount of the general reserve before doing this was £20,000, the account would look like this:

General reserve

	1988			
	1 Jan	Balance	b/d	20,000
	31 Dec	Appropriation	a/c	4,000

The decision as to how much ordinary dividend to declare is one for the directors to take. In the case of the preference shares, provided there is enough profit, the decision is easy because the amount of the dividend is fixed. This is how the above figures were calculated:

Company XYZ authorised share capital:
200,000 £1 15% preference shares   500,000 £1 ordinary shares.

Company XYZ issued share capital:
100,000 £1 15% preference shares   400,000 £1 ordinary shares.

Proposed preference share dividend = 15% × *Issued* preference share capital
= 15% × £100,000 = £15,000

The authorised capital information has been included only to show you that it is **not** used in this calculation. The authorised capital is the amount that the company is legally allowed to issue. Dividend will only be paid on the amount actually issued.

As the directors have proposed a dividend of £40,000 on the ordinary shares and as we know that the Issued Ordinary Share Capital is £400,000 we can see that the dividend they have declared is ten per cent:

$$\frac{£40,000}{400,000} \times 100 = 10\%$$

As these amounts will be paid to the various holders of the shares in the near future they will be credited to current liability accounts:

Preference share dividend

	1988		
	31 Dec	Appropriation a/c	15,000

Ordinary share dividend a/c

	1988		
	31 Dec	Appropriation a/c	40,000

When these amounts are paid the accounts will be debited and closed until next year. The credit entry wil be in the cash book.

The £6,000 closing balance in this year's appropriation account will be added to next year's profits and be available for distribution then if required.

SELF-CHECK ▶
12.2

Company ABC Ltd had the following balances in its accounts at 31 December 1988:

	£ cr
Ordinary share capital	300,000
Preference share capital	200,000
General reserve	50,000
Debentures 11%	100,000
Profit and loss account (1 Jan 88)	7,000

Additional information:
(*a*)   Authorised share capital: 800,000 ordinary shares at 50p; 300,000 12% preference shares at £1.

(b)   Net profit for the year amounted to £58,000 and the directors decided the following:

     (i) to recommend payment of the preference dividend;

     (ii) to recommend an ordinary dividend of 9%;

     (iii) to transfer £6,000 to general reserve.

Select the information that is relevant and prepare an appropriation account for the year ended 31 December 1988.

SOLUTION ▶

Appropriation account of ABC Ltd for the year ended 31 December 1988

	£	£
Net profit b/d	58,000	
Profit and loss a/c balance b/d (from last year)	7,000	
Profit available for distribution		65,000
General reserve	6,000	
Proposed dividends:		
Preference	24,000	
Ordinary	27,000	
		57,000
Profit and loss account balance c/d (to next year)		8,000

COMMENT ▶

The information not relevant was:

(a)   The details about the debentures – as debenture interest is an expense that would be included with the other expenses in the profit and loss account it would *already* have been dealt with in arriving at the net profit figure.

(b)   The amount of the authorised capital – dividends are paid on the issued share capital not the authorised capital.

12.3 COMPANY BALANCE SHEETS

Most of the items in the balance sheet of a company will be the same as in that a sole trader or partnership. The amounts of money involved will usually be larger and columns are often headed £000 so that the figures below can be kept smaller. In the current liabilities you will find any dividends due to shareholders that have not yet been paid and possibly interest due to debenture holders that may not have been paid. Watch out for these!

The major difference will occur in the finance section of the balance sheet. The following example is fairly typical:

Balance Sheet (extract) of ABC Ltd as at 31 December 1988

	£(000)	£(000)
Financed by:		
Long term Liabilities:		
11% Debentures		100
Issued share capital:		
600,000 50p ordinary shares	300	
200,000 12% £1 preference shares	200	
		500
Reserves:		
General reserve	56	
Profit and loss a/c balance	8	
Share premium account	50	
		114
		714

Notes to the balance sheet
Authorised share capital:
800,000 ordinary shares at 50p; 300,000 12% preference shares at £1.

COMMENT ▶

From this example you can deduce that in the top half of a vertical balance sheet the fixed assets + working capital = £714,000. Most of the figures for the above balance sheet extract were taken from the last self-check. The following points are worth emphasizing:

1 Company accounts often contain debentures. These should be inserted under the heading of long term liabilities. Any interest due to the holders that had not been paid by the date of the balance sheet should be placed with the current liabilities because it will be paid soon.

2 It is the issued share capital that counts in the balance sheet. It is normal practice to include a note of the authorised capital for information. At one time this was often done inside the balance sheet and great care had to be taken *not* to add this figure into the finance as it is only memorandum information. Today most companies prefer to show the authorised capital as a note following the balance sheet where it is less likely to cause confusion.

3 In reserves the figures for general reserve and balance on profit and loss account have been taken from the information in the last self-check. The general reserve was £50,000 before completing the appropriation account and as the directors decided to place £6,000 of this year's profits into the general reserve its value will now be £56,000. Care must be taken to use the closing balance on the appropriation account and not the opening balance which would have been the

figure used last year. Thus £8,000 and not £7,000 is the profit and loss account reserve at 31 December 1988.

The figure you will not find in the last self-check is the one for share premium account. This arises when a company issues some of its shares at a price higher than the face or nominal value (i.e. at a premium). The excess of the price at which they are issued over the nominal value is credited to a share premium account and should be shown with the reserves.

4 Sometimes you may meet shares that have been issued but have not yet been fully paid for. The most likely reason for this is that the purchasers of the shares are being allowed to pay by instalments. If 100,000 £1 ordinary shares were issued as partly paid – say 50p each – then the amount of finance raised would be £50,000 and it is this amount that should be shown in the finance section of the balance sheet. Any dividends on such shares would only be paid as a percentage of the shares that have been paid for.

SELF-CHECK ▶
12.3

Conniford Ltd has an authorised capital of £600,000 divided into 300,000 £1 ordinary shares and 300,000 8% £1 preference shares. Of these 200,000 ordinary shares and 100,000 preference shares have been issued and fully paid. It had £32,000 general reserve on 31 December 1987 and a profit and loss account balance of £16,000 on that date. For the financial year ended 31 December 1988 the following information was available:

(a)   Net profit for the year was £56,000. The directors recommended a transfer of £17,000 to general reserve, and proposed the payment of the preference dividend and an ordinary dividend of fourteen per cent.

(b)   The *other* closing balances in the books were:

Fixed assets	£350,000
Current assets	£100,000
Current liabilities	£46,000

Prepare the company's profit and loss appropriation account for the year ended 31 December 1988 and a vertical style balance sheet at that date.

SOLUTION ▶

Appropriation account of Conniford Ltd for the year ended 31 December 1988

		£	£
Net profit	b/d	56,000	
Profit and loss account balance	b/d	16,000	
Profit available for distribution			72,000
General reserve		17,000	
Proposed preference dividend		8,000	
Proposed ordinary dividend		28,000	
			53,000
Profit and loss account balance	c/d		19,000

Balance Sheet of Conniford Ltd as at 31 December 1988

	£	£	£
Fixed assets			350,000
Current assets		100,000	
Less current liabilities:			
Ordinary dividend proposed	28,000		
Preference dividend proposed	8,000		
Others	46,000		
		82,000	
Net current assets (working capital)			18,000
Total assets *less* current liabilities			368,000
Financed by:			
Issued share capital:			
200,000 £1 ordinary shares		200,000	
100,000 8% £1 preference shares		100,000	
			300,000
Reserves:			
General reserve		49,000	
Profit and loss account balance		19,000	68,000
			368,000

COMMENT ▶	It is important that you realise that the entries in the appropriation account for the appropriation of the profits will be accompanied by credit entries in general reserve, ordinary dividend and preference dividend accounts. The existing finance balance in the general reserve will thus be increased from £32,000 to £49,000. The proposed ordinary and preference dividends are current liabilities and must be added to the total of the other current liabilities.

EXERCISES

12.1

Biltor Ltd has an authorised capital of £400,000 divided into 300,000 £1 ordinary shares and 100,000 6% £1 preference shares. Of these, 250,000 ordinary shares and 60,000 preference shares have been issued and fully paid. It had no general reserve on 31 December 1987 but had a profit and loss account balance of £36,000 on that date.

For the financial year ended 31 December 1988 the following information was available:

(a)   Net profit for the year was £80,000. The directors recommended a transfer of £15,000 to general reserve, and proposed the payment of the preference dividend and an ordinary dividend of fifteen per cent.

(b)   The *other* closing balances in the books were:

Fixed assets	£350,000
Current assets	£126,000
Current liabilities	£50,000

Prepare the company's profit and loss appropriation account for the year ended 31 December 1988 and a vertical style balance sheet at that date.

12.2

The following trial balance was obtained from the books of Acme Ltd at 31 December 1988.

	£ dr	£ cr
£1 ordinary shares, issued and fully paid		30,000
6% £1 debentures		15,000
Freehold buildings at cost	80,000	
Purchases	91,000	
Sales		165,000
Debtors and creditors	8,900	7,400
Rent receivable		450
Salaries	18,000	
Rates and insurance	500	
Motor expenses	1,000	
Directors' remuneration	19,000	
General expenses	2,500	
Motor vans at cost	5,200	
Provision for depn on motor vans (1.1.88)		3,000
Stock (1.1.88)	1,200	
Bank and cash	5,400	
Debenture interest paid (to 30 June)	450	
Bad debts	600	
Profit and loss account balance (1.1.88)		12,900
	233,750	233,750

The following additional information was available at 31 December 1988:
(a)   Stock valuation £1,400.
(b)   General salaries due £200.
(c)   Rent receivable due £150.
(d)   Rates paid in advance £50.
(e)   Debenture interest is due for the last six months of the year.
(f)   Depreciation is to be charged at 25% per annum on the cost of the motor vans.
(g)   The directors propose to transfer £5,000 to a general reserve and pay a 10% dividend on the ordinary shares.
Note: The authorised share capital is 50,000 £1 ordinary shares.
Prepare the trading profit and loss and appropriation account for the year ended 31 December 1988 and a balance sheet at that date.

12.3

An investor in Apex Glass PLC has received the final accounts and the balance sheet.

Apex Glass PLC balance sheet as at 31 December 1985

	£	£
Fixed assets		275,000
Current assets		
Stock	92,000	
Debtors	64,000	
Cash at bank	46,000	
	202,000	
Less current liabilities		
Trade creditors	47,000	
		155,000
		430,000
Financed by:		
Share capital		
Authorized and issued		
£1 ordinary shares	160,000	
£1 10% preference shares	40,000	
		200,000
Reserves		
Share premium	41,000	
General reserve	45,000	
Unappropriated profits	44,000	
		130,000
		330,000
Long term liabilities		
11% Debentures 1985/89		100,000
		430,000

(*a*)   (i) Why does PLC appear beside the name of the company?
(ii) Explain the difference between:
    (*a*) Authorised and issued capital

(b) Preference and ordinary shares

(c) Shares and debentures

(iii) What does the ten per cent represent in relation to preference shares and why is there no percentage beside the ordinary shares?

(iv) How would the share premium account have arisen?

(v) For what purpose are reserves generally created?

(vi) A significant balance appears in the profit and loss account. Would it be possible in this case to distribute a large proportion of it by declaring an additional dividend?

(vii) In relation to the debentures:

(a) What does the eleven per cent represent?

(b) What is meant by 1985/89?

(b)   What is the company's working capital and what is the importance of this figure?

(c)   The investor also tells you that his shares are listed in daily newspapers at £2 each, but that they still only appear on the balance sheet at £1 each. He feels that his investment should be updated.

Explain to him why it is likely that the market price of the ordinary shares will differ from their nominal value.

(NISEC specimen paper)

12.4   From the following information prepare a trading and profit and loss account of The Deer's Leap Hotel for the year ended 31 March 1988 and a balance sheet at that date.

Trial balance as at 31 March 1988

	Dr £(000)	Cr £(000)
Sales		750
Purchases	296	
Stock (31.3.87)	10	
Wages and salaries	83	
Directors' remuneration	65	
Overheads	210	
Premises	258	
Furniture and equipment at cost	98	
Provision for depn on furniture (31.3.87)		34
Glass, china and cutlery at cost	14	
Provision for depn on china etc. (31.3.87)		5
Debtors	16	
Creditors		19
Debentures (15%)		90
General reserve		50
Issued ordinary shares (£1)		80
Issued preference shares (14% £1)		40
Bank	22	
Profit and loss a/c (31.3.87)		4
	1,072	1,072

Notes:

(a)   Stock at 31.3.88 was valued at £12,000.

(b)   The overheads balance does not include the depreciation for the year to 31.3.88. Furniture and equipment should be depreciated by ten per cent on cost and glass etc. by fifteen per cent on cost.

(c)   The debenture interest is due on 31.3.88. This should be dealt with as an accrual.

(d)   The directors have recommended that £17,000 should be allocated to general reserve; payment of the dividend on the preference shares; and payment of an ordinary dividend of eighteen per cent.

(e)   Authorised share capital: 120,000 ordinary shares at £1 and 60,000 preference shares at £1. All the issued capital is fully paid.

12.5

From the following information prepare the profit and loss account of Duchy Ltd for the year ended 30 November 1988 and a balance sheet at that date.

Trial balance as at 30 November 1988

	Dr £(000)	Cr £(000)
Gross profit		412
Stock (30.11.88)	23	
Wages and salaries	67	
Directors salaries	45	
Auditor's fees	5	
Overheads	198	
Premises	167	
Machinery at cost	80	
Provision for depn on machinery (30.11.87)		22
Furniture and equipment at cost	7	
Provision for depn on furniture (30.11.87)		3
Debtors	9	
Creditors		17
Debentures (15%)		80
General reserve		34
Ordinary shares (£1)		75
Bank	48	
Profit and loss a/c (30.11.87)		6
	649	649

Notes

(*a*)   The trading account has already been completed, hence the stock in the trial balance is the closing stock.

(*b*)   The overheads balance does not include the depreciation for the year ended 30 November 1988. Machinery should be depreciated by twelve per cent on cost and furniture and equipment by ten per cent on cost.

(*c*)   Debenture interest is due on 30 November 1988 and should be treated as an accrual.

(*d*)   The directors have decided to allocate £20,000 to general reserve and recommend an ordinary dividend of eighteen per cent.

(*e*)   Authorised share capital is 120,000 £1 ordinary shares. The issued share capital is fully paid.

MANUFACTURING ACCOUNTS

CONTENTS

All the business accounts we have dealt with so far have involved trading, i.e. the buying and selling of goods. In this chapter you are going to see how to adapt your knowledge to deal with the accounts of businesses that make goods for resale from raw materials and components. We will concentrate on the final accounts. From these you will be able to see what additional ledger accounts will be needed.

The final accounts of a manufacturer will comprise the following:

1   Manufacturing account in two parts:
    (a)   the prime cost section and
    (b)   the cost of manufactured goods section.
2   Trading account which includes all the warehouse costs.
3   Profit and loss account, which in the case of partnerships and companies will include an appropriation section.
4   Balance sheet.

Owing to the time it would take to produce a full set of final accounts and the fact that the profit and loss account and balance sheet are little different from those of traders, examination questions in this area usually concentrate on the manufacturing account and the trading account.

13.1 TERMS AND DEFINITIONS

Prime costs As the name suggests, these are the first costs associated with making anything. They include **direct materials** – those materials used in making the finished product and **direct labour** – the wages paid to the workers directly involved in production.

Factory overheads or **indirect factory expenses** These are costs which are not directly traceable to the finished product but which nonetheless must be incurred for production to take place. In fact, they are the type of costs which will be incurred even if no production is taking place. Common examples are factory rent and rates; repairs and depreciation of machinery; and the salaries of the management of the factory.

The **total cost of production** is made up of:

▶   prime costs + factory overheads

Therefore   direct materials + direct labour + factory overheads
                = total cost of production

The total cost of production is also known as the cost of manufactured goods or factory cost of goods completed.

Since a manufacturer is turning raw materials into finished products he will have stocks of both of these at all times. He is also likely to have a stock of partly finished goods. These are known as **work in progress**.

SELF-CHECK ▶
13.1

Learn the definitions of the terms in bold type and test yourself until you know them.

13.2 THE MANUFACTURING ACCOUNT

The following information has been taken from the books of Finepine plc, a furniture manufacturer:

	£
Stocks at 1 January 1987	
Raw materials	7,000
Work in progress (valued at factory cost)	4,500
Finished goods	12,000
Sales	98,750
Purchases	20,000
Factory:	
Wages (direct)	20,000
Power	4,000
Salaries	15,000
Rent and rates	1,000
Heating and lighting	1,500
Repairs	400
Depreciation	2,400
Warehouse:	
Wages	9,000
Rates	500
Stocks at 30 June 1987:	
Raw materials	9,500
Work in progress (valued at factory cost)	8,600
Finished goods	15,000

You may assume that expenses not labelled 'direct' are all indirect, i.e. overheads. From the above information the following manufacturing account has been prepared:

FINEPINE PLC

Manufacturing account for the six months ended 30 June 1987

	£	£
Opening stock of raw materials	7,000	
add Purchases of raw materials	20,000	
	27,000	
less Closing stock of raw materials	9,500	
Cost of raw materials used	17,500	
Direct wages	20,000	
Prime cost		37,500
Factory overheads:		
Power	4,000	
Salaries	15,000	
Rent and rates	1,000	
Heating and lighting	1,500	
Repairs	400	
Depreciation	2,400	
		24,300
		61,800
add Opening work in progress		4,500
		66,300
less Closing work in progress		8,600
Cost of manufactured goods	c/d	57,700

It is important to obtain separate subtotals for the prime costs and the indirect costs or overheads. An adjustment must be made to allow for the fact that there will be a change in the valuation of work in progress from the opening to the closing date. The information that the work in progress is valued at factory cost is significant. It means that a share of all the factory costs has been built into the valuation. The adjustment for the change therefore takes place *after* prime costs have been calculated. In some companies work in progress is calculated on the basis of prime costs only, with no share of the overheads built into the valuation. When this is the case the adjustment for work in progress changes should be shown in the prime cost section. The work in progress is basically like any other stock adjustment, i.e. the opening value is added to costs and the closing value is deducted.

The trading account can now be completed. It is similar to the trading accounts prepared earlier but the cost of manufactured goods will replace purchases because manufacturers *make* the goods they sell and do not merely buy them. Also the manufacturer's trading account will include any expenses designated as warehouse expenses.

Trading account, six months ended 30 June 1987

	£	£
Sales		98,750
Less Cost of goods sold:		
Opening stock of finished goods	12,000	
add Cost of manufactured goods b/d	57,700	
	69,700	
less Closing stock of finished goods	15,000	
	54,700	
add Warehouse expenses:		
Wages	9,000	
Rates	500	
		64,200
Gross profit c/d		34,550

The gross profit will then be brought down to the profit and loss account which will contain the remainder of the expenses of the business together with any other income. It will thus be similar to all the other profit and loss accounts you have prepared and result in the calculation of net profit. The balance sheet of a manufacturer is also basically the same as the other balance sheets you have prepared. The main difference will be in the current assets where there will be three stock figures: raw materials, finished goods and work in progress. Because the final accounts of manufacturers are split up into so many sections it is permissable to omit the name of the business in the sections following the manufacturing account.

SELF-CHECK ▶
13.2

The following information has been taken from the books of Robson Ltd, a manufacturer:

Stocks at 1 January 1987:	£
Raw materials	6,000
Work in progress (valued at factory cost)	3,500
Finished goods	14,000
Sales	96,600
Purchases	19,200
Factory:	
Wages (direct)	20,000
Power	3,900
Salaries	18,000
Rates	600
Heating and lighting	900
Depreciation	2,100
Warehouse:	
Wages	12,000
Rates	300
Stocks at 31 March 1987:	
Raw materials	10,500
Work in progress (valued at factory cost)	6,800
Finished goods	16,800

Prepare manufacturing and trading accounts for the three months ended 31 March 1987.

SOLUTION ▶

ROBSON LTD

Manufacturing account for the three months ended 31 March 1987

	£	£
Opening stock of raw materials	6,000	
add Purchases of raw materials	19,200	
	25,200	
less Closing stock of raw materials	10,500	
Cost of raw materials used	14,700	
Direct wages	20,000	
Prime cost		34,700
Factory overheads		
Power	3,900	
Salaries	18,000	
Rates	600	
Heating and lighting	900	
Depreciation	2,100	
		25,500
		60,200
add Opening work in progress		3,500
		63,700
less Closing work in progress		6,800
Factory cost of goods completed c/d		56,900

Trading account, three months ended 31 March 1987

	£	£
Sales		96,600
less Cost of goods sold:		
Opening stock of finished goods	14,000	
add Factory cost of goods completed b/d	56,900	
	70,900	
less Closing stock of finished goods	16,800	
	54,100	
add Warehouses expenses:		
Wages	12,000	
Rates	300	
		66,400
Gross profit c/d		30,200

COMMENT ▶ This self-check is very similar to the example in the text. The alternative title for cost of manufactured goods has been used at the end of the manufacturing account and again in the trading account. It is advisable to be aware of valid alternative terms.

13.3 COLUMNAR LAYOUT

Many manufacturers make a large number of products. It is useful to be able to adapt your layout of the accounts to show as much information as possible. This is often done best by using vertical layout and having a set of money columns for each product. There is no need to repeat the description.

Example
The following account will show the differences in prime costs for two different products: X and Z.

Manufacturing account, year ended 31 December 1987

	Product X £	Product Z £
Opening stock of raw materials	6,000	5,000
add Purchases of raw materials	19,200	14,000
	25,200	19,000
less Closing stock of raw materials	(10,500)	(3,500)
Cost of raw materials used	14,700	15,500
add Direct wages	20,000	14,000
Prime cost	34,700	29,500

This could be continued to show the whole of the manufacturing account and the trading and profit and loss account as well if it was desired.

The same method is also used in other types of businesses. For example, a retailer with four departments could use four columns to obtain separate gross profit figures for each product in the same trading account. This is known as **departmental accounting**. Once you have mastered a technique it is always possible to make use of it in other circumstances.

SELF-CHECK ▶ 13.3 Helios Ltd manufacture two different types of product A1 and A2. The following information relates to the financial year ended 31 December 1988:

	A1 £	A2 £
Opening material stocks (1 Jan 1988)	6,000	8,500
Purchases of materials	56,150	77,500
Direct wages cost	75,000	89,500
Depreciation: plant and machinery	1,200	1,800
Direct expenses	600	450
Factory rent and other indirect expenses	1,350	2,120
Closing material stocks (31 Dec 1988)	6,300	9,650

Prepare a manufacturing account in columnar form for the year ended 31 December 1988, one column for A1 and one for A2. Show clearly:

(i) the prime cost;
(ii) the factory cost of goods completed.
Note: there were no stocks of work in progress.

SOLUTION ▶

Manufacturing account, year ended 31 December 1988

	Product A1 £	Product A2 £
Opening stock of materials	6,000	8,500
add Purchases of materials	56,150	77,500
	62,150	86,000
less Closing stock of raw materials	(6,300)	(9,650)
Cost of materials used	55,850	76,350
add Direct wages	75,000	89,500
Direct expenses	600	450
Prime cost	131,450	166,000
add Depreciation on plant	1,200	1,800
Rent and other indirect expenses	1,350	2,120
Factory cost of goods completed	134,000	170,220

13.4 CAPITALISATION OF REVENUE EXPENDITURE

Sometimes an expenditure which is normally quite correctly classified as revenue is turned into capital expenditure. The most common example involves maintenance workers who spend most of their time repairing and maintaining fixed assets. Their earnings will normally be recorded in a wages account and deducted from income to obtain net profit. Occasionally, however, they might be employed to *improve* a fixed asset and not merely to restore its value. If this happens their earnings, while performing this task, should be removed from the wages account, which counts as revenue expenditure, and transferred to an account for the fixed asset that has increased in value.

Example

The maintenance staff at Tom Brown's engineering works used waste material to build shelves in a storeroom. Their total wages for the period when the shelves were being erected amounted to £250. If this is allowed to remain in the wages account it will be deducted (as part of the total wages paid during the year) from income to obtain net profit. Clearly this would not be fair as £250 of the expenditure on wages resulted in an increase in the value of an asset which will last for some considerable time. The £250 should be transferred from the wages account to an account for fixtures and fittings. As it is a relatively unusual transaction it would probably be recorded in the journal before being posted to the ledger.

Journal

Date	Description	dr	cr
...	Fixtures and fittings	250	
	Wages		250
	Capitalisation of revenue expenses in improving the storeroom.		

While this kind of transaction can occur in all types of business it is perhaps more common in manufacturing.

SELF-CHECK ▶ 13.4

Tom's maintenance men are used to build a storage bunker which increases the value of the premises. They use materials purchased by the business for production purposes worth £400 and while building it are paid wages of £300. Show the journal entries necessary to capitalise the revenue expenditure involved. A narrative is not required.

COMMENT ▶

As well as transferring the £300 wages it is also necessary this time to transfer the materials. If this were not done materials worth £400 would be included as an expense in this manufacturing account where it would incorrectly reduce profit.

SOLUTION ▶

Journal

Date	Description	dr	cr
...	Premises	700	
	Wages		300
	Purchases		400

13.1

The following information has been taken from the books of Jonas Ltd.

Stocks at 1 June 1987:	£
Raw materials	14,000
Work in progress (valued at prime cost)	7,500
Finished goods	9,000
Sales	88,250
Purchases	19,460
Factory:	
Wages (direct)	22,196
Power	3,260
Salaries	16,150
Rates	750
Heating and lighting	1,210
Repairs	240
Depreciation	1,345
Warehouse:	
Wages	11,000
Rates	400
Stocks at 31 August 1987:	
Raw materials	16,250
Work in progress (valued at prime cost)	9,800
Finished goods	13,000

(a) Prepare a manufacturing account for the quarter ended 31 August 1987 clearly showing the prime cost and factory cost of goods completed.

(b) Prepare a trading account for the quarter ended 31 August clearly showing cost of goods sold and gross profit.

13.2

S. Thorn manufacture soft toys. The following is the manufacturing, trading and profit and loss account for the year ended 31 December 1984.

	£	£	£
Sales			105,000
less Cost of sales:			
Opening stock raw materials		2,000	
Purchases raw materials		20,000	
Carriage on raw materials		1,000	
		23,000	
less Closing stock raw materials		2,500	
		20,500	
Direct wages		35,500	
		56,000	
Factory indirect expenses:			
Factory rates, light and heat	3,000		
Factory power	2,500		
Factory insurance	500		
Depreciation of factory machinery	900		
		6,900	
		62,900	
Opening stock finished goods		5,000	
		67,900	
less Closing stock finished goods		6,000	
			61,900
			£43,100

(a)   What is the purpose of a manufacturing account?

(b)   Why do retailers not need to prepare a manufacturing account?

(c)   What is the distinction between direct and indirect factory expenses?

(d)   Using the information given in the above account, state clearly the following amounts:

        (i) Cost of raw materials consumed

        (ii) Prime cost

        (iii) Factory cost of goods completed

        (iv) Cost of sales

        (v) Gross profit   (NISEC specimen paper)

13.3

The following figures relate to the production of one edition of a school magazine.

	£
Opening stock of paper valued at cost	30.00
Purchases of paper, paid for in cash	270.00
Paper unused, values at cost	50.00
Payment to a member of staff for collecting supplies using his own car	5.00
Wages paid:	
William Gee editor	20.00
Brian Doe printer	14.00
Ruby Grand sales manager	24.00
John Ward cleaner	9.00
Charge made by school for electricity	30.00
Rent of the room used, charged by school	40.00
Hire of school's printing machine	50.00

2,000 copies of the magazine were produced and sold for 50p each.

(a)   Draw up a cash account showing the cash received and paid. Any remaining balance in hand is to be banked in a special school magazine account.

(b)   Prepare accounts to show (i) prime cost, (ii) cost of production and (iii) net profit on this edition of the magazine.

(c)   The head teacher wants to know the reason for the difference (if any) between the profit made and the amount of cash placed in the bank account. Write a short explanation to the head teacher.

(LEAG specimen paper)

13.4

Jack Thomas owns a small factory in which he manufactures footballs in two qualities, 5 star and 3 star. The following information is available for his financial year to 30 June 1986.

	£
Stocks at 1 July 1985:	
Raw materials	3,860
Finished goods:	
5 star	1,225
3 star	3,200
Purchase of raw materials	124,514
Carriage on raw materials	320
Workshop wages:	
5 star	16,000
3 star	48,000
Workshop light and heat	1,300
Workshop general expenses	800
Workshop rent and rates	1,800
Raw materials returned	480
Sales:	
5 star	100,000
3 star	200,000
Stocks at 30 June 1986:	
Raw materials	1,300
Finished goods:	
5 star	594
3 star	2,125

Workshop records show that, of the raw materials consumed in production in the year ended 30 June 1986, £50,894 was used in the production of 5 star and the remainder in the production of 3 star. All workshop costs not allocated are to be apportioned one quarter to the production of 5 star and three quarters to the production of 3 star.

You are required to prepare for the year ended 30 June 1986:

(a)   a manufacturing account showing clearly the prime cost and the factory cost of goods manufactured for each grade of product;

(b)   a trading account for each grade of product;

(c)   a brief explanation of the significance of the factory cost of goods manufactured.

Note:

You are recommended to adopt the columnar form of presentation for the manufacturing and trading accounts.

(WJEC specimen paper)

13.5 Witch and Warlock Ltd manufacture two different types of cauldron –
C1 and C2.

Cauldron C1 was sold at factory cost plus 25%.

Cauldron C2 was sold at factory cost plus 10%.

During the year ended 31 October 1986 the following costs were
incurred.

	C1 £	C2 £
Commencing material stocks (1 Nov 1985)	7,000	10,500
Purchases of materials	16,150	27,500
Direct wages cost	15,000	19,500
Depreciation: plant and machinery	1,500	2,600
Wage costs: plant maintenance	750	1,100
Factory rent and other indirect expenses	1,100	2,000
Closing material stocks (31 Oct 1986)	6,500	9,200

Number of cauldrons produced during the year: C1 – 7,000; C2 –
27,000. There was no work in progress.

You are required to:

(a)   Prepare two distinct manufacturing accounts (which may be
presented in columnar form) for the year ended 31 October 1986, one
for C1 and one for C2. You must show clearly:

(i) the prime cost;

(ii) the factory cost of cauldrons completed.

(b)   Calculate the selling price of the two types of cauldron. (All
calculations must be shown.)

(c)   What would the gross profit of Witch and Warlock have been
for the year ended 31 October 1986 if 6,000 C1 cauldrons and 25,000
C2 cauldrons had been sold? (Assume remaining stocks are valued at
factory cost.)   (NEA specimen paper)

INCOMPLETE RECORDS

CONTENTS

The accounting records of a business may be incomplete for a number of reasons. Whatever the reason it is likely that HM Customs and Excise will not be happy if a business is registered for VAT and the necessary information is missing. Even businesses not registered for VAT have to satisfy the Inland Revenue with regard to tax. The Inspector of Taxes is likely to impose a high tax demand on businesses that do not keep proper records in order to encourage them to do better in the future! The main problem as far as incomplete records is concerned is with calculating the net profit. There are two basic situations. In the first the information available is limited to the assets and liabilities of the firm. In the second some kind of cash book has been kept so it can be seen how much money has been received and paid during the year and to what the money related.

14.1 CALCULATING NET PROFIT THROUGH CHANGES IN OWNER'S CAPITAL

Read sections 1.5 and 1.6 again, paying particular attention to the equation developed in section 1.6. This equation summarised the effects of profit, loss, input of capital and drawings on the capital of a business over a period of time. The equation that was developed may be written like this:

Initial Capital (IC) − Losses (L) + Input (IN)
+ Profit (P) − Drawings (D) = Final Capital (FC).

There are both profits and losses in this equation because it was used to see how capital could change over several years. Normally we will be dealing with only one year at a time. We can assume for the moment that a profit has been made. If we get rid of the losses from this equation it will now look like this:

Initial Capital (IC) + Input (IN) + Profit (P)
− Drawings (D) = Final Capital (FC).

Suppose we are in a situation where we know all the figures for the items in the equation except profit. It will be possible to find the profit by changing the equation around. The rule about doing this is that when you change an item from one side of an equation to another you must change the sign. Thus if the equation is re-written to find profit it will look like this:

Profit (P) = Final Capital (FC) + Drawings (D)
— Input (IN) − Initial Capital (IC).

The addition of drawings and the subtraction of input from the final capital reveals what the final capital would have been if there had been no drawings and no input. Taking the initial capital away from this adjusted final capital gives the profit made in the year.

```
        FINAL CAPITAL
    +   DRAWINGS
    −   INPUT
        ADJUSTED FINAL CAPITAL
    −   INITIAL CAPITAL
        NET PROFIT
```

This equation will also reveal a loss. It will show up as a negative or minus figure for profit.

SELF-CHECK ▶
14.1

Learn the equation: PROFIT (P) = FINAL CAPITAL (FC) + DRAWINGS (D) − INPUT (IN) − INITIAL CAPITAL (IC) and then use it to complete the following table:

	FC	D	IN	IC	P
	£	£	£	£	£
(a)	10,000	2,000	3,000	7,000	
(b)	13,000	4,000	—	8,000	
(c)	12,000	1,000	2,000	15,000	

SOLUTION ▶

(a) Profit £2,000; (b) Profit £9,000; (c) Loss £4,000.

COMMENT ▶

(a) fits nicely with the above explanation; in (b) there is no input of capital so you just omit it from the calculation; and in (c) the answer comes to −£4,000 which means that a loss has been made.

14.2 CALCULATING THE CAPITAL FIGURES

Using the above equation is normally made a little more difficult because it requires you to find the initial and final capital figures. Section 1.3 will remind you how to do this. Provided you have information about the assets and liabilities it is possible to calculate the capital at any date by using the book-keeping equation:

Capital + Liabilities = Assets
Therefore: Assets − Liabilities = Capital

In order to find a capital figure using this equation you could simply list the assets and liabilities then deduct the total liabilities from the total assets. This could be done in a balance sheet. A balance sheet is usually prepared in a formal manner with headings for the types of assets and liabilities. It might be better to omit this kind of detail to arrive at the answer more quickly. The name 'statement of affairs' is usually given to a balance sheet which has been drawn up without the usual headings. For example, you are told that a trader has the following assets and liabilities on 1 January 1988, the beginning of his financial year:

Premises £50,000; equipment £10,000; stock £5,000; creditors £3,000; debtors £2,000; bank £4,000; mortgage £20,000.

A statement of affairs to calculate the initial or opening capital will look like this:

Statement of affairs of a trader as at 1 January 1988

Assets	£	Liabilities	£
Premises	50,000	Mortgage	20,000
Equipment	10,000	Creditors	3,000
Stock	5,000		23,000
Debtors	2,000	∴ Capital	48,000
Bank	4,000		
	71,000		71,000

The purpose of this statement of affairs is solely to find the capital. If the assets total £71,000 and the liabilities £23,000 then the capital must equal £48,000 on 1 January 1988. Always take care with the date because you often have to calculate the closing capital as well.

SELF-CHECK ▶
14.2

The above trader was found to have the following assets and liabilities on 31 December 1988:

Premises £50,000; equipment £12,000; stock £9,000; creditors £6,000; debtors £5,000; bank overdraft £1,000; mortgage £19,000.

Draft a statement of affairs to calculate the final capital.

SOLUTION ▶

Statement of affairs of a trader as at 31 December 1988

Assets	£	Liabilities	£
Premises	50,000	Mortgage	19,000
Equipment	12,000	Creditors	6,000
Stock	9,000	Bank overdraft	1,000
Debtors	5,000		26,000
		∴ Capital	50,000
	76,000		76,000

14.3 STATEMENT OF PROFIT OR LOSS

It is now possible to calculate the net profit or loss for the year. To do so you will need to know whether there have been any increases or decreases of capital caused by reasons other than profits and losses, i.e. whether there have been any drawings or inputs. We will assume that the owner had withdrawn £7,000 of assets for his private use and that he had invested £2,000 in the business from his private resources. The equation used in the last section will provide the net profit or loss:

$$FC \; £50,000 + D \; £7,000 - IN \; £2,000 - IC \; £48,000$$
$$= P \; £7,000$$

This would be fine if you are asked merely to calculate the profit. If, however, you are asked to prepare a statement to show the profit then something a little more formal would look better. A heading and full information makes the presentation better. For example:

Statement of a trader's profit and loss for the year ended 31 December 1988

	£
Final Capital	50,000
add Drawings	7,000
	57,000
less Input	2,000
	55,000
less Initial Capital	48,000
Net Profit	7,000

If you are asked to find the net profit or loss and are given insufficient information to do a profit and loss account, but are provided with enough information about assets and liabilities, you should approach the problem in three stages.

Stage 1: Calculate the initial or opening capital.

Stage 2: Calculate the final or closing capital.

Stage 3: Use the equation FC + D − IN − IC = P to find the net profit. (Remember if the answer is negative a loss has been made.)

SELF-CHECK ▶
14.3

M. Tyson is a trader who has not kept proper books of account. At 1 July 1987 his assets and liabilities were:

Bank £1,500; fixtures £4,900; stock £8,700; loan £12,000; debtors £900; creditors £5,500; motor vehicle £2,900; prepaid expenses £600.

During the year to 30 June 1988 his drawings amounted to £9,750 and a legacy of £1,600 was invested in the business.

At 30 June 1988 he decided that he should depreciate his fixtures by ten per cent and his motor vehicle by twenty per cent. Other assets and liabilities were valued as follows:

Bank £4,550; stock £9,500; loan £10,000; debtors £1,400; creditors £4,340; accrued expenses £200.

Prepare a statement to show Tyson's profit or loss for the year.

SOLUTION ▶

Statement of Tyson's affairs at 1 July 1987

	£		£
Bank	1,500	Loan	12,000
Stock	8,700	Creditors	5,500
			17,500
Debtors	900		
Prepayments	600		
Fixtures	4,900	∴ Capital	2,000
Motor vehicle	2,900		
	19,500		19,500

Statement of Tyson's affairs at 30 June 1988

	£		£
Bank	4,550	Loan	10,000
Stock	9,500	Creditors	4,340
Debtors	1,400	Accrued expenses	200
			14,540
Fixtures (£4,900−£490)	4,410		
Motor vehicle (£2,900−£480)	2,420	*Hence* Capital	7,740
	22,280		22,280

Statement of profit and loss for M. Tyson for the year ended 30 June 1988

	£
Final Capital	7,740
add Drawings	9,750
	17,490
less Input	1,600
	15,890
less Initial Capital	2,000
Net Profit	13,890

COMMENT ▶ Although it is not absolutely essential to calculate the initial and final capital by using a statement of affairs it probably will help you to get the answer right. You are especially advised not to complicate the final statement of affairs by including the drawings and input. It is best to use it solely to find the final capital. This will be the capital *after* all changes have taken place, i.e. drawings, input and profit or loss. The profit or loss is then calculated in its own statement where you will have to adjust the final capital figure to allow for the drawings and input.

14.4 SINGLE ENTRY RECORDS

Many businesses, especially small ones, do not have their accounts kept on a double entry basis. In section 9.6 we saw how an analysed cash book could provide some of the advantages associated with a full ledger system. Most small businesses manage with even simpler types of cash book. The term single entry is applied to these systems because for every transaction only the money aspect is recorded. There is no double entry in, for example, a debtor's or creditor's account.

Whatever type of cash book is used it is usually possible to prepare an actual trading and profit and loss account to calculate the net profit of the firm. It will not be as easy as under a double entry system because there will be no accounts for such items as purchases, sales and expenses. For example, the cash book may reveal how much money has come in from customers in the year but this will not necessarily be the same as the amount of sales. This is because some of the money that has come in may be for last year's sales. It is also possible that sales made this year have not yet been paid for; in this case there will be no entry relating to the sale in the cash book. Similarly, the amount paid to suppliers shown in the cash book may include payments for last year's purchases and will not include purchases made at the end of the year which have not yet been paid for. The expenses figure too, will be the money amount and not the real amount.

Provided enough information is known, however, it is usually possible to calculate enough of the information that is needed to complete a trading and profit and loss account. The degree of incompleteness of the records is not as great as in the previous section.

14.5 CALCULATING PURCHASES AND SALES

A trader's cash book revealed that in the year ended 31 December 1988 payments to suppliers totalled £7,200. It is also known that trade creditors totalled £400 on 31 December 1987 and £650 on 31 December

1988. There are two methods of calculating the purchases: firstly in the form of a statement and secondly in the form of an account.

	£
Amount paid to suppliers in 1988	7,200
less Payments made for goods bought in 1987 (opening creditors)	400
	6,800
add Purchases made in 1988 not paid for (closing creditors)	650
Purchases made in 1988	7,450

The above statement is self-explanatory because of the detail it contains. Normlly it is sufficient just to write: *less* opening creditors and *add* closing creditors. The same information may be obtained by completing a total creditors account. All the information that is known can be fitted in the right places making it possible to calculate the item that is missing. Remember it is the purchases figure we need to find.

Total creditors account

1988			£	1988			£
....	Cash book		7,200	1 Jan	Balance	b/d	400
31 Dec	Balance	c/d	650	....	∴ Purchases		7,450
			7,850				7,850
				1989			
				1 Jan	Balance	b/d	650

To use this method you need to remember your double entry bookkeeping and how accounts are balanced. The £400 owing to creditors at the end of 1987 will be shown as a credit (liability) balance brought down to the start of 1988. The amount paid to suppliers will have been credited in the cash book and would have been debited in the creditors account during the year. The closing balance of £650 is a liability and will be shown carried down from the debit side and brought down, after the account has been totalled, on the credit side. It will then be possible to insert the **purchases** figure. For the account to balance at £650 with totals of £7,850 the only figure that fits this jigsaw is purchases £7,450.

You have a similar choice when calculating the sales figures. For example, suppose the trader's cash book showed that he had received £10,000 from his customers in 1988 and that trade debtors totalled £1,100 on 31 December 1987 and £1,320 on 31 December 1988.

	£
Amount received from customers in 1988	10,000
less Amount received for goods sold in 1987 (opening debtors)	1,100
	8,900
add Sales made in 1988 not paid for (closing debtors)	1,320
Sales made in 1988	10,220

Or:

Total debtors account

1988			£	1988			£
1 Jan	Balance	b/d	1,100	....	Cash book		10,000
....	∴ **Sales**		10,220	31 Dec	Balance	c/d	1,320
			11,320				11,320
1989							
1 Jan	Balance	b/d	1,320				

This time it was the **sales** figure that was missing from the above account. By inserting all the other known figures in their proper positions it was possible to deduce that **sales** must be £10,220. No other figure would have made the account balance at £1,320 – the figure we know is the correct closing balance.

SELF-CHECK 14.5(a)

Calculate the purchases and sales figures for the year ended 30 June 1988 from the following information:

1 July 1987–30 June 1988   Received from customers £14,560;
1 July 1987–30 June 1988   Paid to suppliers £9,340;
1 July 1987   Trade debtors £1,530;   30 June 1988   Trade debtors £980;
1 July 1987   Trade creditors £2,420;   30 June 1988   Trade creditors £2,570.

SOLUTION ▶

	£		£
Received from customers	14,560	Paid to suppliers	9,340
less Opening debtors	1,530	*less* Opening creditors	2,420
	13,030		6,920
add Closing debtors	980	*add* Closing creditors	2,570
Sales	14,010	Purchases	9,490

COMMENT ▶

You would have obtained the same answers by using the total debtors and total creditors account method. Use whichever method you find easier. If you have any doubts check your answer by using the alternative method.

One thing to look out for is any additional information about the debtors or creditors that will have affected the final debtors' or creditors' balance. For example, if you were given the additional information that cash discounts allowed to debtors for prompt payment during 1988 totalled £400, this must be taken into consideration. While discounts allowed reduces the amount of money coming in it does not reduce the value of the sales that took place. Any discounts allowed should therefore be added on to the money received like this:

	£
Received from customers	14,560
add Discounts allowed	400
	14,960
less Opening debtors	1,530
	13,430
add Closing debtors	980
Sales	14,410

Bad debts that have been written off the debtors' account during the year will also have reduced the final debtors balance but will not have affected the sales figure. This too should therefore be added back into the amount received from customers. If we assume that in the above example the £250 bad debts were written off during 1988 the sales figures would have been £250 higher again, i.e. £14,660. This is what the total debtors' account would look like if both discounts allowed and bad debts have to be taken into account:

Total debtors a/c

1987/88			£	1987/88			£
1 Jul	Balance	b/d	1,530	....	Cash/bank		14,560
....	∴ **Sales**		14,660	....	Discounts allowed		400
				....	Bad debts		250
				30 Jun	Balance	c/d	980
			16,190				16,190
1988/89							
1 Jul	Balance	b/d	980				

As before, all entries are inserted in their correct positions. The missing **sales** figure then completes the jigsaw. If you are told that cash discounts were received from suppliers during the year you would have to take that into consideration when calculating the purchases figure in a similar way. The amount paid to the creditors will have been reduced by the amount of the discount received. This must therefore be added back in to find the purchases.

SELF-CHECK ▶ 14.5(b)

State the purchases figure from the facts contained in self-check 14.5(a) together with the information that discounts received from suppliers during the year totalled £360.

SOLUTION ▶

	£
Paid to suppliers	9,340
add Discounts received	360
	9,700
less Opening creditors	2,420
	7,280
add Closing creditors	2,570
Purchases	9,850

You could, of course, complete a total creditors account to obtain the same answer.

14.6 CALCULATING BUSINESS EXPENSES

A similar procedure needs to be followed in order to calculate the *real* amount of a business expense for a period. The cash book will only reveal the amount of cash paid for an expense during a period. To calculate the actual expense you need to know if any of this payment was for last year or next year. If it was, then it must be excluded. On the other hand, if any payment was made last year for this year or if there is an amount due at the end of the year that has not been paid it must be included.

Example

A trader's cash book showed that in the year ended 31 December 1988 he paid £4,900 rent and rates. You are also told that on 1 January 1988 rent prepaid had been £400 and rates accrued were £250; while on 31 December 1988 rent prepaid was £150 and rates accrued was £300. The real amount of rent and rates to be included in the profit and loss account can be calculated like this:

	£
Rent and rates paid in 1988	4,900
add rent paid in 1987 for 1988 (opening prepayment)	400
	5,300
less rates paid in 1988 for 1987 (opening accrual)	250
	5,050
less rent paid in 1988 for 1989 (closing prepayment)	150
	4,900
add rates owing at 31 December 1988 for 1988 (closing accrual)	300
REAL amount of rent and rates for year ended 31 Dec 1988	5,200

The order in which you do the calculation does not matter. Once you have mastered it you will not need to write the explanation so fully. Basically, you add opening prepayments and closing accruals whilst you should deduct opening accruals and closing prepayments. It is possible to obtain the same answer by completing a ledger account for rent and rates. Inserting all the known information in the right places will enable you to deduce the missing figure – the amount to be transferred to the profit and loss account. Accounts with four balances in them often lead to confusion, I therefore recommend that you use the calculation method for the above. If there is only one opening and one closing balance it is not so difficult to complete a ledger account. Reading chapter six again should be of benefit.

SELF-CHECK ▶ 14.6

A trader's cash book shows that during the year ended 31 December 1988 he paid business expenses of £26,000. You are also told that on 1 January 1988 total expenses prepaid had been £1,400 and total expenses accrued were £1,250; while on 31 December 1988 total expenses prepaid were £650 and total expenses accrued were £1,340.

(*a*)   Calculate the amount of business expenses to be included in the profit and loss account for the year ended 31 December 1988.

(*b*)   Show relevant balance sheet entries at 31 December 1988.

SOLUTION ▶

(*a*)

	£
Business expenses paid in 1988	26,000
add expenses paid in 1987 for 1988 (opening prepayment)	1,400
	27,400
less expenses paid in 1988 for 1987 (opening accrual)	1,250
	26,150
less expenses paid in 1988 for 1989 (closing prepayment)	650
	25,500
add expenses owing at 31 Dec 1988 for 1988 (closing accrual)	1,340
Business expenses to profit and loss a/c for the year ended 31 Dec 1988	26,840

(*b*)   Balance Sheet of a trader as at 31 December 1988

	£
Current assets	
Prepaid expenses	650
Current liabilities	
Expenses accrued	1,340

COMMENT ▶

This is a timely reminder that prepayments and accruals at any date should be shown in the balance sheet for that date.

14.7 FINAL ACCOUNTS AND BALANCE SHEET

By completing all the calculations required you should now be able to put together a trading and profit and loss account for a trader who does not keep double entry records. You should also be able to prepare a balance sheet. The final accounts are no different to those you have prepared for traders who do keep double entry records. The extra work lies in the calculations that have to be completed before you begin.

SELF-CHECK ▶
14.7

B. Powell is a café owner who does not keep a full set of accounts. His assets and liabilities on 1 January 1988 and 31 March 1988 were:

	1 January £	31 March £
Premises	30,000	30,000
Trade creditors	180	380
China and utensils	220	220
Furniture and equipment	2,000	2,000
Stock	900	1,200
Accrued expenses	640	880
Prepaid expenses	80	40
Trade debtors	30	50
Cash in bank	1,100	1,320

His bank account contained the following information:

Bank account summary

1988			£	1988			£
1 Jan	Balance	b/d	1,100	....	Drawings		1,250
....	Total sales receipts		22,720	....	Business expenses		4,140
				....	Wages		7,220
				....	Trade creditors		9,840
				....	Bank charges		50
				31 March	Balance	c/d	1,320
			23,820				23,820

You are asked to prepare Powell's trading and profit and loss account for the quarter ended 31 March 1988 and a balance sheet at that date taking into account the following *additional* information:
(*a*)   Furniture should be depreciated by £35 and china/utensils by £30 at 31 March.
(*b*)   Discounts received from suppliers totalled £50 during the quarter.
(*c*)   Bad debts of £40 had been written off during the quarter.

SOLUTION ▶

Calculations and notes for guidance

In this question you have enough balance sheet information to calculate the profit or loss by using the equation developed in section 14.1. However, as the question asks for a trading and profit and loss account you would not earn many marks for finding the profit in another way.

	£		£
Paid to trade creditors	9,840	Sales receipts	22,720
add Discounts received	50	*add* Bad debts	40
	9,890		22,760
less Opening creditors	180	*less* Opening debtors	30
	9,710		22,730
add Closing creditors	380	*add* Closing debtors	50
Purchases	10,090	**Sales**	22,780
Business expenses paid	4,140	**Statement of affairs 1.1.88**	
less Opening accrual	640	Premises	30,000
	3,500	China and utensils	220
less Closing prepayment	40	Furniture	2,000
	3,460	Stock	900
add Opening prepayment	80	Bank	1,100
	3,540	Prepayments	80
add Closing accrual	880	Debtors	30
Real business expenses	4,420	Total assets	34,330
		less liabilities:	
		creditors	180
		accruals	640
			820
		CAPITAL	33,510

Besides calculating the purchases and sales you will see that I have also calculated the opening capital figure. This was not given in the information and is frequently left for you to calculate using the accounting equation. It will not be needed until you get to the balance sheet but it is useful to organise yourself to make all the calculations in advance. It is always a good idea to show your calculation for any question. In this type of question it is even more important than usual. Once the calculations have been done the trading and profit and loss account and balance sheet may be completed in the usual manner.

Trading and profit and loss account of B. Powell for the three months ended 31 March 1988.

	£	£
Sales		22,780
less Cost of sales:		
Opening stock	900	
add Purchases	10,090	
	10,990	
less Closing stock	1,200	
		9,790
Gross profit		12,990
add Discounts received		50
		13,040
less Expenses:		
Wages	7,220	
Bank charges	50	
Business expenses	4,420	
Depreciation on furniture	35	
Depreciation on china	30	
Bad debts	40	
		11,795
Net profit		1,245

It is important to remember to include the expenses and income you have not calculated but were given in the question. Wages and bank charges were in the summary of the bank account while bad debts, depreciation and discount received were given as additional information.

Balance Sheet of B. Powell as at 31 March 1988

Fixed assets	£	£	£
Premises		30,000	
Furniture		1,965	
China		190	
			32,155
Current assets			
Stock	1,200		
Trade debtors	50		
Prepayments	40		
Bank	1,320		
		2,610	
less Current liabilities			
Creditors	380		
Accruals	880		
		1,260	
Working capital			1,350
Total assets *less* current liabilities			33,505
Financed by:			
Owner's capital 1.1.88		33,510	
add Net profit		1,245	
		34,755	
less Drawings		1,250	
			33,505

EXERCISES

14.1

Calculate the profit or loss for each of the following traders:

	Final Capital	Drawings	Input	Opening Capital	Profit/Loss
	£	£	£	£	£
(a)	30,000	6,000	5,000	17,000	
(b)	12,000	4,350	—	8,950	
(c)	22,500	—	7,000	25,000	
(d)	6,000	3,000	1,000	10,000	

14.2   M. Hagler is a trader who has not kept proper books of account. At 1 July 1987 his assets and liabilities were:

Bank £2,550; equipment £6,940; stock £8,320; loan £2,000; debtors £670; creditors £4,500; motor vehicle £3,500; accrued expenses £250.

During the year to 30 June 1988 his drawings amounted to £6,250 and a legacy of £2,100 was invested in the business.

At 30 June 1988 he decided that he should depreciate his equipment by 20% and his motor vehicle by 25%. Other assets and liabilities were valued as follows:

Bank overdraft £1,600; stock £13,250; loan £2,000; debtors £1,600; creditors £3,240; prepaid expenses £120.

Prepare a statement to show Hagler's profit or loss for the year.

14.3   Calculate the purchases and sales figures for the year ended 30 June 1988 from the following information:

1 July 1987–30 June 1988   Received from customers £112,365;
1 July 1987–30 June 1988   Paid to suppliers £59,243;

1 July 1987   Trade debtors £11,632;   30 June 1988   Trade debtors £9,850;
1 July 1987   Trade creditors £12,342;   30 June 1988   Trade creditors £10,457.

14.4   A trader's cash book shows that during the year ended 31 December 1988 he paid business expenses of £43,540. You are also told that on 1 January 1988 total expenses prepaid had been £1,140 and total expenses accrued were £3,176; while on 31 December 1988 total expenses prepaid were £250 and total expenses accrued were £1,960.
(a)   Calculate the amount of business expenses to be included in the profit and loss account for the year ended 31 December 1988.
(b)   Show relevant balance sheet entries at 31 December 1988.

14.5   Calculate the purchases and sales figures for the year ended 31 July 1988 from the following information:

1 August 1987–31 July 1988   Received from customers £72,265;
1 August 1987–31 July 1988   Paid to suppliers £39,543;

1 August 1987   Trade debtors £6,325;   31 July 1988   Trade debtors £6,985;
1 August 1987   Trade creditors £8,234;   31 July 1988   Trade creditors £9,245.

During the year bad debts of £356 had been written off, discounts received from suppliers totalled £1,100 and discount allowed to customers totalled £2,456.

14.6

S. Hunt does not keep a full set of accounts. His assets and liabilities on 1 January 1988 and 30 June 1988 were:

	1 January	30 June
	£	£
Premises	50,000	50,000
Trade creditors	480	530
Equipment	2,320	2,320
Furniture	6,000	6,000
Stock	4,900	5,250
Accrued expenses	564	488
Prepaid expenses	180	240
Trade debtors	1,303	1,500
Cash in bank	2,500	?

His bank account revealed the following information:

Bank account summary

1988			£	1988		£
1 Jan	Balance	b/d	2,500	....	Drawings	5,990
....	Total sales			....	Business expenses	14,640
	Receipts		42,472	....	Wages	11,520
				....	Trade creditors	9,840

You are asked to prepare Hunt's trading and profit and loss account for the six months ended 30 June 1988 and a balance sheet at 30 June 1988 taking into account the following *additional* information:

(a)   Furniture should be depreciated by £125 and equipment by £90 at 30 June.

(b)   Discounts received from suppliers totalled £145 during the period and discounts allowed to customers totalled £258.

(c)   Bad debts of £144 had been written off during the period.

CLUB ACCOUNTS

CONTENTS

There is a very large number of social, sports and general interest clubs that do not seek to make a profit but exist for the benefit of their members. Honorary Treasurer is the title usually given to the person responsible for looking after the finances of the club. The members will expect him to be honest and to be able to account for the income earned and expenditure made on their behalf. Club accounts are kept in a variety of ways depending largely on the accounting knowledge of the treasurer. Provided you understand the accounts of businesses and, in particular, the way in which final accounts can be prepared for businesses that do not keep their accounts by means of double entry book-keeping, you should not experience any difficulty.

15.1 TERMS USED IN CLUB ACCOUNTS

It is unlikely that a club will have its accounts kept by double entry book-keeping. Usually a cash book is the only record kept of transactions. This may be written up weekly or perhaps even monthly. At the end of the year the cash book is usually summarised. The name given to this summary is the **receipts and payments account**.

Once a year clubs hold a general meeting known as the **Annual General Meeting** or **AGM**. The end of year accounts are usually presented to members at this meeting. There are two parts to the final accounts:

First, the **Income and Expenditure Account**. This is the club's equivalent of a profit and loss account. As such it contains all items of revenue and revenue expenditure for the year. If the club has a major income earner such as a bar it may begin with a trading account for this item in the same way that a business's profit and loss account is preceded by a trading account. Confusion often arises between a receipts and payments account and an income and expenditure account, perhaps because their names seem so similar. If you think of the receipts and payments account as the equivalent of a cash book and the income and expenditure account as the same as a profit and loss account, it will help to avoid confusion. The main purpose of a club is not to make a profit. If the income of the club is greater than its expenditure it will, however, have done so. In order to distinguish this kind of organisation from one which seeks to make a profit the term **surplus** is used instead of net profit. The surplus is a surplus of income over expenditure. If the expenditure for the year is greater than the income, the term **deficit** is used instead of net loss.

The second part to the final accounts is the **balance sheet**. This is the same as the balance sheet of any business, as it contains the assets of the club together with any liabilities. The finance invested by the club's members which would be called the capital if it was a business is known as the **accumulated fund**. This will be increased by a surplus and decreased by a deficit just as a business has its capital increased by a profit and decreased by a loss. In club accounts, however, there will be no drawings.

SELF-CHECK ▶
15.1

(a)   Learn the meaning of the terms in bold type.
(b)   State whether you would expect to find the following items in an athletic club's receipts and payments account, income and expenditure account or balance sheet:
   (i) weekly wages of groundsman
   (ii) total wages for the year
   (iii) purchase of new javelin
   (iv) total value of field events equipment – hammers, shot, javelins etc.
   (v) surplus
   (vi) accumulated fund

SOLUTION ▶

Item (i) would be in the receipts and payments account. At the end of the year the total amount paid in wages (ii) would be totalled in the receipts and payments account and this total placed in the income and expenditure account as it is revenue expenditure. Item (iii) is an example of capital expenditure. As such its purchase must **not** be shown in the income and expenditure. Payment for it will appear in the receipts and payments account and at the end of the year it will be added to the value of the equipment in (iv) and be shown in the balance sheet. Item (v) will appear in the income and expenditure account and then be added to item (vi) in the balance sheet.

15.2 INCOME AND EXPENDITURE ACCOUNTS

The receipts and payments account will provide the starting point when preparing an income and expenditure account.

Receipts and payments account of Newton Social Club

	£		£
Balance at 1.1.88	960	Bar purchases	14,000
Subscriptions	2,500	Cost of socials	2,600
Receipts from socials	2,900	Bar wages	4,000
Bar takings	25,000	Purchase of furniture	1,500
Donations	350	General expenses	2,800
		Repairs to premises	650
		Balance at 31.12.88	6,160
	31,710		31,710

Receipts are entered on the left-hand side and payments on the right as in the cash book but it is unlikely that they will be known by the terms debit and credit. The closing balance is often not shown brought down to its correct side but it is important to realise that as the receipts plus the opening balance is greater than the payments the closing balance is an asset. It represents the amount of money that the social club has in hand at 31 December 1988.

There will be some items of income in club accounts that are unlike those of businesses. Most clubs obtain the majority of their income from subscriptions paid by members. They frequently also receive donations from well-wishers. Expenditure items are basically the same as those of businesses.

As it is unlikely that a club will have ledger accounts you are not likely to have all the information neatly presented in a trial balance at the end of the year. The situation is more similar to that of a trader who does not keep a full set of accounts. A certain amount of 'detective work' is therefore needed to calculate some of the figures you need.

Example
During the year ended 31 December 1988 the treasurer of Newton Social Club had received subscriptions totalling £2,500. On 1 January 1988 £25 subscriptions were due for the previous year and £50 subscriptions had already been paid in 1987 for 1988. At the end of 1988 subscriptions due for 1988 totalled £30 and £260 had been paid in advance for 1989.

Calculating the subscriptions for 1988 is similar to the calculations made in the last chapter. Anything relating to last year or next year must be excluded and the *real* amount for 1988 calculated.

	£
Subscriptions received in 1988	2,500
add Subs received in 1987 for 1988 *prepaid*	50
	2,550
less Subs received in 1988 for 1987 *easy*	25
	2,525
add Subs due at end of 1988 for 1988 *accrued*	30
	2,555
less Subs paid in 1988 for 1989 *prepaid*	260
Real amount of subscriptions for 1988	2,295

Further calculations must be made if information is provided to show that the money amount in the receipts and payments summary is not the real amount. For example, suppose the Newton Social Club owed £2,000 for bar supplies on 1 January 1988 and £1,300 on 31 December 1988. Bar purchases for the year will be calculated as follows:

	£
Paid for bar purchases in 1988	14,000
less Opening creditors (due for 1987)	2,000
	12,000
add Closing creditors (due for 1988)	1,300
Purchases for 1988	13,300

If we assume that the only other information needed to be taken into account is that:

     (i) Furniture should be depreciated by £200 and

     (ii) Opening and closing bar stocks were £6,000 and £7,000 respectively

an income and expenditure account can then be prepared.

    As the bar is clearly a major part of the club's activities a bar trading account precedes the income and expenditure account.

Bar trading account of Newton Social Club for the year ended 31 December 1988

	£	£
Takings		25,000
less Cost of goods sold:		
Opening stock	6,000	
add Purchases	13,300	
	19,300	
less Closing stock	7,000	
	12,300	
add Bar wages	4,000	
		16,300
Profit on bar		8,700

Income and expenditure account of Newton Social Club for the year ended 31 December 1988

	£	£
Income:		
Bar profit	8,700	
Subscriptions	2,295	
Donations	350	
Profit on socials	300	
		11,645
Less expenses:		
Depreciation on furniture	200	
General expenses	2,800	
Repairs to premises	650	
		3,650
Surplus for the year		7,995

A number of variations could be made. For example the cost of socials has been deducted from the receipts for socials and the net amount entered as a profit. You would get the same answer if the cost was entered as an expense and the receipts as an income. It is also possible that a bar trading account would not be shown as such in the final accounts. The bar profit would have to be worked out, of course, but this would be done as a calculation and only the bar profit shown to members on the income and expenditure account. You can also expect to see different styles of layout. The vertical format has been kept here because that is the one we have used the most but others are perfectly acceptable.

Once the income and expenditure account has been completed the surplus will be added to the accumulated fund of the club in the balance sheet. This is similar to a business balance sheet, where the profit would be added to the capital of the owner. As usual you will need to remember to make entries in the balance sheet for any adjustments at the end of the year. From the information given about the Newton Social Club this will include:

(*a*)   Adding the new £1,500 of new furniture to the previous balance in the fixed assets and deducting the £200 depreciation.

(*b*)   Entering the £30 subscriptions due at 31 December as a current asset. From the club's point of view this money is owed to it by some of the members. We always assume that debts will be paid.

(*c*)   Entering the £260 subscriptions received in advance for 1989 as a current liability. The club owes its members who have paid in advance.

(*d*)   Entering the £7,000 closing bar stock figure as a current asset.

(*e*)   Entering the £1,300 closing bar creditors as a current liability.

(*f*)   Entering the end of year cash balance of £6,160 as a current asset.

SELF-CHECK ▶ 15.2	At 31 December 1987 the balance sheet of Fleetley Sports Club was summarised as follows:

	£		£
Premises	20,000	Accumulated fund	31,000
Furniture	2,000	Creditors for bar supplies	2,600
Equipment	4,000	Subscriptions in advance	300
Bar stocks	3,900		
Bank	4,000		
	33,900		33,900

The cash book for the year to 31 December 1988 had been summarised as follows:

Receipts and payments account

	£		£
Balance at 1 Jan	4,000	Bar purchases	15,000
Subscriptions	3,960	Bar wages	5,000
Bar takings	29,000	General expenses	3,740
Receipts from socials	3,650	Costs of socials	3,840
		Purchase of equipment	2,000
		Balance at 31 December	11,030
	40,610		40,610

At 31 December 1988 the following additional information is also available:

(*a*)   Bar stocks are valued at £4,500.

(*b*)   £4,200 was owed to creditors for bar supplies.

(*c*)   £200 subscriptions had been received in advance.

(*d*)   Depreciation was estimated at £200 on furniture and £500 on equipment.

Prepare a bar trading account and an income and expenditure account for the year ended 31 December 1988 and a balance sheet at that date.

SOLUTION

Calculations

	£
Paid for bar purchases in 1988	15,000
less Opening creditors (due for 1987)	2,600
	12,400
add Closing creditors (due for 1988)	4,200
Purchases for 1988	16,600

	£
Subscriptions received in 1988	3,960
add Subs received in 1987 for 1988	300
	4,260
less Subs received in 1988 for 1989	200
1988 subscriptions	4,060

	£
Receipts from socials	3,650
less Costs of socials	3,840
Loss on socials	190

Bar trading account of Fleetley Sports Club for the year ended 31 December 1988

	£	£
Takings		29,000
less Cost of goods sold:		
Opening stock	3,900	
add Purchases	16,600	
	20,500	
less Closing stock	4,500	
	16,000	
add Bar wages	5,000	
		21,000
Profit on bar		8,000

Income and expenditure account of Fleetley Sports Club for the year ended 31 December 1988

Income:	£	£
Bar profit	8,000	
Subscriptions	4,060	
		12,060
less Expenses:		
Loss on socials	190	
Depreciation on furniture	200	
Depreciation on equipment	500	
General expenses	3,740	
		4,630
Surplus for the year		7,430

Balance Sheet of Fleetley Sports Club as at 31 December 1988

Fixed assets		£	Accumulated fund		£
Premises		20,000	Opening accumulated fund		31,000
Furniture		1,800	*add* Surplus		7,430
Equipment		5,500	Closing accumulated fund		
		27,300			38,430
Current assets	£		**Current liabilities**	£	
Bar stocks	4,500		Bar creditors	4,200	
Bank	11,030		Subs in advance	200	
		15,530			4,400
		42,830			42,830

EXERCISES

15.1   The cash book of Oldtown Athletic Club for the year to 31 December 1988 has been summarised as follows:

Receipts and payments account

	£		£
Balance at 1 Jan	1,000	Bar purchases	5,000
Subscriptions	3,960	Affiliation fees	120
Bar takings	9,540	General expenses	1,140
Receipts from socials	350	Costs of socials	340
		Purchase of equipment	2,000
		Travelling expenses	1,986
		Balance at 31 December	4,264
	14,850		14,850

On 31 December 1987 the balance sheet of Oldtown Athletic Club contained the following information:

	£		£
Premises	20,000	Accumulated fund	25,730
Mini bus	2,000	Creditors for bar supplies	1,640
Equipment	2,340	Subscriptions in advance	160
Bar stocks	2,190		
Bank	1,000		
	27,530		27,530

At 31 December 1988 the following additional information is also available:
(a)   Bar stocks are valued at £2,450.
(b)   £2,320 was owed to creditors for bar supplies.
(c)   £120 subscriptions had been received in advance.
(d)   Depreciation was estimated at £400 on the minibus and £275 on equipment.
    Prepare an income and expenditure account for the year ended 31 December 1988 and a balance sheet at that date.

15.2

You are the secretary of the Students' committee entrusted with the arrangements for the end-of-term Christmas party. You have hired the hall, booked the disco and purchased the refreshments.

Expenses:	£
Hire of hall	20
Cost of Disco	40
Refreshments	35
Ballot tickets	24
Prizes	16

It is necessary to set aside a further ten per cent of the total of their expenses in case of unforeseen items. You would also like to make a small profit to enable you to make a donation to charity.

Requirements:
(a)   What price would you have to charge for the tickets to enable you to do this if you expect to sell 150 tickets?
(b)   After the party, you will need to present an account to your fellow members. Set this account out in the style and with the title normally used by a club or society.   (NISEC specimen paper)

15.3

(a)   The following figures relate to the snack bar of the Penguin Social Club for the year ended 31 December 1980:

	£
1 January – Stock	1,400
1 January – Creditors	470
Cash paid for purchases during the year	56,000
Sales for cash during the year	88,000
31 December – Stock	2,400
31 December – Creditors	800
Steward's wages for the year	5,000

Prepare a trading account for the bar to show the amount of profit.

(b)　　The following figures relate to the *main* bank account of the club:

	£
Balance at bank 1 January 1980	5,316
Subscriptions received during year	6,300
Secretary's expenses paid	3,318
Purchase of new equipment	6,500
Repairs to property	1,800
Bar profits handed over by steward [as calculated in part (a)]	?

Prepare a receipts and payments account for the year ended 31 December 1980.

(c)　　Prepare an income and expenditure account for the year ended 31 December 1980, taking into consideration items (i) and (ii) below:

(i) Rent for the year unpaid　　　　　　£1,200

(ii) Subscriptions unpaid for the year　　　360

(LEAG specimen paper)

ASSET VALUATIONS

CONTENTS

Throughout this book you have been given the value of opening and closing stock at cost price to enable you to calculate the cost of the goods sold when combined with the purchases figure. Placing a value on stock is by no means an easy task, particularly in a business that sells a large range of items very quickly. Some businesses rely solely on an annual stock take at the end of their financial year.

Example

The financial year of a trader ends on 31 December. The following are his stock take figures at that date:

Year ended 31 Dec	Stock valued at cost price
	£
1986	4,000
1987	5,000
1988	6,000

There is enough information here about stock to be able to complete two trading accounts, one for the year ended 31 December 1987 and the other for the year ended 31 December 1988. The closing stock for 1986 will be the opening stock for 1987 and the closing stock for 1987 will be the opening stock for 1988.

The importance of obtaining the correct valuation of stock can be seen by the effect of a valuation mistake on the profits of a firm. Consider the following trading account in which the stock has been *correctly* valued:

Correct trading account of Jones, year ended 31 December 1987

	£	£
Sales		20,000
less Cost of goods sold:		
Opening stock	4,000	
Purchases	9,000	
	13,000	
less Closing stock	5,000	
		8,000
Gross profit		12,000

We can see the effect of stock taking errors on the profits by making two separate mistakes:

> Suppose a mistake had been made in calculating the closing stock figure (either accidentally or deliberately) and that it had been valued at £6,000. The *incorrect* trading account would have looked like this:

Incorrect trading account of Jones, year ended 31 December 1987

	£	£
Sales		20,000
less Cost of goods sold:		
Opening stock	4,000	
Purchases	9,000	
	13,000	
less Closing stock	6,000	
		7,000
Gross profit		13,000

Adding £1,000 to the value of the closing stock has decreased the cost of sales by that amount and increased the gross profit by the same amount.

SELF-CHECK ▶
16.1(a)

Using the figures in the above *correct* trading account, rewrite it using a mistaken figure of £3,000 for the closing stock. Then state the effect on profits of an error which reduces the value of closing stock.

SOLUTION ▶

Incorect trading account of Jones, year ended 31 December 1987

	£	£
Sales		20,000
less Cost of goods sold:		
Opening stock	4,000	
Purchases	9,000	
	13,000	
less Closing stock	3,000	
		10,000
Gross profit		10,000

Reducing the value of the closing stock by £2,000 has increased the cost of sales by that amount and decreased the gross profit by the same amount.

The effect of a mistake in the closing value of stock will also have an effect on the next period's profits. The following is the *correct* trading account for the trader:

Correct trading account of Jones, year ended 31 December 1988

	£	£
Sales		24,000
less Cost of goods sold:		
Opening stock	5,000	
Purchases	11,000	
	16,000	
less Closing stock	6,000	
		10,000
Gross profit		14,000

If we take the mistake of overvaluing the closing stock of 1987 by £1,000 and carry this mistake into 1988 the trading account would look like this:

Incorrect trading account of Jones, year ended 31 December 1988

	£	£
Sales		24,000
less Cost of goods sold:		
Opening stock	6,000	
Purchases	11,000	
	17,000	
less Closing stock	6,000	
		11,000
Gross profit		13,000

Overvaluing the opening stock by £1,000 has increased the cost of sales and decreased the gross profit by this amount.

SELF-CHECK ▶ 16.1(b)

Using the figures in the above *correct* trading account for the year ended 31 December 1988, rewrite it using the mistaken figure of £3,000 for the opening stock. Then state the effect on profits of an error which reduces the value of opening stock.

Incorrect trading account of Jones, year ended 31 December 1988

	£	£
Sales		24,000
less Cost of goods sold:		
Opening stock	3,000	
Purchases	11,000	
	14,000	
less Closing stock	6,000	
		8,000
Gross profit		16,000

Undervaluing the opening stock by £2,000 has decreased the cost of sales and increased the gross profit by this amount.

The above examples and self-checks show that:

1 An overvaluation of stock at the end of one period increases profit in that period by that amount and reduces it in the following period by the same amount.

2 An undervaluation of stock at the end of one period decreases profit in that period by that amount and increases profit in the following period by the same amount.

16.2 STOCK RECORDS

Keeping the right amount of stock in a business is essential to the success of that business. Running out of stock could delay production in a manufacturing firm and lose sales. It could also lose sales for a trader as customers are likely to shop elsewhere. On the other hand, holding too much stock is expensive. It has to be paid for and no money will be received for it until it is sold. On top of that, storage costs money and the longer it is stored the greater the chance that it will deteriorate, become obsolete or be stolen. In order to keep a close control on stock many firms keep record cards for each item similar to the one below.

STOCK RECORD CARD					
Item		Maximum Stock....................		Minimum Stock....................	
Date	Receipt		Issues		Balance
	Qty	Invoice No	Qty	Reqn No	

When stock is received the stores will have recorded the receipt and an invoice (or delivery note) number. It will issue stock to departments requiring it in return for a requisition note made out by that department and signed by someone in authority. The effect on the balance of stock in hand for that item of each receipt or requisition can be recorded in the balance column. A check can then be made as to whether the balance fits within the maximum and minimum limits for this item.

16.3 LIFO AND FIFO

It is not always possible to identify which items of stock go into which sale. A greengrocer may be selling oranges from a box on his stall at 10p each. Some of these may have been purchased at 5p and some at 6p. At the end of the day's trading he may have six oranges left. What is the value of his stock? The correct answer will depend on how many of the oranges left cost 5p and how many cost 6p. As it is not likely that he will have marked the cost price on each orange he will not know. The scale of this problem will be even greater for a manufacturer who is using a large number of components to produce his finished products.

There are two basic ways around this problem. You can either assume that the stock that comes in first is used first. This is known as 'first in first out' or FIFO. Alternatively you can assume that the stock that has come in most recently is used first. This is known as 'last in first out' or LIFO. The method chosen will affect the stock valuation figure and hence the profits. Whichever method is chosen should be consistently applied.

Example

On 1 January 1987 a trader had 50 units of item X in stock at a cost of £10 per unit. During 1987 the following purchases and sales took place:

Purchases			Sales	
Jan	50 units @ £11		Feb	30 units
April	20 units @ £12		May	40 units
Sept	40 units @ £9		Nov	20 units
Oct	20 units @ £10		Dec	30 units
Total	130		Total	120

You are asked to find the value of the stock at 31 December using both FIFO and LIFO methods.

Calculation of closing stock using FIFO

Total units sold in 1987:		120
These would comprise: the opening stock		50
+ January purchases		50
+ April purchases		20
		————
		120
		————

Stock remaining at 31 December 1987:

September purchases 40 units @	£9	=	£360
October purchases 20 units @ £10		=	£200
Total closing stock of X			£560

Calculation of closing stock using LIFO

Total sales 120 units comprising:

Feb – 30 units of the Jan purchases
May – 40 units (20 Apr + 20 Jan)
Nov – 20 units of Sept purchases
Dec – 30 units (20 Oct + 10 Sept)

Balance remaining

20 Jan @ £11 + 50 Op Stock @ £10
50 Op Stock @ £10
50 Op Stock @ £10 + 20 Sept @ £9
50 Op Stock @ £10 + 10 Sept @ £9

Total stock remaining at 31 December 1987:

10 units of September purchases @ £9	=	£90
50 units of opening stock @ £10	=	£500
Total closing stock		£590

As you can see, calculating the stock value of LIFO is more complicated than with FIFO and greater care needs to be taken with it.

SELF-CHECK
16.3

On 1 January 1987 a trader had 30 units of item Z in stock at a cost of £12 per unit. During 1987 the following purchases and sales took place:

Purchases		Sales	
Jan	20 units @ £11	Feb	40 units
April	30 units @ £12	May	20 units
Sept	50 units @ £10	Nov	60 units
Oct	20 units @ £10	Dec	10 units

Find the value of the stock at 31 December using (*a*) FIFO and (*b*) LIFO.

SOLUTION ▶   (*a*)   FIFO

Total sales 130 units comprising:

Opening stock – 30 units @ £12
January purchases – 20 units @ £11
April purchases – 30 units @ £12
September purchases – 50 units @ £10

Total stock remaining at 31 December 1987:

October purchases – 20 units @ £10 = £200

(b)   LIFO

Total sales 130 units comprising:

Feb – 40 units (20 Jan + 20 op stock)
May – 20 April units
Nov – 60 units (50 Sept + 10 April)
Dec – 10 Oct units

Balance remaining

10 op stock @ £12
10 April @ £12 + 10 op stock @ £12
10 op stock @ £12
10 op stock @ £12 + 10 Oct @ £10

Closing stock at 31 December 1987:

10 Opening stock @ £12	=	£120
10 Oct purchases @ £10	=	£100
Total		£220

16.4 GOODWILL AND THE VALUE OF A BUSINESS

Putting a value on a business is not an easy matter but so many businesses are bought and sold it must be possible to arrive at a value that satisfies both the purchaser and seller. The starting point for valuing a business will be the balance sheet. Consider the following summary.

Balance Sheet of Ruth Turner, retailer, as at 30 June 1987

	£		£
Fixed assets	36,000	Owner's capital	45,000
Current assets	10,500	Current liabilities	1,500
	46,500		46,500

To agree a price for this business the purchaser and seller would first have to agree on three matters:

1 Whether the items in the balance sheet are correctly valued. If not, correct valuations should be obtained and a new balance sheet drawn up. We will assume that the above balance sheet is correct.

2 Whether the above balance sheet contains an amount for the goodwill and if not whether an amount for goodwill should be included.

Goodwill is the benefit obtained from purchasing a business with connections and reputation. The value of this asset is not easy to assess because it can fluctuate a great deal. For example, a successful restaurant might lose goodwill through the bad publicity associated with an outbreak of food poisoning or through a competitor opening up near by.

As the value of goodwill is difficult to assess it will not normally appear in a balance sheet. When a business is to be sold it will be necessary to include an amount for goodwill if the business possesses any. We will assume that Ruth Turner and the prospective purchaser of her business, Tom Grade, have agreed that a figure of £6,000 should be incorporated into the above balance sheet for goodwill. The new balance sheet would look like this:

Balance Sheet of Ruth Turner, retailer, as at 30 June 1987

	£		£
Fixed assets	36,000	Owner's capital	51,000
Current assets	10,500	Current liabilities	1,500
Goodwill	6,000		
	52,500		52,500

The effect of including the goodwill is to increase the assets by £6,000 and at the same time increase the owner's capital by the same amount. Clearly, the goodwill belongs to the current owner.

3 Whether the purchaser is taking over responsibility for the liabilities of the business. If he is, and if the above is a correct valuation of the business, Tom would be expected to pay £51,000 – the value of the net assets of the business or the value of the business to the owner. If, however, Ruth is going to pay off her current liabilities herself then she would charge Tom £52,500 for the business, i.e. the full value of the assets he is obtaining, including the goodwill. We will assume that Tom takes over the current liabilities and only pays £51,000 to Ruth. If he starts trading the following day his opening balance sheet will look like this:

Balance Sheet of Tom Grade, retailer, as at 1 July 1987

	£		£
Fixed assets	36,000	Owner's capital	51,000
Current assets	10,500	Current liabilities	1,500
Goodwill	6,000		
	52,500		52,500

The only difference between Tom's first balance sheet and Ruth's last one is the date and the name. This is because Tom has taken over the business completely, i.e. liabilities as well as assets. If Tom is going to keep a set of ledger accounts he will now have open an account for each asset (including the goodwill) and each source of finance.

GOODWILL

Goodwill is known as an intangible asset. Unlike the other assets, it has

no physical existence. Because of this, and the problems associate
with valuing it, the usual practice is to get rid of it from the books a
soon as possible. This is done by depreciating it as you would an
fixed asset. To do so at the end of one year's trading might have a
unfair effect on the accounts for that year, so normally it is written of
over a period of a few years. The entries are the same as for any othe
depreciation on fixed assets, i.e. credit the asset account and debit th
depreciation account. The amount of the depreciation will then b
transferred to the profit and loss account as an expense. Thus profit i
reduced and the value of the goodwill in the balance sheet is reduced
If Tom wrote off the goodwill over four years it would reduce hi
profit by £1,500 per annum until the goodwill account was closed
This if you see goodwill in a set of accounts you may assume that the
business is being sold or has been sold fairly recently.

SELF-CHECK ▶
16.4

G. Wade is in the process of selling her business. It has the following
assets and liabilities: fixed assets £40,000; current assets £23,000; current liabilities £5,000. A. Hobbes has agreed that these values are
correct and is going to buy it for £72,000.

Calculate the amount that Hobbes is paying for the goodwill if:
(*a*)   the purchase price does not require her to take over the
liabilities;
(*b*)   the price does involve taking over the liabilities.

SOLUTION ▶

(*a*)

	£
Purchase price	72,000
less Total value of assets purchased	63,000
Goodwill	9,000

(*b*)

	£
Purchase price	72,000
less Net value of assets purchased	58,000
Goodwill	14,000

16.1

For the year ended 31 December 1988 the closing stock value was overstated by £4,000. What would be the effect of this error on gross profit in (*a*) the 1988 final accounts and (*b*) the 1989 final accounts.

16.2

On 1 January 1988 a trader had 30 units of item K in stock at a cost of £14 per unit. During 1988 the following purchases and sales took place:

Purchases			Sales	
Jan	40 units @ £13		Feb	60 units @ £15
April	20 units @ £12		May	10 units @ £16
Sept	50 units @ £11		Nov	50 units @ £15
Oct	20 units @ £13		Dec	15 units @ £16

(*a*)   Find the value of the stock at 31 December using (i) FIFO and (ii) LIFO.
(*b*)   Prepare a trading account for this item of stock using (i) FIFO and (ii) LIFO.

16.3

You are working in the stock records section of a wholesale firm during the month of May and you have been asked to complete the stock card for item number 24. The name of suppliers should be shown against receipts, and the requisition number against issues.

Item number 24
1 May 1984   Balance in stock   500

Receipts
 2 May 1984   Moonlight Co Ltd   300
 8 May 1984   Starbeam and Sons   200
24 May 1984   Moonlight Co Ltd   350

Issues
 9 May 1984   Requisition Number 740   173
10 May 1984   Requisition Number 810   294
14 May 1984   Requisition Number 976   104
28 May 1984   Requisition Number 981   206

Requirement:
Complete the stock record card for May and show clearly how many items are in stock at the end of the month.

Appendix for question 16.3

STOCK RECORD CARD

Item _____   Maximum stock _____
                                            Minimum stock _____

Date	RECEIPT			ISSUES			Balance
	Qty.	Invoice No.	Supplier	Qty.	Department	Reqn. No.	

(NISEC specimen paper)

MANAGEMENT ACCOUNTING

CONTENTS

Most of the GCSE syllabuses are concerned mainly with record-keeping, i.e. book-keeping, and preparing final accounts and balance sheets, i.e. financial accounting. There are, however, some aspects of management accounting in the syllabuses and these aspects will be covered in this chapter. Management accounting is concerned with the ways in which accounting information can be used as an aid in controlling a business. I will also take this opportunity to review the accounting concepts and conventions that have been referred to (explicitly or implicitly) in this book and to give some examples of the short answer type questions you may encounter.

17.1 PROFITABILITY RATIOS

These use information about profit to measure the success of a business.

If you knew that business A had made a net profit of £1 million and that business B had made a profit of £2 million you might be tempted to say that B has done twice as well as A. This would be a mistake. It is possible that Business A made its profit on sales of £10 million while B's sales were £100 million. You might now feel that perhaps A has done substantially better than B. If, however, further information became available you might change your mind again. In order to use profit as a measurement of success you need to know something more than the profits figure. You need something to which the profit figure can be related so that a genuine comparison can be made. Relating profits to another factor is known as profitability measurement. The result is known as a profitability ratio though in practice this ratio is usually turned into a percentage. There are **four** commonly used profitability ratios:

1. Gross profit margin (%) $= \dfrac{\text{Gross profit}}{\text{Sales}} \times 100$

2. Mark up on cost (%) $= \dfrac{\text{Gross profit}}{\text{Cost of goods sold}} \times 100$

3. Net profit margin (%) $= \dfrac{\text{Net profit}}{\text{Sales}} \times 100$

Calculating these three should not cause any major problem, as they involve relating a profit figure to other figures you have met already.

Calculate the net profit margin for businesses A and B above.

$$A = \frac{£1m}{£10m} \times 100 = 10\% \qquad B = \frac{£2m}{£100m} \times 100 = 2\%$$

The superior profitability of A is clear from this calculation.

While calculating the ratios might not cause problems, interpreting them is sometimes a lot more difficult. There are three legitimate comparisons. Firstly, to compare a ratio with another firm in the same kind of business; secondly, to compare this year's performance of a firm with a previous performance; and thirdly, to compare this year's performance with a target for the year. Without such comparative figures it is difficult to make valid judgements because what is acceptable to one firm in one industry in a particular economic climate might not be acceptable to another.

4   Return on capital employed (%) $= \dfrac{\text{Net profit}}{\text{Capital employed}} \times 100$

This measurement does cause more difficulty because there is no accepted definition of what is meant by capital employed. Some people use it to mean the net value of the assets, i.e. total assets less current liabilities, while others use the total asset value without allowing for the liabilities. It is important, therefore, when using this measurement of profitability to make certain that you are consistent. Once you have selected your base, stick to it.

Relating profit to a figure for capital employed does make it a little easier to make judgements on the result. It is possible to compare the percentage achieved with a percentage that might be achieved if the capital had been employed by being invested in a bank deposit account or a building society account. Such comparisons are fraught with difficulty because like is not necessarily being compared with like. There is obviously a bigger risk associated with business investment than with placing money in a bank or building society. It does, however, enable us to state that a business is failing to achieve a reasonable return on the assets invested or that it is achieving a very good return. It is in the middle ground that the real problems arise, as the following self-check should show.

SELF-CHECK ▶ 17.1(b)

Using the following information calculate the return on capital employed (ROCE) for firm X in each of the three years:

Year	Net profit	Capital employed	ROCE
	£	£	%
1	16,000	400,000	
2	40,000	400,000	
3	80,000	400,000	

SOLUTION ▶

Year 1 – four per cent seems low; year 2 – ten per cent seems acceptable; and year 3 – twenty per cent seems excellent. In all three cases, however, to make a valid judgement you really need further information about the firm, its market, the prevailing economic climate, and its targets. For example, four per cent in year 1 may have followed a year in which the firm made a loss and came close to extinction! Similarly although the twenty per cent in year 3 seems excellent, if the firm was a computer firm and year 3 was a successful year for such firms, its competitors might have been achieving a return of fifty per cent.

17.2 LIQUIDITY RATIOS

These are used to measure the ability of a business to pay its immediate debts, i.e. its current liabilities. To be able to do so quickly it needs sufficient current assets.

Through using vertical balance sheets we have already encountered one measurement of ability to meet current liabilities from current assets. This is the calculation of working capital, i.e. current assets less current liabilities. We would expect a well run business to have current assets that are greater in value than current liabilities, i.e. a positive working capital. If the current liabilities were greater than the current assets (negative working capital) it might mean that creditors pressing for payment would not be able to be satisfied. It would be difficult to obtain further credit and, if it was not possible to remedy the situation the business might be forced to close.

Two ratios are used to measure liquidity:

1 Current ratio $\dfrac{\text{Current assets}}{\text{Current liabilities}}$

Unlike the profitability ratios the convention is not to express this ratio as a percentage. Thus if a firm had current assets of £30,000 and current liabilities of £15,000, the current ratio would be written as:

$$\frac{\text{Current assets}}{\text{Current liabilities}} = \frac{30,000}{15,000} = \frac{2}{1} \quad \text{Or it could be written as 2:1}$$

To have current assets that are twice as high as the current liabilities would be regarded as safe by most people. It is not always easy to say what the minimum ratio is for safety but most would agree that about 1.8:1 is acceptable. You should not just think in terms of a ratio being too low, and therefore risky, if asked to comment on a firm's liquidity. Too high a ratio indicates that a firm has too much money tied up in current assets. For example, it might have an excessive amount of stock which is not being sold quickly enough or money in a bank current account that is not being used to its best advantage.

2   Acid test ratio $\dfrac{\text{Current assets} - \text{stock}}{\text{Current liabilities}}$

This ratio is also known as the liquid ratio. It is used as an alternative measurement of liquidity or to supplement the current ratio. It takes a tougher line on whether a firm can pay its current liabilities by excluding the stock from the amount available to pay. This is done mainly for firms that take a long time to turn their stock into cash. Thus the only assets that usually count are cash, bank and debtors. You might think that a ratio of 1:1 would be expected here. However, because it is unlikely that all the creditors are demanding immediate payment, a ratio of 0.8:1 is usually regarded as satisfactory.

As with profitability ratios it is dangerous to make comments that are too definite without access to further information about the business. Access to the final accounts and balance sheet will enable both profitability and liquidity ratios to be calculated and a more thorough evaluation of the performance of the business to take place. It is usually considered sufficient to calculate these ratios correct to one place of decimals.

SELF-CHECK ▶
17.2

Using the following information calculate and comment on the liquidity position of firm X:

Balance Sheet (extract) of X as at 31 December 1987

Current assets:	£	Current liabilities:	£
Stock	16,000	Trade creditors	9,000
Debtors	4,000	Expense creditors	2,000
Bank	1,000		

$$\dfrac{\text{Current assets}}{\text{Current liabilities}} = \dfrac{21,000}{11,000} = 1.9:1$$

The current ratio shows the firm to be in a relatively safe liquidity position. Using this ratio, however, hides the influence of the very high stock figure. If the acid test is ratio used the result is less than satisfactory:

Acid test ratio $\dfrac{\text{Current assets} - \text{stock}}{\text{Current liabilities}} = \dfrac{5{,}000}{11{,}000} = 0.5{:}1$

To be able to comment further you would need more information. For example, what kind of business is it? How quickly could the stock be turned into cash? The latter question will be considered in the next section.

17.3 PRODUCTIVITY RATIOS

These help to measure the efficiency of a firm and, when used in conjunction with the profitability and liquidity ratios, enable a more complete evaluation of performance to be made.

1   Sales per employee (£) $\dfrac{\text{Sales}}{\text{Number of employees}}$

This measures the productivity of employees and the efficient use of the labour force by management. As with the profitability ratios valid comparisons can only be made with other similar firms, targets or past performances.

2   Stock turnover (times) $= \dfrac{\text{Cost of goods sold}}{\text{Average stock at cost price}}$

or

$$= \dfrac{\text{Sales}}{\text{Average stock at selling price}}$$

This measures the speed with which stock is being sold or 'turned over'. Information is usually given about stock at cost price since that is how it is valued for the final accounts. If, however, stock is given at selling price, the second formula will be quicker to use. If you have information about both the value of stock at selling price and cost price you should obtain the same answer whichever formula you use.

Calculating the average stock will usually be done by:

$$\dfrac{\text{Opening stock} + \text{Closing stock}}{2}$$

If you have access to monthly stock figures you would, of course, be able to take them all into account and divide by twelve to obtain an average for that year.

     The rate of stock turnover is usually expressed as so many times per annum. For example, firm Z's opening stock is valued at £5,000 and its closing stock at £7,000 – both at cost price. For the year ended 31 December 1987 its cost of goods sold was £36,000. Its rate of stock turnover for the year is:

$$\dfrac{36{,}000}{6{,}000} = 6$$

This means that on average during 1987 the firm turned its stock over six times. This can be used to calculate how long on average the stock was in the business before being sold. As there are twelve months in a year and the firm turned over its stock six times it is easy to see that the stock was in the business for two months on average before being sold. Whether this is a good rate of turnover will depend on what kind of things firm Z sells. Whether it is satisfactory to Z will also depend on what other firms have been achieving, what Z achieved last year and what target Z had set for this year.

It now becomes possible to say a little more about firm X in the last self-check. The acid test ratio revealed a dangerous level of illiquidity because stocks were very high. If the turnover rate for that firm was six times per annum it would re-inforce the concern. However, if the firm had a stock turnover rate of twenty-four, i.e. about every two weeks, there would be less reason to be concerned.

3   Debtor turnover (times) $= \dfrac{\text{Sales}}{\text{Debtors}}$

Debtor collection period (days) $= \dfrac{\text{Debtors}}{\text{Average sales per day}}$

These ratios measure the speed with which money owing from customers is collected. The higher the rate of collection or the lower the number of days it takes to collect the debts the better. It is a good way of assessing the efficiency of the arrangements for collecting debts and credit control. The debtor's figure used will be an average if more than one figure is available. It is usual to assume a 365-day year even if a business is only open for six days per week so the average daily sales is obtained by dividing the annual sales by 365.

Example
Firm Q had sales of £100,000 in 1987 and its average debtors were £8,000. Its debtors are being turned over 12.5 times per annum:

$$\frac{100,000}{8,000} = 12.5 \text{ times}$$

This would be considered very satisfactory by most firms as it means they are being paid on average within less than a month (a rate of 12 would be exactly one month). We can check this by using the alternative formula. First find the average daily sales:

$$\frac{100,000}{365} = £274 \text{ per day then:} \qquad \frac{8,000}{274} = 29 \text{ days.}$$

As with the other ratios we have used there is a danger in placing too much significance on it without further information. It is only an average. This could mean that some customers are paying up within a week while others are taking three months or more!

4 Creditor turnover (times) $= \dfrac{\text{Purchases}}{\text{Creditors}}$

Creditor payment period (days) $= \dfrac{\text{Creditors}}{\text{Average purchases per day}}$

This is similar in concept to the debtors ratios explained above. While a business would normally want its debtors to pay as promptly as possible it is advantageous to obtain as long a period of credit as possible in which to pay creditors. If a monthly figure is required, substitute the monthly figure in the second equation for both debtors and creditors.

SELF-CHECK ▶ 17.3

Learn all the profitability, liquidity and productivity ratios. You could practise using them on any of the final accounts contained in this book.

17.4 CASH FLOW STATEMENTS

When analysing the accounts of a business attention is often drawn to the fact that although a healthy profit may have been made this is not always reflected in a healthy cash balance. Preparing a cash flow statement to summarise the effects of cash inflows and outflows will show how this has happened. The following list contains the main **sources of cash**:

1 Trading profit before depreciation is deducted. Cash is generated from trading if there is an excess of cash received from sales over the cash paid out on operating expenses. Depreciation is not a cash expense, but involves the reduction in value of a fixed asset. The amount of depreciation for the year should therefore be excluded from the calculation of profit when profit is being used to assess the cash flow of a business. Trading profit is usually the most important cash source for a business.

2 Inputs of capital by the owner or owners.

3 Money borrowed by means of loans, debentures, mortgages etc., i.e. increases in long term liabilities.

4 Proceeds from the sale of fixed assets such as property.

5 Decreases in other current assets. By reducing the amount of money tied up in other current assets a business can increase its cash balance. For example, it could reduced the level of its debtors by persuading them to pay more promptly and thus generate more cash. Similarly it could reduce the level of stock by not replacing it when sold to generate more cash.

6 Increases in current liabilities. Delaying payment to creditors keeps cash in the business for a longer period.

The **uses** or **applications of cash** are the opposite events to the above:

1 Trading losses – where the cash paid for expenses is greater than the income from sales. (Remember to exclude the depreciation from the expenses.)
2 Drawings by the owner or owners.
3 Repayment of long term liabilities.
4 The purchase of fixed assets.
5 Increases in other current assets. For example, investing more money in stock.
6 Decreases in current liabilities. For example, using cash to reduce the amount owed to creditors.

When asked to prepare a cash flow statement you are normally given two balance sheets which contain information about the profit earned in a period. For example, suppose you are asked to construct a cash flow statement for Terry Yeo whose balance sheets have been summarised on page 343. These have been presented vertically for your convenience.

If the balance sheets are not arranged like this in a question it is worthwhile re-arranging them. Leave space alongside the balance sheet to analyse the applications and sources, using the lists above. It is then simply a question of finding the differences in each item for the liabilities and assets. You could do the same for the final capital figures, for these are the ones that count in the balance sheet. If you did so the change in capital would be a source of £7,000 because capital has increased from £57,000 to £64,000. However, since profit is usually the main source of funds and it is desirable to show it as an individual item it is better to show the whole profit as a source, i.e. £17,000 and the drawings for the year, £10,000 as an application. The net result is the same, i.e. an overall source of £7,000.

The bank figures have not been analysed because this is the change to which we are reconciling all the others. The cash flow statement can then be written out as on page 343.

Balance sheet of T. Yeo at 31 December

	1987	1988	Movement	
Fixed assets	50,000	65,000	15,000	A**
Current assets				
Stock	6,000	8,000	2,000	A
Debtors	3,000	4,000	1,000	A
Bank	2,000	....		*
	61,000	77,000		
Owner's capital at 1 Jan	55,000	57,000		
Profit for the year	6,000	17,000	17,000	S
	61,000	74,000		
less Drawings	4,000	10,000	10,000	A
Owner's capital at 31 Dec	57,000	64,000		
Current liabilities				
Creditors	4,000	6,000	2,000	S
Bank overdraft	....	7,000		*
	61,000	77,000		

Cash flow statement of T. Yeo for the year ended 31 December 1988

	£	£
Sources of cash		
Trading profit	17,000	
Increase in creditors	2,000	
		19,000
Applications of cash		
Drawings	10,000	
Purchase of fixed assets	15,000**	
Increase in stock	2,000	
Increase in debtors	1,000	
		28,000
Decrease in cash		9,000*

* The decrease in cash of £9,000 is accounted for by the reduction of the positive cash balance of £2,000 to an overdraft of £7,000. Questions involving overdraft situations at a time of profit are common in this area, as they highlight the fact that making good profits does not necessarily results in a healthy cash position.

** There is an assumption here that the £15,000 increase in fixed assets is the purchase figure and therefore an application. It is possible that depreciation on fixed assets for the year ended 31 December 1988 was, say, £5,000. If this is the case the application of finance to increase the fixed assets is really £20,000 and should be shown as such. For the fixed assets to have increased in value from £50,000 to £65,000 at a time when they have depreciated by £5,000 the purchase must have been £20,000. The amount of the depreciation should then be added back into the profit figure because depreciation is not a cash expense and should not be allowed to influence the amount of this source of cash. If you were told that depreciation for the year was £5,000, the cash flow statement would look like this:

Cash flow statement of T. Yeo for the year ended 31 December 1988

	£	£
Sources of cash		
Trading profit (17,000 + 5,000)	22,000	
Increase in creditors	2,000	
		24,000
Application of cash		
Drawings	10,000	
Purchase of fixed assets	20,000	
Increase in stock	2,000	
Increase in debtors	1,000	
		33,000
Decrease in cash		9,000

SELF-CHECK ▶ 17.4

Prepare S. Perks' cash flow statement for the year ended 31 December 1988 from the following information:

Balance Sheet of S. Perks as at 31 December

	1987	1988
Fixed assets	30,000	35,000
Current assets		
Stock	7,000	8,000
Debtors	6,000	4,000
Bank	3,000	....
	46,000	47,000
Owner's capital at 1 Jan	37,000	39,000
Profit for the year	8,000	14,000
	45,000	53,000
less Drawings	6,000	9,000
Owner's capital at 31 Dec	39,000	44,000
Current liabilities		
Creditors	7,000	2,000
Bank overdraft	....	1,000
	46,000	47,000

Note: Fixed assets had been depreciated by £3,000 during the year.

SOLUTION ▶

Balance Sheet of S. Perks as at 31 December

	1987	1988	Movement	
Fixed assets	30,000	35,000	5,000 + 3,000 depn	A
Current assets				
Stock	7,000	8,000	1,000	A
Debtors	6,000	4,000	2,000	S
Bank	3,000	.....		
	46,000	47,000		
Owner's capital at 1 Jan	37,000	39,000		
Profit for the year	8,000	14,000	14,000	S
	45,000	53,000		
less Drawings	6,000	9,000	9,000	A
Owner's capital at 31 Dec	39,000	44,000		
Current liabilities				
Creditors	7,000	2,000	5,000	A
Bank overdraft	....	1,000		
	46,000	47,000		

Value of fixed assets at 31.12.87	£30,000
less Depreciation for year to 31.12.88	3,000
Value of *same* fixed assets at 31.12.88	27,000
Value of fixed assets at 31.12.88	35,000
Therefore new fixed assets purchased =	8,000

Cash flow statement of S. Perks for the year ended 31 December 1988

	£	£
Sources of cash		
Trading profit before depreciation (14,000 + 3,000)	17,000	
Decrease in debtors	2,000	
		19,000
Application of cash		
Drawings	9,000	
Purchase of fixed assets	8,000	
Increase in stock	1,000	
Decrease in creditors	5,000	
		23,000
Decrease in cash		4,000

17.5 BREAK-EVEN ANALYSIS

This analysis may be very useful in management accounting. The break-even point is the output or sales at which neither a profit nor a loss is being made, i.e. total costs incurred are exactly equal to the total revenue earned. It is a key point because in most businesses losses are made initially. Profits are gained only when production expands. The arrival of the break-even point thus signals the end of the loss making stage and the arrival of profits. A break-even chart contains a great deal of information about a business or one product of a business. For example, a manufacturer is considering whether to go ahead with production of a new product called Diaron. The following information has been obtained:

Expected sales: 20,000 at £5 per unit.
Total fixed costs: £20,000.
Variable costs: £3 per unit.

The management would like to know how many Diarons have to be sold before it breaks even. This information can be calculated by the following formula:

$$\text{Break-even point in numbers of units} = \frac{\text{Total fixed cost}}{\text{Contribution per unit}}$$

Contribution per unit refers to the amount of the selling price that contributes towards meeting the fixed costs. In order to contribute towards the fixed costs the variable cost of one unit must first be met.

Thus contribution per unit = selling price of one unit less variable cost of one unit.

Using the above figures the contribution per unit will be:

£5 (selling price) − £3 (variable cost of one unit) = £2.

Therefore break-even point = $\dfrac{£20,000 \text{ (fixed costs)}}{£2 \text{ (contribution per unit)}}$ = 10,000 units.

The same information can be shown by constructing a break-even chart. Study the example below which has been constructed from the figures relating to the Diaron product.

Figure 17.5 Break-even chart for Diaron

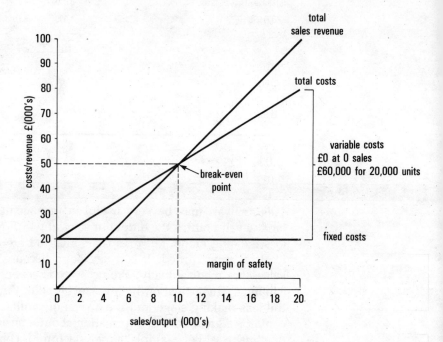

The horizontal axis is always used to show the number of sales and the vertical axis to show sales and costs in money values. After choosing suitable scales, the chart is prepared as follows:

1 The fixed costs are shown as a straight line parallel to the horizontal axis. In this case it shows that whatever the output the total fixed costs are £20,000.

2 The easiest way to plot the total revenue line is to calculate the total revenue obtained from selling all of the product – 20,000 × £5 = £100,000. Plot this point against the numbers of diarons to be sold (20,000). A straight line joining this point to 0 will show the revenue for any number of sales at any point on the line.

3 The total cost line is obtained by adding on the variable costs to the fixed cost. The easiest way to do this on the chart is to do so for 20,000 sales. With a variable cost of £3 per unit the total variable cost for 20,000 sales will be £3 × 20,000 = £60,000. As fixed costs are £20,000 this means that the total costs for 20,000 sales will be £80,000. (Fixed

costs £20,000 + variable costs £60,000 = total costs £80,000.) Plot this point against 20,000 sales and draw a line to the fixed cost line. Where it meets the fixed cost line at 0 sales the total cost is only the fixed cost. There is no variable cost until one unit is produced.

4   The break-even point will be where the total revenue line and the total cost line cross, i.e. the point at which they are equal. This illustrates the calculation made earlier. In terms of sales, break-even is obtained at 10,000. In terms of revenue, or costs, the vertical axis shows it takes place at £50,000, i.e. 10,000 × £5 selling price.

As well as showing the break-even point this chart also shows:

(a)   The loss made up to this point. This is given by the area of the triangle made between the total sales revenue line and the total cost line *before* break-even.

(b)   The profit made after this point. This is given by area of the triangle between total sales revenue and total cost lines *after* break-even.

(c)   The variable costs at any sales level. This can be seen as the difference between the total costs and fixed cost at the sales level.

(d)   The margin of safety. This is the difference between the total expected sales and the break-even point. In this case 20,000 less 10,000 = 10,000. In other words the company could sell 10,000 less than it hopes and still not actually make a loss.

The usefulness of the break-even chart can be seen if it is necessary to vary any one of the predicted facts: variable cost, fixed cost, selling price or sales target.

SELF-CHECK ▶
17.5

Calculate the break-even point for expected sales of 20,000 diarons if selling price remained at £5 and variable costs at £3 per unit but fixed costs were: (a) £30,000 or (b) £10,000.

SOLUTION ▶

$$\text{Break-even point in numbers of units} = \frac{\text{Total fixed cost}}{\text{Contribution per unit}}$$

(a) $\dfrac{£30,000}{£5-£3} = \dfrac{30,000}{2} = 15,000 \text{ units}$

(b) $\dfrac{10,000}{5-3} = \dfrac{10,000}{2} = 5,000 \text{ units.}$

COMMENT ▶

You might find it useful to draw a chart for each of these situations to re-inforce the technique.

17.6 PERSONAL MONEY MANAGEMENT AND HOUSEHOLD ACCOUNTS

It is important to realise that there is nothing so special about accounting that it must be done only by accountants. Recording transactions (book-keeping); reporting to others about financial matters (financial accounting); and controlling and planning (management accounting) are all undertaken by individuals in their ordinary daily lives. Provided you understand the techniques of business accounting, household accounts should cause no problem. Of course, the system of book-keeping used is more likely to be a simple cash book than double entry. Keeping some sort of record of receipts and payments is the starting point. When a bank statement arrives it is very useful to be able to reconcile it with your records. A student who wishes to justify to his parents that he can afford to run a motor cycle might prepare a statement of his income and expenditure similar to a profit and loss account to back his argument. He will be carrying out the role of a financial accountant though he might think that this is too grand a name for what he is doing. Similarly, a housewife who is trying to plan a future holiday for her family will be acting as a management accountant when she costs out various alternative ways of saving money. For example, deciding whether her children should have school lunches or take their own. If faced with a problem involving personal money management you are advised to use the same techniques you have learnt to handle business affairs. Just adapt them to suit the circumstances of the case.

SELF-CHECK ▶
17.6

Review the business accounting procedures you have encountered and list the areas which have greatest relevance to personal money management and household accounts.

17.7 ACCOUNTING CONCEPTS AND CONVENTIONS

Accounting concepts are the rules that are followed to ensure objectivity when preparing and using accounting records. The way in which these concepts are interpreted is governed by conventions. These are practices which are both generally accepted and applied. Although a number of these have already been referred to specifically, it will be useful to summarise them here.

CONCEPTS OF ACCOUNTING

(a)   **Business entity concept** refers to the need to regard the owner or owners of a business as completely separate to the business.

(b)   **Money measurement concept** refers to the fact that accounts can only show items that have a money value.

(c)   **Cost concept** refers to the basis of valuation for assets. This should be at cost price except for special cases; for example, the need to increase the valuation of premises to reflect changing property values; or to value stock below cost price if the replacement price is lower.

(d)   **Going concern concept** refers to the fact that when accounts are prepared it is assumed that the business will continue to operate indefinitely.

(*e*)   **Realization concept** refers to the fact that profit is regarded as having been earned at the time when the goods or services are supplied to the customer.

(*f*)   **Accruals (matching) concept** refers to the need to charge expenses against profits in the period that the profits have been earned.

CONVENTIONS OF ACCOUNTING

(*a*)   **Materiality** refers to the need to decide for each business when to record a purchase as an expense and when to record it as an asset. For example, a small garage may decide to include purchases of a small number of new spanners as equipment and therefore as a balance sheet item, whereas a large national organisation might regard such a small purchase as an expense to be charged against profits.

(*b*)   **Conservatism** refers to the need for caution, especially with regard to profits. Profit should not be anticipated; for example, by valuing unsold stock at its *expected* selling price.

(*c*)   **Consistency** refers to the need for the same methods to be used when completing accounts. For example, if LIFO is the basis of stock valuation that method should not be changed unless there is good reason and the change is clearly shown.

SELF-CHECK ▶
17.7

Learn the above concepts and conventions.

17.8 REVIEW QUESTIONS

Most of the GCSE examination papers contain a number of short answer questions of various types. These questions tend to range over the whole syllabus area and provide a useful revision tool. If you are not able to answer them immediately you should be able to find solutions within the book.

1   (*a*)   What is the difference between VAT inputs and VAT outputs?

(*b*)   What is the purpose of a credit note?

(*c*)   S. Jones, a trader, has received an invoice for £350 from one of her suppliers. Name the subsidiary book in which this invoice will be recorded.

(*d*)   J. Brown has balanced his cash book for the month of March and he finds that the bank column has a balance of £250 which has been carried down to the credit side of the account. What does this balance represent?   (NISEC specimen paper)

2   From the list of items at the end of this question, select the correct word or phrase to complete each of the following blanks in the

sentences. Write your answers in the spaces provided in each sentence.

(*a*)   The amount by which a club's income exceeds its expenditure is known as a ~~Surplus~~ but if the expenditure exceeds the income the difference is called a ~~deficit~~.

(*b*)   Carriage inwards is an _____ item which when preparing the final accounts should always be entered on the _____ side of the _____ account.

(*c*)   The difference between the current assets and the current liabilities of a business is known as _____ but the total of all the money invested in the business is known as the _____.

(*d*)   When stock taking, goods should be valued at _____ price or _____ price, whichever is the lower.

(*e*)   The purchase of fixed assets is known as _____ expenditure but the payment of expenses is _____ expenditure.

(*f*)   The cost of goods sold divided by the average stock indicates the _____.

(*g*)   When a trial balance does not agree, and the error cannot be found, the difference is placed in a _____ account.

(*h*)   If the purchase of an asset, e.g. machinery, is debited in error to an expense account the _____ account will be understated in the profit and loss account, and the total of _____ will be understated in the balance sheet.

Surplus	Manufacturing	Deficit
Suspense	Net profit	Fixed assets
Debit	Cost	Selling
Trading	Capital employed	Rate of stock
Expense	Capital	turnover
Revenue	Working capital	

(London and East Anglian Group)

3   (*a*)   What type of discount is **not** recorded in the ledger accounts?

(*b*)   Explain the term 'error of commission'.

(*c*)   Where is a prepayment shown in the balance sheet?

(*d*)   What is meant by an accrual?

(*e*)   When partners adopt the 'fixed capital method', what additional partners' accounts are used?

(*f*)   By what name is the excess of the current assets over current liabilities known?

(MEG specimen paper)

17.1

The following details relate to J. King's business for the year ending 31 December 1986.

Trading and profit and loss account of J. King for year ending 31 December 1986

		£			£	£
Stock (1.1.86)		7,000	Sales		42,000	
add Purchases	(i)		less Returns		2,000	40,000
		35,000				
less Stock (31.12.86)	(ii)					
Cost of goods sold	(iii)					
Gross profit		10,000				
		40,000				40,000
Expenses	(iv)		Gross profit			10,000
Net profit		4,000				
		10,000				10,000

(a)   Write in the missing values at (i), (ii), (iii) and (iv) above.
(b)   Calculate the following:
(i) Rate of stock turnover
(ii) Gross profit as a percentage of turnover
(iii) Net profit as a percentage of turnover.

(NEA specimen paper)

17.2

The following balances at 31 December 1985 have been extracted from the books of F. Lion.

	£
Premises at cost	70,000
Wages and salaries	21,000
Rates	1,500
Electricity	520
Purchases	49,000
Stock at 1 January 1985	2,600
Carriage outwards	96
Sales	84,690
Returns inwards	71
Motor vans at cost	5,000
Provision for depreciation on motor vans at 1 January 1985	3,000
Mortgage on premises	20,000

Administration expenses	11,200
Creditors	2,690
Insurance	240
Debtors	3,140
Cash in hand	526
Bank overdraft	1,400
Capital at 1 January 1985	66,226
Drawings	13,113

The following additional information relates to the year ended 31 December 1985:

	£
Electricity accrued at 31 December 1985	300
Insurance prepaid at 31 December 1985	120
Motor vans to be depreciated by	1,000
A provision for bad debts of 5% is to be created on debtors at 31 December 1985	
Stock at 31 December 1985	3,200

Required

(a)   For F. Lion, making year end adjustments, where needed
(i) a trading account for the year ended 31 December 1985
(ii) a profit and loss account for the year ended 31 December 1985
(iii) a balance sheet as at 31 December 1985 distinguishing between fixed and current assets and long term and current liabilities.

Required

(b)   (i) An assessment of the profitability and liquidity of F. Lion's business.
(ii) Your opinion on the profitability of F. Lion's business, giving reasons to support your argument.
(iii) TWO other bases of comparison (not available in the data given in this question) that would make an overall appraisal of F. Lion's business more meaningful.

(SEG specimen paper)

17.3   The following are the summarised trading and profit and loss accounts for the year 1985/6 and the balance sheets as at 30 June 1986 of Fox Ltd and Badger Ltd.

Trading and profit and loss account (1986/7)

	Fox £	Badger £		Fox £	Badger £
Stock (1.7.85)	48,000	8,000	Sales	360,000	360,000
Purchases	319,000	324,000	Stock (30.6.86)	52,000	12,000
Gross profit	45,000	40,000			
	412,000	372,000		412,000	372,000
Expenses	16,200	17,600	Gross profit	45,000	40,000
Net profit	28,800	22,400			
	45,000	40,000		45,000	40,000

Balance Sheet

	Fox £	Badger £		Fox £	Badger £
Issued share capital	100,000	100,000	Fixed assets	127,800	107,500
Reserves	80,000	16,000	Stock	52,000	12,000
Profit and loss account	60,000	24,000	Debtors	40,000	24,000
Creditors	63,800	40,500	Bank	84,000	37,000
	303,800	180,500		303,800	180,500

You are required to set out and complete a table in the following form:

	Fox Ltd	Badger Ltd
(i) Gross profit as percentage of sales		
(ii) Stock turn		
(iii) Debtors ratio (in months)		
(iv) Creditor ratio (in months)		
(v) Current ratio		
(vi) Liquid ratio		
(vii) Working capital		
(viii) Return on total assets employed		

You may assume that the stock of each company has been built up from an amount at 1 July to the amount at 30 June at an even rate during the year.

In relation to the liquid ratio trade debtors are to be treated as liquid assets. Calculations to two decimal places.

(WJEC specimen paper)

17.4 Smith and Jones, accountants, receive a message from Mr B. Ward, a client who has just completed his second year of trading.

'I just don't understand this Balance Sheet you have sent me. What is a Balance Sheet? And why are last year's figures shown?

'I have worked really hard this year to reduce my overdraft and debtors so as to give me more working capital. What have I done wrong?

'Finally, please explain why my capital is less when my total assets have increased.

'I look forward to receiving your report.'

Balance Sheet of B. Ward as at 31 May 1986 (and 1985)

	1986 £	(1985) £		1986 £	(1985) £
Fixed assets (at cost)	6,500	5,000	Capital	12,100	12,000
Additions during year	2,800	1,500	Net profit/loss	(700)	1,600
	9,300	6,500		11,400	13,600
less Depreciation	1,800	1,300	Drawings	1,700	1,500
	7,500	5,200		9,700	12,100
Current assets			Bank loan	2,300	1,000
Stock	4,200	5,000			
Debtors	3,300	5,050	**Current liabilities**		
Bank balance	1,000	—	Creditors	4,000	1,650
			Bank overdraft	—	500
	16,000	15,250		16,000	15,250

You are required to write a reply in report form (i.e. numbered points) answering Mr Ward's queries. (NEA specimen paper)

17.5

Plowden Manufacturing PLC has produced the following information from which to produce a cash budget for the six months ended 30 June 1985.

Sales	Oct	Nov	Dec	Jan	Feb	Mar	Apr	May	June	July	Aug
(Units)	90	80	70	60	90	120	140	150	180	—	—
Production (units)	100	90	60	90	110	130	160	200	210	230	200

(i) The selling price of £18 per unit is received three months after the sale.

(ii) Raw materials used in production cost £6 per unit, and are paid for two months before being used in the factory.

(iii) Direct labour of £4 per unit is paid for in the same month as the unit is produced.

(iv) Other variable expenses of £3 per unit are paid for, ⅔ in the same month as production, and ⅓ in the month following.

(v) Fixed expenses of £150 per month are payable one month in arrears.

(vi) New equipment is to be installed in December 1984 and paid for in March 1985, £3,400.

Requirement:

(a)   Produce the relevant receipts and payments schedules.

(b)   Produce the firm's cash budget for the six months ended 30 June 1985.

(c)   Offer advice which you consider might be helpful to management as a result of what your cash budget reveals.

(NISEC specimen paper)

17.6

(a)   Mr and Mrs Pearson keep a detailed record of their personal income and expenditure. The following record is available for the first two weeks of May 1981. Write up a two-column cash book, and balance it.

		£
May 1	Cash in house	2.69
	Cash at bank	506.50
2	Drew from the bank current account	50.00
	Paid the following:	
	Grocer	25.00
	Butcher	9.35
	Greengrocer	4.77
4	Bought petrol for car (cash)	9.00

May 5	Paid by cheque rates for the half year	176.48
	9 Drew from bank current account	60.00
	Paid the following:	
	Grocer	26.50
	Butcher	8.50
	Greengrocer	3.75
	Chemist	1.50
	11 Petrol for car (cash)	9.00
	Car service paid by cheque	22.50
	13 Shoe repairs paid in cash	4.30

14 Bought a new suit for Mr Pearson. The suit cost £95 and the amount was paid through a credit card account.
Received notice that two weeks' wages had been paid into the bank … £210.

(b)   Prepare an analysed statement of income and expenditure for the period 1 May to 14 May 1981. In your statement use the following headings:

Food; Medical; Travel; Clothing; Housing.

(c)   Write a brief explanation of your treatment of the £95 paid for the suit.   (LEAG specimen paper)

17.7   Jenny White proposes to set up her own business making soft toys. She has approached department stores and specialist shops and has been assured of orders. Based on this canvassing, she is confident that the following forecasts are reasonably accurate for the four months 1 July 1986 to 31 October 1986.

1   She will be able to put £5,000 cash into the business on 1 July 1986.
2   Sales:

July	Aug	Sept	Oct
£	£	£	£
1,250	2,900	3,300	3,600

Two month's credit will have to be given to buyers.
3   Purchases of raw materials:

July	Aug	Sept	Oct
£	£	£	£
1,000	1,200	1,250	1,350

These are paid for one month after purchase.
4   Wages costs will be £600 per month, payable the same month.
5   Fixed expenses £200 per month will be paid one month in arrears.
6   Other expenses will be £120 per month for July and August and £160 per month thereafter. One quarter of these monthly expenses will be paid in the following month.

7   Sewing machines costing £1,550 will be paid for in August.

QUESTIONS

(a)   Prepare a forecast cash budget for the four months ending 31 October 1986 showing clearly the cash balance at the end of each month.

(b)   Suggest how the problem of a forecast cash deficit could be dealt with, assuming that the problem, if it arises, is short term.

(MEG specimen paper)

17.8   Carol McNeill is employed as a sales representative earning £10,000 per annum. Her husband has a full-time job as a word processor operator at a salary of £4,000 per annum. They have savings of £10,000 in a building society account at an interest rate of 10% per annum.

Carol's grandfather died recently and Carol will receive the sum of £30,000 under the terms of her grandfather's will.

Carol and her husband have been discussing what to do with the money. They decide that it must be ONE of the following three alternatives.

Either   Option A

Add it to their existing savings and continue their jobs.

or   Option B

Buy a retailer's business which operates from rented premises. The price for the goodwill, fittings and stock is £40,000. They would not wish to borrow any money to finance the purchase. Mr and Mrs McNeill would not continue to employ the assistant who is helping the present owner but would run the business themselves. The assistant earns £2,500 per year but any redundancy money due would be paid by the present owner. The summarised figures taken from the recent audited accounts are:

Annual sales	£140,000
Gross profit margin	30%
Overhead expenses	£22,500

or   Option C

Invest the late grandfather's money in a friend's company which requires funds for expansion. Carol has the opportunity to buy one third of the issued ordinary share capital. This would enable the company to increase its sales and her friend estimates that the net profit would rise by 50% from its present level of £20,000. It is the company's policy to pay out half the profits to its shareholders and this policy would continue. Neither Carol nor her husband would take any part in running the company.

QUESTIONS

(*a*)   Prepare financial summaries for each of these three possible courses of action so that Carol and her husband can compare the total incomes they would receive under each option.

(*b*)   Comment on the results obtained in part (*a*) and outline any other factors which you feel the McNeills should consider before making a final decision.

(*c*)   Indicate which course of action you would recommend. Give reasons.

(MEG specimen paper)

17.9   The balance sheets below are those of Winston Baines, who prepares his accounts annually to 31 December.

Balance Sheet as at 31 December

	1984 £	1985 £		1984 £	1985 £
Capital, 1 January	8,000	8,200	Fixed assets, at cost	5,800	8,800
Profit for the year	2,600	3,200	*less* Provision for depreciation	600	1,200
Additional capital introduced	—	1,200			
				5,200	7,600
	10,600	12,600	Stock	2,600	2,200
less Drawings	2,400	3,000	Debtors	1,400	1,800
			Bank	800	
	8,200	9,600			
Creditors	1,800	1,400			
Bank overdraft	—	600			
	10,000	11,600		10,000	11,600

Winston cannot understand why his bank balance is now overdrawn at 31 December 1985.

QUESTIONS

(*a*)   Prepare an appropriate financial statement to explain to Winston Baines how, despite additional capital and profit, his bank balance has become overdrawn.

(b)   The following additional information is available:

Sales   £16,000

Cost of sales   £9,600

Calculate

(i) the average collection period for debtors.

(ii) the rate of stock turnover (stock turn).

(iii) the gross profit mark up.

(MEG specimen paper)

FOREWORD TO
SOLUTIONS

Lack of space means that it is not possible to provide fully worked answers to all exercises. In addition, not all the examining boards permit the publication of solutions or guidance. The solutions that follow are the author's responsibility and do not necessarily constitute the only acceptable solution. Solutions to questions requiring a balance sheet have been given on the assumption that a vertical balance sheet has been prepared and that the equation used is:

Fixed assets + Current assets − Current liabilities = Long term Liabilities + Capital.

SOLUTIONS TO EXERCISES

1.1 (a) Capital £10,710
     (b) Assets £29,620
     (c) Capital £26,187
     (d) Liabilities £29,170
     (e) Deficiency of capital £13,040.

1.2 (a) £56,550
     (b) (i) Totals £72,300; (ii) Totals £71,550.

1.3 Balance Sheet items 6 June: Equipment £3,000; Fittings £400; Stock £6,000; Bank £4,000; Cash £600; Creditor £4,000; Capital £10,000.

1.4 Balance Sheet items 5 March: Cash £12,800; Capital £12,800.

1.5 Capital £44,800.

1.6 Capital £55,631; Totals £63,631.

1.7 £10,000.

2.1 Items (*b*), (*d*) and (*f*) are capital expenditure. The others are revenue expenditure and will be used in measuring profit.

2.2 Items (*a*) and (*c*) are capital receipts. Items (*b*) and (*d*) are revenue receipts.

2.3 Net profit £16,659.

2.5 Items (*a*), (*d*) and (*g*) are capital expenditure. The others are revenue expenditure.

CHAPTER 3

3.1 Premises a/c: Dr M1 balance £33,000.
Equipment a/c: Dr M1 balance £15,000; M2 bank £1,500. Cr M4 bank £2,000.
Debtors a/c: Dr M1 balance £5,500.
Stock a/c: Dr M1 balance £17,000.
Bank a/c: Dr M1 balance £1,250; M4 equipment £2,000; M7 sales £500.
Cr M2 equipment £1,500; M6 creditors £300.
Creditors a/c: Dr M6 bank £300. Cr M1 balance £6,750.
Capital a/c: Cr M1 balance £65,000.
Purchases a/c: Dr M3 AJK £950.
AJK a/c: Cr M3 purchases £950.
Sales a/c: Cr M7 bank £500.

3.2

Bank a/c

Date			Date		
1 April	Balance	1,560	2 April	Rates	250
4 April	Rent received	60	3 April	Wages	620
7 April	Insurance	12	5 April	Insurance	120
			6 April	Rent received	10
			8 April	Drawings	100

3.3   (a)   DIY Supplies Ledger

Bill Lewis a/c

1 June	Balance	250	6 June	Returns in	75
3 June	Sales	458	9 June	Bank	240
			9 June	Discount allowed	10

(b)   Bill Lewis' Ledger

DIY Suplies a/c

6 June	Returns out	75	1 June	Balance	250
9 June	Bank	240	3 June	Purchases	458
9 June	Discount received	10			

3.4   (a)   Zoe Clough's Ledger

Peter Blake a/c

5 April	Bank	441	1 April	Balance	450
5 April	Discount received	9	3 April	Purchases	356
6 April	Returns out	20			

(b)   Peter Blake's Ledger

Zoe Clough a/c

1 April	Balance	450	5 April	Bank	441
3 April	Sales	356	5 April	Discount allowed	9
			6 April	Returns in	20

3.5   Tom Scott a/c

3 May	Sales	450	29 May	Cash	150
			31 Aug	Bad debts	300
		450			450

Bad debts a/c

31 Aug	Tom Scott	300			

3.7

VAT a/c

7 Jan	T. Rees	18	5 Jan	B. Dale	42
9 Jan	D. Wilkins	21	8 Jan	H. Davies	39

CHAPTER 4

4.1

(a)   £276 dr balance means that Smith is a debtor to Highgate for that amount.

(b)   1 Feb   Smith owed Highgate £350

4 Feb   Highgate sold £234 goods to Smith on credit

7 Feb   Smith returned £58 goods to Highgate

9 Feb   Smith paid Highgate £243 by cheque, having deducted £7 discount.

4.2

(a)   Balance sheet should show owner's capital, £14,178.

(d)   Trial Balance

	Dr	Cr
Bank	1,130	
Stock	8,575	
Cash	695	
F & F	9,000	
Loan		5,000
Capital		14,178
Sales		1,421
Purchases	1,544	
Creditors		660
Rent	160	
Trade debtors	20	
Wages	90	
Insurance	45	
	21,259	21,259

4.3

Suspense a/c

31 July	Error in books	124	19 Aug	Country supplies	124

Country Supplies a/c

19 Aug	Suspense a/c	124			

4.5

John Evans a/c

1 April	Evans owes Eastern £600
10 April	Eastern sold £600 goods on credit to Evans
12 April	Evans paid Eastern £580 by cheque, having deducted discount allowed of £20. This settled the amount due on 1 April
16 April	Evans returned £10 worth of goods to Eastern
30 April	Evans owes Eastern £590

Welsh Meat Supplies PLC a/c

1 April	Eastern owes WMS £650
18 April	Eastern paid WMS £600 by cheque, having deducted £50 discount received. This settled the amount due on 1 April
20 April	Eastern purchased £400 worth of goods on credit from WMS
30 April	Eastern owes WMS £400

Vehicles and Equipment

1 April	Eastern possesses V&E valued at £10,000
10 April	Eastern sold V&E for £2,000, received by cheque
28 April	Purchased V&E for £5,000 from MTSA on credit
30 April	Eastern possesses V&E valued at £13,000

4.6   (*a*)   (ii) Trial balance totals £13,215.

CHAPTER 5

5.1   Gross profit £24,680; Net profit £22,355.

5.2   Gross profit £48,497.

5.3　Gross profit £51,915; Net profit £28,381; Balance Sheet totals £49,881 (note: depreciation has already been deducted from fixed assets).

5.4　(a) and (b)　Gross profit £24,512.
(c)

Stock a/c

1 May	Balance	b/d	4,870	31 Oct	Trans. to Trading a/c		4,870
31 Oct	Trading	a/c	6,870	31 Oct	Balance	c/d	6,870
1 Nov	Balance	b/d	6,870				

5.5　Gross profit £39,187 (note: wages in trading a/c); Net profit £26,074; Balance Sheet totals £70,074.

5.6　(a)　(i) £10,390; (ii) £11,790; (iii) £1,400; (iv) £1,000.
(b)　(i) £4,000; (ii) £2,880; (iii) £3,270; (iv) £4,810.

CHAPTER 6

6.1

Rent a/c

1987/8			£	1988			£
1 July	Cash book		300	30 June	Profit and loss a/c		1,200
5 Oct	Cash book		300	30 June	Balance prepaid c/d		300
4 Jan	Cash book		300				
4 April	Cash book		300				
6 June	Cash book		300				
			1,500				1,500
1988							
1 July	Balance prepaid	b/d	£300				

Balance Sheet: Current assets – rent prepaid £300.
Profit and loss a/c: Expenses – rent £1,200.

6.2
- (b)   P&L a/c £285; BS £165
- (c)   prepaid £71; BS £71
- (d)   Dr £10,096; BS £264
- (e)   Dr £1,556; Prepaid £300
- (f)   Prepaid £125; P&L £871.

6.3   Profit and loss a/c: Expenses – wages £54,191; Balance Sheet: Current liabilities – wages due £735.

6.4
- (b)   P&L a/c £728; BS £232
- (c)   Accrued £225; BS £225
- (d)   Cr £9,301; BS £156
- (e)   Cr £18,738; Accrued £830
- (f)   Accrued £129; P&L a/c £692.

6.5   P&L a/c: Rent received £1,050; BS: Current liabilities – rent received in advance £200.

6.6   £889.

6.7   Gross profit £47,250; Net profit £26,780; BS totals £123,980.

CHAPTER 7

7.1

Bad debts a/c

1987		£	1987		£
....	Sundry debtors	165	31 Dec	Trans to P&L a/c	165

Provision for bad debts a/c

1987			£	1987			£
31 Dec	Balance	c/d	138	31 Dec	Profit & loss a/c		138
				1988			
				1 Jan	Balance	b/d	138

Profit and Loss a/c

Expenses:	£
Bad debts	165
Provision for bad debts	138

Balance Sheet

Current assets:	£	£
Debtors	2,760	
less PBD	138	2,622

7.2

Provision for bad debts a/c

1987			£	1987			£
....	Sundry debtorts		110	1 Jan	Balance	c/d	145
31 Dec	Balance	c/d	225	31 Dec	Profit & loss a/c		190
			335				335
				1988			
				1 Jan	Balance	b/d	225

Profit and loss a/c

Expenses:	£
Provision for bad debts	190

Balance Sheet

Current asssets:	£	£
Debtors	4,500	
less PBD	225	4,275

7.3   Provision for bad debts a/c

1987			£	1987			£
....	Bad debts		540	1 Jan	Balance	b/d	450
				....	Bad debts recovered		70
31 Dec	Balance	c/d	384	31 Dec	Profit & loss a/c		404
			924				924
				1988			
				1 Jan	Balance	b/d	384

Profit and loss a/c   Balance Sheet

Expenses:	£	Current assets:	£	£
Provision for bad debts	404	Debtors	9,600	
		less PBD	384	9,216

CHAPTER 8

8.1   1985: £2,500; £2,500; £7,500
1986: £1,875; £4,375; £5,625
1987: £1,406; £5,781; £4,219

8.2   Depreciation £2,500 per annum; accumulated depreciation to 31 Dec 1987 £7,500; asset value at 31 Dec 1987 £2,500.

8.5
(a)   Motor vehicle disposal a/c

	£		£
Motor vehicle at cost	9,000	Accum depn to date	4,750
		Sale of vehicle	4,000
		Loss on sale	250
	9,000		9,000

Profit and loss a/c: Expenses – loss on sale of vehicle £250.

(b)   Motor vehicle disposal a/c

	£		£
Motor vehicle at cost	9,000	Accum depn to date	4,750
Profit on sale	750	Sale of vehicle	5,000
	9,750		9,750

Profit and loss a/c	£
Gross profit	×
Add Profit on sale of vehicle	750

8.7   Gross profit £19,010; Net profit £9,230; Balance Sheet totals £14,230.

CHAPTER 9

9.1   (a)   GL;
                 (b)   CB;
                 (c)   GL;
                 (d)   PL;
                 (e)   GL.

9.2   (a)   Personal;
                 (b)   Nominal;
                 (c)   Real;
                 (d)   Real;
                 (e)   Nominal;
                 (f)   Personal;
                 (g)   Nominal;
                 (h)   Personal.

9.3   Discount allowed total £14.00; Discount received total £30.00; Cash balance £395.83 (dr); Bank balance £365.63 (dr).

9.4

Bank reconciliation statement

	£
Balance as per cash book	2,800
add: Receipt from debtor	500
Dividend	100
	3,400
less Charges	25
*Amended cash book balance	3,375
add: Unpresented cheques	3,500
Direct debit	50
Standing order	75
Balance as per bank statement	7,000

*Note: In this question you were not asked to bring the cash book up to date before doing the bank reconciliation. It is therefore possible to bring the cash book up to date within the reconciliation statement.

9.6

(a)　Closing balance £4.17; Total expenses £40.83; Canteen total £11.34; Travelling total £10.35; Postage total £11.60; Cleaning total £7.54.

9.8

(c)　Total expenses £28.76; Postages total £14.30; Stationery £6.50; Office expenses £7.96.

9.9   (b)   (ii)

Bank reconciliation statement

	£
Amended cash book balance	654
add Unpresented cheques:	109
	72
	835
less Lodgement	186
Balance as per bank statement	649

9.10   (a)   Discount allowed total £38; Cash balance £109 (dr); Bank balance £1,580 (dr).
(d)   Actual bank balance £1,550.

CHAPTER 10

10.1   (a)   Purchases journal:
(b)   Returns outward journal;
(c)   Sales journal;
(d)   Returns inward journal.

10.2   Sales journal total £921.29; Sales a/c Cr £921.29; Baxter a/c Dr £218.35; Carter a/c Dr £134.43 etc.

10.3   Returns inward journal total £262.25; Returns inward a/c £262.25; Gregg a/c Cr £28.79; Hector a/c Dr £79.78 etc.

10.4   (a)   Dr Motor vehicles; Cr Abbot Motors
(b)   Dr Sales; Cr Trading a/c
(c)   Dr T. Hall £1,200; Cr Delivery vehicle £1,000; Cr Profit on sale of vehicle £200.
(d)   Dr Bad debts; Cr Sundry debtors

(e)   Dr Bly £390, Dr Loss on sale of equipment £60; Equipment £450.

10.5   Totals equal – no error revealed.

10.6   Dr total £80,035; Cr total £82,035 – therefore error in books.

10.7   (a)   Capital £48,050;
(b)   Sales day book total £1,340; Purchases day book total £276; Sales returns book £72 (note: do not allow the list price for returns as trade discount has been deducted).

10.9 (c)   (i)   Journal

	Dr £	Cr £
1. Suspence a/c	180	
Motor van a/c		180
2. Purchases a/c	90	
Suspense a/c		90
3. Drawings a/c	140	
Wages a/c		140
4. Diane Jones (creditor)	25	
Suspense a/c		25

(ii)   Suspense a/c

	£		£
Motor vehicle	180	Error in books	65
		Purchases	90
		D. Jones	25
	180		180

(iii)   Trial balance totals £232,850.

CHAPTER 11

11.1   (*a*)   Appropriation a/c: share of profits R £4,500; B £3,000; G £1,500.

(*b*)   Current a/cs: R £6,100 Cr balance; B £4,250; G £2,350.

11.2   (*a*)   Appropriation a/c: share of profits   B $\frac{4}{9}$ £8,000

L $\frac{3}{9}$ £6,000

W $\frac{2}{9}$ £4,000

Current a/cs: B £9,800 Cr balance; L £7,790 Cr balance; W £3,100 Cr balance.

11.3   (*c*)   Current a/cs: Exworth £3,920 Cr; Young £2,140 Cr.

(*d*)   Balance sheet totals £96,060.

CHAPTER 12

12.1   Profit and loss a/c balance £59,900; Balance Sheet totals £384,900.

12.2   Gross profit £74,200; Net profit £30,850; Appropriation a/c balance £35,750; Balance Sheet totals £85,750.

12.3   (*b*)   Working capital £155,000.

12.4   Appropriation a/c balance £39,600; Balance Sheet totals £316,600.

12.5   Appropriation a/c balance £47,200; Balance Sheet totals £256,200.

CHAPTER 13

13.1   (*a*)   Prime cost £37,106; Factory cost of goods completed £60,061
      (*b*)   Cost of goods sold £67,461; Gross profit £20,789.

13.2   (*d*)   (i) £20,500
             (ii) £56,000
             (iii) £62,900
             (iv) £61,900
             (v) £43,100

13.3   (*a*)   Cash balance to be banked £538.00
      (*b*)   (i) £269.00 (ii) £398.00 (iii) £558.00.
      (*c*)   £20 increase in stock of paper causes the difference.

13.4   (*a*)   Prime costs: 5 Star £66,894; 3 Star £124,020; Factory cost of goods manufactured: 5 Star £67,869; 3 Star £126,945.
      (*b*)   Gross profits: 5 Star £31,500; 3 Star £72,980.

13.5   (*a*)   (i) Prime costs: C1 £31,650; C2 £48,300
             (ii) Factory cost of goods completed: C1 £35,000; C2 £54,000
      (*b*)   C1 £6.25; C2 £2.20
      (*c*)   C1 £7,500; C2 £5,000.

CHAPTER 14

14.1   (*a*)   £14,000 Profit;
      (*b*)   £7,400 Profit;
      (*c*)   £9,500 Loss;
      (*d*)   £2,000 Loss.

14.2   Net profit £5,227.

14.3   Purchases £57,358; Sales £110,583.

| 14.4 | (a) | £43,214; |
| | (b) | Current asset: expenses prepaid £250; Current liability: expenses accrued £1,960. |

14.5   Purchases £41,645; Sales £75,737.

14.6   Gross profit £33,386; Net profit £6,890; Balance Sheet totals £67,059.

CHAPTER 15

15.1   Bar profit £4,120; Surplus £4,209; Balance Sheet totals £29,939.

15.2   (a)   Answer depends on how much is to be donated to charity. Ticket price of £1 would provide a donation of £1.50.

15.3	(a)	£27,670 bar profit;
	(b)	£27,668 closing balance;
	(c)	£28,012 surplus.

CHAPTER 16

| 16.1 | (a) | Gross profit overstated by £4,000; |
| | (b) | Gross profit understated by £4,000. |

| 16.2 | (a) | (i) £315; (ii) £325. |
| | (b) | (i) £18,375 gross profit; (ii) £18,385 gross profit. |

16.3   573 items.

17.1 (a) (i) £28,000; (ii) £5,000; (iii) £30,000; (iv) £6,000.
(b) (i) 5; (ii) 25%; (iii) 10%.

17.2 (a) (i) Gross profit £36,219; (ii) Net profit £326; (iii) Balance sheet totals £73,439.

17.3

	Fox	Badger
(i)	12.5%	11.11%
(ii)	6.3	32
(iii)	1.33 months	0.8 month
(iv)	2.4 months	1.5 months
(v)	2.76	1.80
(vi)	1.94	1.51
(vii)	£112,200	£32,500
(viii)	9.48%	12.41%

17.5 (b) Cash balances: Jan £90; Feb £330 O/D; March £4,710 O/D; April £6,130 O/D; May £7,400 O/D; June £8,050 O/D.

17.6 (a) Cash balance £11.02; Bank balance £407.52
(b) Expenditure analysis: Food £ 77.87
Medical £ 1.50
Travel £ 40.50
Clothing £ 99.30
Housing £176.48

INDEX